# Stages of Play

# Stages of Play

## Shakespeare's Theatrical Energies in Elizabethan Performance

# Michael W. Shurgot

DELAWARE

Newark: University of Delaware Press
London: Associated University Presses

Associated University Presses
440 Forsgate Drive
Cranbury, NJ 08512

Associated University Presses
16 Barter Street
London WC1A 2AH, England

Associated University Presses
P.O. Box 338, Port Credit
Mississauga, Ontario
Canada L5G 4L8

The paper used in this publication meets the requirements of the American National Standard for Permanence of Paper for Printed Library Materials Z39.48–1984.

**Library of Congress Cataloging-in-Publication Data**

Shurgot, Michael W., 1943–
   Stages of play : Shakespeare's theatrical energies in Elizabethan performance / Michael W. Shurgot.
      p.   cm.
   Includes bibliographical references and index.
   ISBN 0-87413-614-8 (alk. paper)
   1. Shakespeare, William, 1564–1616—Stage history—To 1625.
   2. Shakespeare, William, 1564–1616—Stage history—England—London.
   3. Shakespeare, William, 1564–1616—Dramatic production.   4. Great Britain—History—Elizabeth, 1558–1603.   5. Theater—England—History—16th century.   I. Title.
   PR3095.S58   1998
   792.9′5′0942—dc21                                          97-12163
                                                                CIP

*To*
*Gail, Mara, and Nicholas*

# Contents

# Acknowledgments

This book began as a seminar paper on Elizabethan staging of eavesdropping scenes in *Twelfth Night* and *Troilus & Cressida* for Miriam Gilbert's 1981 National Endowment for the Humanities (NEH) Summer Seminar at the University of Iowa. Seven years later, at Arthur Kirsch's NEH Summer Seminar at the University of Virginia, I presented the initial draft of the present *Hamlet* chapter. Arthur's positive reception of that paper convinced me that this larger project would be worth pursuing. I sincerely thank Professors Gilbert and Kirsch for their initial interest in my approach to Elizabethan staging.

As this book assumed a shape in my mind, several other scholars have encouraged its development. During a long bus ride through Tokyo at the 1991 International Shakespeare Congress, Charles Frey judiciously tempered my untutored enthusiasm for predicting Elizabethan audiences' responses to performance, and my revisions have benefited from his remarks. I am especially indebted to Philip C. McGuire, H.C. Coursen, and Jay L. Halio. For several years, Philip has generously given his time, knowledge, and friendship to my work, especially to early efforts on *Troilus & Cressida* and *Hamlet*. Herb Coursen carefully reviewed the entire initial draft, and his critical wisdom now informs every page of this book. While precariously balancing a cup of coffee and several papers during a break at the 1994 Teaching Shakespeare Conference in Stratford-upon-Avon, Jay Halio agreed to read the manuscript for the University of Delaware Press. Jay's criticism, especially of the early chapters, was extremely helpful, as was his graceful guidance of the manuscript through the publishing process at Delaware.

Donovan Johnson, humanities chairman, Michael Beehler, dean of instruction, and Kenneth Minnaert, president at South Puget Sound Community College in Olympia, Washington, all supported my request for a year's sabbatical leave, which allowed me to complete the manuscript. To all three, I give my sincere gratitude. I also thank my neighbor Harry Bailey, late of Southwark's Tabard Inn, for several stimulating conversations, on his porch and mine, about Chaucer, Shakespeare, and the general state of American higher education during my sabbatical. Finally, a special debt of gratitude to Professor C. Walter Hodges for his kind permission to reprint his sketch "A Playhouse, c. 1595" from his book *The Globe Restored,* which graces the cover of mine. I first read his book at a Princeton NEH seminar in 1978, and my own work is a humble effort to follow the lead Professor Hodges set so well with his. The sketches at the ends of chapters 7 and 8 were drawn especially for this book by Lee Wallat.

I trust the dedication speaks for itself; it is but a small way of acknowledging the three dearest people in my life.

For permission to reprint previously published material, I thank the following:

Material from J. L. Styan's *Shakespeare's Stagecraft* (Cambridge: Cambridge University Press, 1967), reprinted with the permission of Cambridge University Press.

Material from Douglas Sprigg, "Shakespeare's Visual Stagecraft: The Seduction of Cressida," in *Shakespeare: The Theatrical Dimension,* eds. Philip C. McGuire and David A. Samuelson (New York: AMS Press, 1979), reprinted with the permission of AMS Press.

Material from Michael W. Shurgot, "Seing and Believing: Eavesdropping and Stage Groupings in *Twelfth Night* and *Troilus & Cressida,*" in *Shakespeare: Text, Subtext, and Context,* ed. Ronald Dotterer (Selinsgrove: Susquehanna University Press, 1989), reprinted with the permission of Susquehanna University Press.

Material from Michael W. Shurgot, "From Fiction to Reality: Character and Stagecraft in *The Taming of the Shrew,*" *Theatre Journal* 33 (October 1981): 327–40, reprinted with the permission of The Johns Hopkins University Press.

Material from Michael W. Shurgot, "Dramatic Structure and Audience Response in *Twelfth Night,*" *Shakespeare Bulletin* 6 (September/October 1983): 14–20; and "'Get You a Place': Staging the Mousetrap at the Globe," *Shakespeare Bulletin* 12 (summer 1994): 5–9, reprinted with the permission of the editors of *Shakespeare Bulletin.*

Sketch "A Playhouse, c. 1595," in C. Walter Hodges, *The Globe Restored* (1968; reprint, New York: Norton, 1973), reprinted with the permission of C. Walter Hodges, Lewes, Sussex.

Seattle, Wash.
October 20, 1996

# Stages of Play

# 1
# Introduction

THE chapters in this book examine how the theatrical energies of several Shakespearean plays would have provoked spectators' responses in Elizabethan productions. Although the focus of each chapter is different, they nonetheless share several common features. First, each chapter considers a play as a dynamic script written for performance by actors, not as a static literary "text" written for readers. Second, notwithstanding the severe limitations of our knowledge of actual Elizabethan stage practice, each chapter explores selected elements of a Shakespearean play in performance on an Elizabethan stage for which it was initially designed (i.e., those of the Theatre and the Globe). This type of venture is extremely risky, but I believe that our appreciation of Shakespeare as a dramatic artist will be increased by attempting to understand his plays in their initial theatrical settings. Finally, by "dramatic energy" I mean generally the aspect of a Shakespearean script, or part thereof, that engages its spectators and provokes dramatic meaning when played in a theater. The kind of dramatic energy I examine varies from play to play, but each chapter focuses on an element of a Shakespearean script that I believe is especially significant in creating that play's engagement with its Elizabethan theater audience. I thus hope that these chapters will contribute to our collective, growing understanding of Shakespeare's dramatic artistry.[1]

Bernard Beckerman's definition of drama as that which "occurs when one or more human beings isolated in time and space present themselves in imagined acts to another or others"[2] stresses performance and spectators—two elements of Shakespeare's plays that are often ignored when one speaks of them as "texts." A text, as Philip C. McGuire explains, is "Fixed in print . . . static on the page, available like a picture or a building for 'inspection,' (reading) again and again." In the theater, however, a play "does not hold still" for a "second inspection"; rather, "drama calls upon us to open ourselves to an experience that is public and communal in ways that the experience of reading is not."[3] One reads literature; literature is composed of texts. However, as Homer Swander remarks, Shakespeare did not write "literature." He wrote "plays" (i.e., dramatic scripts). Yet "script" is a dangerous and difficult term with which to work because it "cuts all literary moorings and plunges us into an exploration of 'meaning' that has nothing whatever to do with literature but everything to do with *The Tempest* and . . . *Hamlet*."[4] Swander describes the energy of a script as that which "drives towards an aesthetic being, a formal and authentic life, beyond itself: a highly precarious life in the bodies of actors moving in an agreed-upon space as an invitation to spectators to become an audience."[5] As Beckerman's definition shows, a script becomes a play (i.e., becomes drama) only when it is acted before spectators in a theater where, as Michael Goldman writes, it "confronts us with an unparalleled immediacy and inclusiveness."[6]

Each of these essays delves into the precarious life of a Shakespearean script and does so with a clear understanding of the limitations of this entire enterprise. McGuire explains in *Speechless Dialect* that a play is "both its words and its performances," and thus a dramatic script is fundamentally and continually "open" in ways a literary "text" is not. Every new production of a play creates new possibilities of meaning and thus new ways of "seeing" the dramatic potential inherent within the script. McGuire insists that this fact about dramatic scripts creates both frustrations and opportunities. "If we are to understand the multiplicity generated by the freedom inherent in Shakespeare's plays, we must put aside assumptions and methods shaped by the themata of simplicity, completeness, and causality."[7] He adds that rather than insisting, as literary approaches often do, on completeness in our critical formulas, we must realize that a Shakespearean play "does not exist in a single mode—as a playtext—but as an ensemble of various possibilities that may overlap and even conflict with one another."[8] Performance criticism thus attempts to describe what is constantly in motion, the actual performance of a play, which will vary, often significantly, from one production to another, one stage to another.[9] The very difficulties of this kind of criticism are also its principal challenge, which Norman Rabkin has articulated in his seminal book *Shakespeare and the Problem of Meaning*:

The challenge to criticism ... is to embark on a self-conscious reconsideration of the phenomena that our technology has enabled us to explore, to consider the play as a dynamic interaction between artist and audience, to learn to talk about the *process of our involvement* rather than our considered view after the aesthetic event.[10] (Emphasis added)

The following essays are responses to Rabkin's challenge to focus on the "dynamic interaction between artist and audience" as created in several Shakespearean plays.

Further, these essays attempt to envision performance of select Shakespearean plays in their initial Elizabethan theatrical settings. Although these essays address individual features of their respective plays and the contemporary theatrical setting differently, each asks that we consider a particular performance feature of the script in a theater in which Shakespeare initially intended his plays to be performed. Homer Swander asserts that consideration of Shakespeare's theatrical "space" is indeed essential to understanding his dramaturgy:

We are used to agreeing, perhaps too readily, that Shakespeare knew what he was doing. If he did, he knew how to write—and did write— for a stage the most prominent feature of which was that it thrust itself out into the very center of the building and radically into the community of the audience. Shakespeare's theatrical language— every element of it, from word to gesture to costume—was native to and developed in a place in which the actors were surrounded by an audience within touching distance. No playwright of genius could fail to include in his plays, in a most basic way, the theatre space and the actor-audience relationship that he knew was a given for him. To the extent that we now exclude such elements, we exclude something Shakespearean, something important. We accept a certain blindness to possibilities that are right before our eyes in the scripts.[11]

Swander's emphasis on the physical features of Elizabethan performance of Shakespeare's plays, especially the "theatre space and the actor-audience relationship," suggests the value of understanding the relationship between Shakespeare's scripts and their initial, intended performance spaces. In the following chapters I will argue that in Shakespeare's imaginative conception[12] of his plays the actual physical shape of the stage in his playhouses, and the actor-audience relationships that this stage created, became increasingly important to his dramaturgy. I shall thus argue that our appreciation of these dramatic scripts will be enhanced by considering them as having been designed for particular theatrical conditions, first at the Theatre and then later at the Globe. The importance of these buildings to Elizabethan drama is thus essential to my approach.

Stephen Orgel makes a seminal point about the Theatre. When James Burbage built it in 1576, it was "either the first or the second permanent theater in Europe after Roman times."[13] Theater in London was now "real," a specific place, a "location, a building, a possession," not just a movable platform on a make-shift cart or a temporary "space" in an innyard. Because theater was now a permanent place, it had a permanent audience: "theaters create not only their drama, but their audiences as well."[14] Harry Berger Jr. writes that the Elizabethan theater established "the primacy of imaginary space time" by marking off an area, walling out the rest of the world, and selling tickets, thus creating "a situation in which an audience [was] brought into a theatrical enclosure for the express purpose of seeing a play."[15] Furthermore, and most important, in the public theaters, unlike the court productions designed by architects such as Inigo Jones, there was no single, dominant visual perspective for spectators. Orgel writes in a later essay that Renaissance popular drama is essentially fluid and disjunctive in nature, and that it depends for its truth on its audience: "Its elements fit together only insofar as a viewer interprets and understands them."[16] Orgel's statement suggests that Elizabethan public theaters superbly incarnated what Marco De Marinis terms a "Dramaturgy of the Spectator." De Marinis writes that theater creates a two-sided "theatrical relationship" between performance and spectators:

> One side of this "theatrical relationship" . . . comprises a manipulation of the audience by the performance. Through its actions, by putting to work a range of definite semiotic strategies, the performance seeks to induce in each spectator a range of definite transformations, both intellectual (cognitive) and affective (ideas, beliefs, emotions, fantasies, values, etc.). The performance may even urge its audience to adopt particular forms of behavior such as in political theatre. . . . The other side . . . consists of an active cooperation by the spectator. More than just a metaphorical coproducer of the performance, the spectator is a relatively autonomous "maker of meanings" for the performance; its cognitive and emotive affects can only be truly actualized by the audience. . . . [T]he spectator's "cooperation" . . . refer[s] to the intrinsically active nature which makes up the spectator's reception of the performance.[17]

The multiplicity of visual perspectives in an Elizabethan public theater intensified the role of each spectator as an autonomous "maker of meanings." In a theater with a thrust stage, its spectators surrounding the platform on three sides and rising far above the stage in galleries, not only does a dominant visual perspective simply not exist, but also the sight lines created by the thrust stage crisscross within the theater, producing far more complex actor-spectator relationships and far more conflicting viewpoints, both literally and metaphorically, than the proscenium arch theater could create.[18] Anyone who has seen plays at the Royal Shakespeare Company's The Other Place or the Swan in Stratford-upon-Avon realizes that, especially at the Swan, many elements of performance, such as actors' gestures, movements, facial expressions, voice inflections, proximity to other actors, and stage position, affect spectators differently in various parts of the theater. Furthermore, if "We are all players, and not such very good ones either, and the theater is the place where we come face to face with our own theatrical selves";[19] if theater spectators too are actors in parts that, like Hamlet's, they may not completely understand, then certainly play watching at the Theatre and the Globe reflexively emphasized the multiplicity of possible views of one's own "roles" in one's life. Just as every actor was seen from many locales and perspectives within the theater, so was every spectator.[20] The chapters in this book explore[21] how the energies of Shakespeare's scripts exploit in various ways these features of thrust stage theaters and the resulting multiplicity of actor-spectator relationships created *by and during* actual performance.

The recent discoveries of the original foundations of the Rose and Globe theaters in London have increased somewhat our knowledge of these two structures. The foundations indicate, for example, that the Rose was definitely smaller than the Globe, but these discoveries have not significantly changed many long-standing assumptions about the design and size of the Globe.[22] Although we no longer speak of "the Elizabethan theater," as if there were an archetypal model (such as the De Witt drawing of the Swan) after which all public theaters were constructed, there is still no convincing evidence that the design of the Globe theater's stage was other than what scholars have deduced it was, based on the wording of the Fortune theater contract. The Globe's stage was large, about 43 feet wide by 27 feet deep, approximately 1161 square feet of playing space. Although we know practically nothing about the actual structure of the Theatre itself, we do know that its timbers were used to construct the first Globe, and because "the timbers would presumably (through attention to "carpenter's marks") have been reassembled in their original relationships so as to take advantage of the original cutting and jointing, we may suppose that the First Globe . . . was of the same size as the Theatre."[23] Although J. L. Styan is right in stating that we do not know exactly where many of Shakespeare's plays were first staged, and Andrew Gurr argues that probably no plays were designed for specific stages before 1594,[24] it is still conceivable that most of Shakespeare's early plays did open at the Theatre or were designed for that playhouse. It is logical to assume, given that the Globe was constructed from the timbers of the Theatre, that Shakespeare's company, or companies, had been associated with the latter playhouse for several years; it is equally logical that for several years Shakespeare had been writing plays that he at least intended to be played in the Theatre when in 1599 the Chamberlain's Men relocated themselves and their timbers across the Thames. Thus, although we cannot be certain about the relative size of the Theatre vis-à-vis the later Globe, and the recent debates about probable design choices for the reconstructed "Third Globe" at Anchor Terrace in Southwark leave several contested questions, nonetheless we can discuss with some certainty the general size and shape of the public theatres for which Shakespeare wrote his plays and on which he intended them initially to be staged, and from these basic assumptions we can then examine how the design of these stages, especially at the Globe, became an integral part of his dramaturgy.

The financial success that we know Shakespeare achieved indicates numerous full houses in his theaters, especially the Globe, and we can assume from his practical success that most spectators at his playhouses were able to see well what they came for. D. A. Latter has argued that sight lines in typical Elizabethan public playhouses were probably adequate for all spectators. Although admitting that Elizabethan theater designers and builders were probably not much concerned with actual sight lines, he argues nonetheless that there is no evidence that spectators anywhere in the theaters could not see the stage. Latter observes that Elizabethan theaters were built, after all, to make money, and it is logical to argue that theaters would have been designed and constructed to maximize spectators' involvement in the plays.[25] Thus, 1/15 Anchor Terrace notwithstanding, although we still possess precious little specific information about the actual dimensions of Elizabethan public theaters, including most ironically the Globe, speculations about staging techniques, including stage blocking and groupings, and the visibility thereof, can nonetheless assume that the theaters allowed maximum visibility of staged action for most spectators, especially for those paying the highest prices. Further, we can assume that this visibility allowed the actors to stage their plays with the greatest possible attention to the intrinsic relationship between script and performance, and with maximum possible actual use of the "flexible, mercurial stage"[26] itself, all approximately 1161 square feet of bare platform that jutted so prominently into the "yard" of the playhouses.

This kind of approach to Shakespeare's dramaturgy necessitates several cautions. First, Peter Thompson asserts flatly that, given production pressures in Elizabethan theaters, "The idolatrous proposition that the text never suffered is absurd."[27] Michael Hattaway adds that "Certainly it is highly unlikely that any Elizabethan performance would be as similar to another as is the case with a modern play enjoying even a modest run."[28] These two statements certainly mandate caution in postulating how any one scene or play would have been produced in an Elizabethan playhouse, just as the production pressures indicated by entries in Henslowe's *Diary* suggest minimal rehearsal. These assertions are credible, and I suspect are widely accepted among Shakespeare scholars and theater historians. My approach to Shakespeare's dramaturgy in this book offers two responses. First, Shakespeare's long association with a steady company in mainly two similar public playhouses could, indeed, have enabled him to write (and help produce) plays for actors he knew well, with whose talents and work habits he was familiar, and, once at the First Globe, in a playhouse whose physical properties and staging possibilities he must have assimilated thoroughly. The Globe, as it were, became second nature to his writing, even though his plays were certainly produced at court and in private theaters. Second, even if one cannot finally be certain about how actors would have been placed on the stage in his scenes, and how they might have moved during performance,[29] one can nonetheless speculate about Shakespeare's *conception* of their staging. I do not claim that one can ever know Shakespeare's exact intentions regarding the staging of his plays. However, by examining his dramatic constructions with the Theatre and especially the Globe stages in mind, one can visualize and thus begin to appreciate how he may have intended to use the shape of the stage to create meanings for his audiences, especially in scenes, such as Hamlet's "Mousetrap" or Cressida's assignation in 5.2, in which multiple perspectives and complex meanings are essential dramatic components. No specific production of any Shakespearean play may have completely mirrored any other specific production; the "script" of *Hamlet* or *King Lear* may have been cut or adjusted, not just for general performance reasons, as the existence of multiple Shakespearean "scripts" strongly suggests, but also from one afternoon to another. The vicissitudes of outdoor theater production are notorious, especially in London's cold, damp winters. Although one can argue that "scripts" were cut from week to week or even day to day, one can also ask whether Shakespeare or Burbage, the most professionally accomplished men of the theater in Renaissance England, would have agreed to enough cutting to dissuade us from postulating how they might have staged their finest scenes to maximize audience attention[30] and thereby pack the playhouses. Under these circumstances, and considering Shakespeare's evolving, vital role in his increasingly prosperous and polished company, investigation of his dramatic intentions regarding staging seems warranted. Emrys Jones asserts that Shakespeare's is an "essentially symbolic mode of poetic drama in which all details aspire towards meaningfulness."[31] Certainly his use of the thrust stage itself to create compelling actor-spectator relationships must be one of those details that aspires toward meaningfulness in his drama.

The most salutary caution against my kind of enterprise is Andrew Gurr's reminder that "The original performance texts, all that intricate interaction between poet's mind and collective audience mind, mediated in the familiar structure of the Globe and its players, can never be reconstructed."[32] Part of our loss, Gurr adds, is that "we are unlikely to know even the scale of our ignorance."[33] Such somber remarks from so accomplished a scholar must give pause. I offer the following explorations into Shakespeare's scripts in the humble belief that while our ignorance may be, and remain, great, nonetheless it will be even greater if we refuse the challenge of trying to understand how every feature of Shakespeare's dramaturgy contributed to his enduring art.

The following essays discuss eight plays ranging from *The Taming of the Shrew* to *Hamlet,* thus covering approximately the first decade of Shakespeare's career. I do not pretend to offer here a "theory" of Shakespearean drama; rather, I seek to discover places in Shakespeare's scripts where performance in Elizabethan playhouses would have generated particular audience responses and thus dramatic meanings in those playhouses. Although this assertion applies most directly to the chapters on *Hamlet* and *Troilus & Cressida,* it is relevant to all of the arguments in this book despite their procedural differences. The essay on *Shrew* focuses primarily on what I call the play's "theatrical energy," establishing what I mean by that term and suggesting how I shall apply it to other plays. The essay on *Love's Labor's Lost* and *A Midsummer Night's Dream* examines how probable stagings of their final scenes on the thrust stage of the Theatre might have influenced spectators' responses to these plays' final moments. The middle essays on *The Merchant of Venice, I Henry IV,* and *Twelfth Night* combine emphasis on each play's theatrical energy, especially as concentrated in Shylock or in Falstaff's and Toby's raucous festivity, with suggestions about how the culmination of these energies complicate spectators' responses to each play's full dramatic design. The final essays on *Hamlet* and *Troilus & Cressida,* focusing primarily on Hamlet's "Mousetrap" in 3.2 and Cressida's "assignation" in 5.2, argue for a particular staging (i.e., blocking) of each scene as being essential to realizing fully each scene's scripted potential for dramatic meaning and spectator involvement during performance at the Globe. These scenes culminate what I see as Shakespeare's continuing exploration (for the purposes of this book, up to ca. 1602) of play writing and scene design for a particular theatre space—that is, his exploring how the actual shape of the thrust stages in his playhouses, especially the Globe, and the crisscross patterns of sight lines and varied actor-audience relationships these stages created, could be incorporated into the full web of the total theatrical phenomenon involving both stage and audience. Thus, although this is not intended primarily as another book about Shakespeare's "development" as a dramatic artist, I conclude with *Hamlet,* and thus defy chronology (*Troilus & Cressida* probably being the later play), because I believe the "Mousetrap" represents Shakespeare's most sophisticated and fascinating use of the Globe stage in the creation of multiple meanings during performance. Indeed, if there is any value in my approach, it ought to be most evident in the book's final two chapters on *Troilus* and *Hamlet.* However, as I examine each of the eight plays differently, these two chapters are far more than simply summations of dramatic techniques I have examined in earlier chapters. Each chapter should contribute to our appreciation of the play or plays it discusses, while also contributing to the book's overall investigation of Shakespeare's creative use of his theaters and their stages for his plays.

All textual references to Shakespeare's plays throughout these essays, unless otherwise stated, are to David Bevington, ed., *The Complete Works of Shakespeare,* 4th ed. (New York: HarperCollins, 1992).

# 2

# From Fiction to Reality: Character and Stagecraft in *The Taming of the Shrew*

MUCH recent criticism of *The Taming of the Shrew* has focused primarily on two issues: the relation between the play's predominantly farcical nature and its characterization, especially of Petruchio and Katharina; and gender relations raised particularly by feminist critics' often severe condemnation of the play. Both of these issues, especially the latter, are distinctively contemporary, and both tend also to treat the play as a literary artifact or, especially regarding the play's gender relations, as a social document indicative of the status of women in early modern England. Although I would not deny that Shakespeare's plays reflect their social and political milieu, this collection of essays begins by focusing on *The Taming of the Shrew* as what, after all, it is: a play written to be performed before a public theater audience in 1591–92.[1] Although performance criticism of *The Shrew* (or any other play) does not obviate recent feminist and new historicist criticism of Shakespeare's plays, I do want to argue that criticism that focuses exclusively on *The Shrew* as a literary or social document fails to appreciate either what Shakespeare wrote—a play—or whether it succeeds as a play, especially one written for an Elizabethan, not a modern, audience. Further, if we can approach the play as a play, perhaps some of the extremely fractious criticism of it will seem less relevant once we appreciate what the play accomplishes in performance rather than attacking it because it does not conform to contemporary views of gender relations or social attitudes.

As Arthur Quiller-Couch once argued, "the trouble about *The Shrew* is that, although it reads rather ill in the library, it goes very well on the stage."[2] Quiller-Couch's remark separates the two distinctly different ways of experiencing a Shakespearean play. The first, "literary," encounters the text as a work of literature to be studied, where such factors as our preconception of the play or knowledge of its sources, our previous "readings"[3] of the play, and our knowledge of its "place" in Shakespeare's "development" all contribute to how we "see" or want to see a particular work. The second, "theatrical," encounters the play as Shakespeare originally intended it to be experienced—on the stage—where the sensory data of the production, including the director's use of lighting, blocking, props, music, his direction of the actors, and their own interpretations of their roles, may forge in our minds a new appreciation and understanding of a play we thought we knew quite well. I would venture that everyone reading this last sentence has had precisely this kind of theatrical experience, and that everyone would attest to its enduring emotional and intellectual impressions.

Although reading (and carefully rereading) Shakespeare's plays is certainly valuable and necessary for the teacher-scholar, nonetheless the "theatrical dimension" of Shakespeare criticism during the past three decades has shown the error of judging how a play "reads" in the library independently of how it "goes" on the stage—or, what is worse, and what is certainly true of much contemporary, ideologically driven criticism, of assuming that the only valid criterion for judging one of Shakespeare's plays, either alone or compared with another, is a "scholarly" reading of the "literary" text. Dramaturgical considerations of Shakespeare's plays demand a more sensuously alert encounter with his words, and ask us to remember that in the theater his scripts create and energize all that we see and hear.[4] Dramaturgical approaches attempt to explain how Shakespeare engages his audience's full participation in his plays, and how the contrasts and emphases of his "visual effects" complement a play's dramatic poetry to create "total theatre."[5]

Theatrical criticism challenges one to perceive the dramaturgy implicit in Shakespeare's script, and meeting that challenge in the script of The Shrew provides a possible solution to Quiller-Couch's dilemma. He is absolutely right about the play's theatrical appeal, yet he fails to see that the reasons for the stage success lie within the very script (Quiller-Couch, I am sure, would have preferred "text") that he finds such a poor companion in the library. Although reading The Shrew may never be as intellectually stimulating as reading, say The Merchant of Venice or Hamlet, nonetheless when we examine The Shrew as a theater script we find ample evidence of why the play—as a play—goes well.[6] To appreciate the theatrical energy of The Shrew, we must begin with Petruchio and Katharina, for throughout the play the dynamics of their roles demonstrate forcefully how characters who may appear simplistic or "one-dimensional"[7] on the page become complex and multidimensional on the stage and thus contribute enormously to a play's stagecraft.

Summarizing Shakespeare's achievement in comic characterization, M. C. Bradbrook writes that, although he adhered to the principle that "comedy portrays character," he "profoundly modified it by deepening and strengthening each separate character, developing the relations between different characters, until the characters *became* the plot."[8] Bradbrook adds that Shakespeare evolved a form of "interior metamorphosis" among his comic figures that permitted them "to develop" rather than being "transformed by some exterior violence" as often happens in earlier (e.g., Lylian) Elizabethan comedy.[9] In the taming plot of *The Shrew*, Shakespeare invests his principal characters with a psychological and physical vitality noticeably lacking in the Bianca plot,[10] and this vitality is the key to appreciating how Shakespeare exploits for maximum theatrical effect the germ of the dramatic ideas and situations contained in his probable folk tale sources.[11] Examining Shakespeare's portrayal of Petruchio and Katharina from a theatrical perspective, the perspective of their dramatized physical relations, reveals how he involves spectators emotionally in their increasingly animated play and thus creates from their stage conflict what Styan calls "total theatre."

The "enormous explosion of energy"[12] in the Induction begins the play in a farcical *media res*. Like Falstaff, Sly is a drunken thief who will not pay for the glasses he has "burst," and like Falstaff he is too exhausted and inebriated to care about the law that the Hostess threatens. Like Hamlet, the Lord who finds Sly is well acquainted with a group of players—"This fellow I remember / Since once he played a farmer's eldest son" (Induction I, ll.82–83)—and like Hamlet, he insists that they be "used well": "Go, sirrah, take them to the buttery, / And give them friendly welcome every one. / Let them want nothing that my house affords" (lines 101–3). The farcical nature of this noisy Induction may function primarily, as H. J. Oliver argues, to "present the story of Kate and her sister as a none-too-serious comedy put on to divert a drunken tinker,"[13] but the Induction's metatheatrical emphasis on play and playing,[14] the evocation of a rough Elizabethan alehouse that is suddenly transformed into a Lord's chamber, and the suggestion of change in Christopher

Sly's "transmutation" into a "lord indeed" suggest that more serious concerns lie beneath the farcical exterior.[15] Whatever the reasons for Sly's disappearance from the Folio script,[16] Shakespeare's play performed by the traveling players bears a brilliantly ironic relationship to its framing Induction. For as the performed play unfolds for the on-stage audience, spectators in the theater realize that Sly's fantasy of easy "transmutation" of human identity and nature is far more complex than the bewildered tinker is led to believe. This irony is most evident in Petruchio's detesting the very means that "Barthol'mew" uses to impersonate, or play, Sly's wife. For Petruchio disdains traditional clothing, social customs and mores, and the conventions of aristocratic behavior by which nobility distinguishes itself from those they consider inferior. To Shakespeare's theater spectators, expecting a play fit only to entertain a drunken rogue wearing borrowed robes, *The Taming of the Shrew* becomes a significant surprise. The traveling players' presentation of "pleasing stuff" with increasingly complex characterization in Petruchio and Katharina exemplifies Shakespeare's own disdain for the limitations of genre and his determination to employ explicitly theatrical means to fracture those limitations. Petruchio and Katharina, "played" by players who arrive on stage in the midst of the Induction's noisy, inebriated setting, modulate into characters who transcend their origins.

Like Sly, both Both Katharina and Petruchio initially explode onto the stage. Katharina reveals her choleric nature in sharp, biting retorts to several other characters: to Hortensio's "No mates for you, / Unless you were of gentler, milder mood" (1.1.59–60), Katharina responds with the threatening, angry, and seemingly irrational aggression that marks her speech and action throughout most of the play:

> I' faith, sir, you shall never need to fear;
> Iwis it is not halfway to her heart.
> But if it were, doubt not her care should be
> To comb your noodle with a three-legged stool,
> And paint your face, and use you like a fool.
>
> (1.1.61–65)

In a scene replete with polite conversation, Petrarchan raptures, and covert scheming for Bianca by Lucentio and Tranio, Katharina's threatened violence[17] announces a socially disruptive, egocentric personality. Clearly she is one of the "raging fires" that are about to consume the stage, although neither Gremio nor Tranio, who label Kate a "fiend of hell" and "stark mad or won-derful froward," consider why Katharina acts as she does. Her exit lines, following her father's polite, but feeble attempt to order her about ("Katharina, you may stay" [1.1.100]), indicate the fierce independence that plagues Baptista (and his tradi-tional wedding formulas) but paradoxically attracts Petruchio in 2.1 : "Why, and I trust I may go too, may I not? / What, shall I be appointed hours, / As though, belike, I knew not what to take, / And what to leave? Ha!" (1.1.102–5). The content of her early speech establishes tension between her and the predomi-nant social environment, even as her tone and staccato rhythm immediately identify her as a major theatrical "force."[18] Clearly, Kate *is* shrewish.

But certainly she has cause, and certainly her shrewishness is far more complex than either Baptista, Gremio, or Tranio per-ceives. Katharina's interest in and jealousy of Bianca's admirers are clearly evident in 2.1, when the bound Bianca enters, naively assuming that her sister covets only her material attractions, her garments and jewels. Kate, however, envies Bianca for her suitors, not just her fine attire: "Of all thy suitors here I charge thee tell / Whom thou lov'st best. See thou dissemble not" (2.1.8–9). Katharina's envy indicates a natural longing for physi-cal affection; hearing and seeing her cruel treatment of Bianca spectators witness her extremely "curst," volatile character.[19] Al-though Katharina may desire the active attention that Bianca receives, she resolutely determines that any such "wooing" will be conducted on her own terms. She will not alter her character to attract the likes of Hortensio or Gremio, yet in her jealous rage she strikes Bianca, attempting to force her to identify her favorite wooer. When Baptista enters, Katharina laments that she must "dance barefoot" on Bianca's wedding day, that she is doomed to "lead apes in hell," and then departs, complaining "I will go sit and weep / Till I can find occasion of revenge" (2.1.35–36). H. B. Charlton thinks Katharina's pathetic claim is "widely out of character,"[20] but he fails to perceive at this moment either the vigorous sincerity of Katharina's desire for masculine com-pany or the complexity of her emotions. Given her intense anger, she may, indeed, seek means of revenge; however, she may very likely "go sit and weep" also, frustrated by Bianca's "silence," and her own solitude and failure to attract suitors.

Katharina is justifiably angry at her father and a social sys-tem[21] that victimizes her. Her shrewishness is a protest and also a defense mechanism, and so leads to her being stereotyped as "fiendish" and "curst" by the men present in 1.1. But her temperament is also partly responsible for her isolation, and whatever contemporary critics may think about Katharina's victimization by her father's patriarchy and obstinate adherence to traditional marriage practices, Katharina's attitude about her situation will not change it. Nor would an Elizabethan audience expect the sheer force of Katharina's shrewishness to change the reigning social system or her place in it. For that, Kate's disruptive theatrical energy needs an ally.

Petruchio's entrance is even more disruptive than Kate's. His impatience with Grumio's word game leads him to "wring" (Bevington, s.d.; Folio "ring") his servant's ear, employing the farcical violence that Katharina merely threatened in her first appearance. As Katharina's aggression and impatience dominate her behavior in 1.1, so Petruchio's description to Hortensio of his travels[22] and his singular attitude regarding women and wooing emphasize his own unruly, indomitable character:

> Signor Hortensio, twixt such friends as we
> Few words suffice. And therefore, if thou know
> One rich enough to be Petruchio's wife—
> As wealth is burden of my wooing dance—
> Be she as foul as was Florentius' love,
> As old as Sibyl, and as curst and shrewd
> As Socrates' Xanthippe, or a worse,
> She moves me not, or not removes, at least,
> Affection's edge in me, were she as rough
> As are the swelling Adriatic seas.
> I come to wive it wealthily in Padua;
> If wealthily, then happily in Padua.
>
> (1.2.64–75)

Grumio's "Nay, look you, sir, he tells you flatly what his / mind is. . . . Why, nothing comes amiss, so / money comes withal" (1.2.76–77, 80–81) informs Hortensio and the audience that Petruchio means exactly what he says. Petruchio's concern with the material rewards of his wooing is central to the play; he is initially interested in Katharina only because her father is wealthy, and he is utterly unconcerned about her being, as Hortensio warns him, "intolerable curst / And shrewd, and froward, so beyond all measure" (1.2.88–89). Instead, he assumes that any woman of any temperament—be she a toothless "old trot" or have as many diseases as "two and fifty horses"—will suit him provided her dowry suffices, an attitude toward marriage consistent with his obstinate, tenacious, and immensely self-confident nature. Petruchio will "board [Kate] though she chide as loud / As thunder when the clouds in autumn crack" (1.2.94–95); having heard lions roar, the sea rage, and "great ordnance in the field" (1.2.202; or so he claims—is all this bragging for effect?),[23] a "woman's tongue" is to him less frightening than "a chestnut in a farmer's fire"; "Tush, tush! Fear boys with bugs" (1.2.208–9).

Intermingled among the various "supposes" and disguises of the developing Bianca plot through 2.1, Petruchio's brash, boasting tone clearly establishes him, like Katharina, as a significant theatrical force. Shakespeare's dramatization of Petruchio's and Katharina's impulsive characters in carefully juxtaposed scenes creates considerable anticipation within a theater audience about the pair's eventual meeting. Katharina's and Petruchio's language and tone exhibit considerable energy, but their interests are diametrically opposed: although marriage is "not half way to [Katharina's] heart," Petruchio's "business asketh haste." Indeed, Petruchio's impatience and bullishness before his meeting with Katharina suggest that his stated willingness to marry her only because of her dowry is just what Grumio says it is: a "humor" that he says Hortensio should allow Petruchio to follow while it "lasts." The sense of spontaneity in this arrangement, and the sheer improbability of its succeeding, are reinforced by Grumio's description of the rhetorical (and possibly physical) violence that Petruchio will use on Katharina; by Petruchio's seemingly preposterous enthusiasm for Katharina after Hortensio enters from her music lesson "with his head broke" (s.d.)—"Now, by the world, it is a lusty wench! / I love her ten times more than e'er I did. / O, how I long to have some chat with her!" (2.1.160–62); and especially by Petruchio's short dialogue with Baptista. To Baptista's sensible caution that "specialities" can be arranged between them only "when the special thing is well obtained, / That is, her love; for that is all in all" (2.1.128–29), which clearly acknowledges Katharina's fierce independence and his realization that the "marriage mart" simply will never entrap her,[24] Petruchio responds: "Why, that is nothing, for I tell you, Father, / I am as peremptory as she proud-minded" (2.1.130–31). Petruchio brashly and rather brutally assumes that both the process of winning Katharina's affections and those affections themselves are "nothing"; he has decided even before meeting her that the actual "taming" of Kate will pose no challenge to his own rough, burly nature. Although contemporary *readers* of the play may find Petruchio terribly offensive here,[25] and may argue that he is emptying Katharina and by extension all women of emotional integrity, the effect in the theater is different. Having *heard* Katharina's scolding tongue and having *seen* two examples of her violent temper in action by this point in the play, theater spectators sense the folly of ignoring the wishes or usurping the will of a woman as independent as she. Petruchio is certainly a braggart soldier, a "madman in his senses";[26] however, the combination of his cavalier attitude toward wooing Katharina and her capacity for violence creates suspense and anxiety about this couple's first meeting that we may not sense when reading the play but that creates in the theater the interplay between stage and audience that keeps spectators alert and receptive.[27] Finally, and equally important for the rest of the play, one must note here the self-conscious "playing" in Petruchio's words and actions, especially in his absurd bragging about his past "masculine" experiences, which he exaggerates (see 2.1.199–205) and thus deliberately ridicules. Dennis Huston emphasizes that the levels of "play" and "playing" evident in the Induction are "relevant to our understanding of Petruchio, whose distinguishing characteristic is his love of play and essential *joie de vivre.* This quality of life he is eventually to impart to Kate, who has to learn to direct her own enormous energies outward into varieties of spontaneous play instead of recalcitrantly forcing them into the narrowly confining roles society would impose on her" (68).

The core of *The Shrew* is the clash between the two irascible individuals whom Shakespeare outlines in the early scenes of the play. Petruchio uses two tactics: first, in their initial encounter, a parody of the courtly Petrarchan lover; and, second, especially at the wedding and later at his estate, a frenetic, strident imitation of Katharina's shrewishness that provides ample comic entertainment on the stage and simultaneously teaches her the social consequences of her habitual behavior. Petruchio's deliberately exaggerated mimicry of Kate supports his contention that he woos "not like a babe"; his well-calculated, ironic tactics indicate some depth in his character, for he has the presence of mind to perceive exactly how Kate must be "tamed." In his soliloquy in 2.1, Petruchio explains his "spirited" wooing:

> Say that she rail, why then I'll tell her plain
> She sings as sweetly as a nightingale.
> Say that she frown, I'll say she looks as clear
> As morning roses newly washed with dew.
> Say she be mute and will not speak a word,
> Then I'll commend her volubility
> And say she uttereth piercing eloquence.

(2.1.170–76)

Petruchio's plan is wholly ironic and playful; in this soliloquy, which sets the comic tone of their entire conflict from acts 2 through 4, Petruchio is instigating a game, imagining his own drama, including dialogue and gesture, and he (and Shakespeare) demands an attentive audience.[28] By deliberately contradicting Katharina's moods and actions, Petruchio intends to exasperate her and so to anger her: the more angry she becomes, the more she "rails," the more he will praise her sweet voice, and thus the angrier she will become because he is not getting angry at her; the more angry she becomes, the more reason he himself will then have to be angry; then the more angry he becomes, the more his behavior will resemble hers; and the more his behavior resembles hers, the more blatant it will be to Kate (so Petruchio confidently asserts) why she must change if she is to have what she wants, including, I shall argue, Petruchio himself. Furthermore, although Petruchio's calculated "wooing" scheme may seem priggish on the page, in the theater it is the perfect prologue to the ensuing debacle; theater spectators, from what they already know of Katharina's character, sense that an explosion between her and Petruchio is imminent. Merely anticipating Kate's reaction to Petruchio's plan increases spectators' uncertainty and anxiety about them and thus stimulates their anticipation of and fascination with their actual encounter. In Petruchio's soliloquy, Shakespeare captures his audience in one of the two most highly charged, tense, and theatrically effective moments in the play; for here the dual energy fields in his script are about to collide.[29]

The collision is violent, explosive, bawdy, and dramatically rich. Shakespeare juxtaposes stichomythia and longer verse paragraphs to create a rhythmic variety in Katharina's and Petruchio's dialogue that directs theater spectators' response to what they see and hear.[30] The violence and bawdiness of their dialogue are confined primarily to the stichomythia of lines 197–

238 and 259–63; within these lines, they exchange increasingly clever sexual puns, and several explicit and implicit stage directions in the script indicate Kate's striking Petruchio, his threat to retaliate, and her attempt to elude him. But the farcical electricity during these few moments is balanced by a series of verse paragraphs, all spoken by Petruchio, that establish his verbal dominance in the scene and emphasize the importance of what he says in them for the rest of the play. "And now, Petruchio, *speak,*" (emphasis added) concludes his first soliloquy. Shakespeare places these verse paragraphs carefully: two frame the stichomythia; the first of these two and another frame the entire scene between Petruchio and Katharina; and, in general, the paragraphs are juxtaposed against Katharina's short, one- or two-line responses so that spectators hear her far less than they hear Petruchio. Thus, Katharina's attempts to respond to his verbal mastery of their encounter, however threatening her words, appear futile. The rhythm of this scene, in other words, tells the audience that Katharina has met her match *verbally;* this rhythm dominates their relationship until the final moment of the play.

Throughout his verse paragraphs, Petruchio ironically praises Kate in a courtly manner, noting her "mildness," her "virtues," and asserting that he finds her "passing gentle" and "courteous." In an attempt to convince her that she may become something more than a shrew detested by every man she has met, he creates an image of something else she may become: a woman praised for her physical beauty, admired for her chastity, and loved for her energetic yet thoroughly compatible, pleasant disposition. To Kate's cry "I chafe you if I tarry. Let me go," Petruchio responds:

> No, not a wit. I find you passing gentle.
> 'Twas told me you were rough, and coy, and sullen,
> And now I find report a very liar,
> For thou art pleasant, gamesome, passing courteous,
> But slow in speech, yet sweet as springtime flowers.
> Thou canst not frown, thou canst not look askance,
> Nor bite the lip, as angry wenches will,
> Nor hast thou pleasure to be cross in talk;
> But thou with mildness entertain'st thy wooers,
> With gentle conference, soft and affable.

(2.1.239–48)

Petruchio's monologue ironically compliments Kate by denying every feature of her speech and action the audience has so far heard and seen, and does so with the repetitive emphasis and exaggeration that characterize not only his speech but also his actions throughout his encounter with her. Petruchio claims that he was told Kate was "rough, coy, and sullen," but he now affirms, with of course absolutely no evidence, that she is "passing gentle ... pleasant, gamesome, passing courteous,"thus adroitly emphasizing the obviously spontaneous "play" in his remarks; he claims she cannot "frown," nor "look askance"; rather than taking pleasure in being "cross in talk," she entertains her wooers[31] with "mildness ... gentle conference, soft and affable." The playfulness in Petruchio's approach shows that, within the limits of an essentially farcical framework, Petruchio is beginning to look much more deeply into Katharina than have the other men of the play. Baptista had insisted that Kate's love was "all in all," and whereas Petruchio had initially insisted that her love, or the winning of it, was "nothing," his promised "roughness" has modulated into an ironic blazon that he knows will anger her and that he hopes will intrigue her.

However, when Petruchio flatly declares "will you, nill you ... upon Sunday is the wedding day" (2.1.268, 295), Katharina angrily responds that she would rather see him "hanged on Sunday first" (line 296) than marry him. Her preference for the gallows is simply another version of her violent reaction to Hortensio's assumption that she might wish to learn the lute. Petruchio's bold declaration that Kate is to marry him, regardless of her wishes, elicits from her precisely his—and the audience's—expected response: Katharina will not allow herself to appear pliant to another's will, and having been challenged by Petruchio's caricature of her own temperament, she responds the only way she (for now) knows: by being as characteristically "curst" as possible. And, one must add here, for good reason, because she is experiencing exactly what she cannot tolerate: the usurpation of her will.

Like Sly the Tinker, Petruchio has little patience with formality; fascinated by Kate's challenging, volatile character, attracted to her beauty, and satisfied with her dowry, he decides for both of them that marriage is imminent:

> Now, Kate, I am a husband for your turn,
> For by this light, whereby I see thy beauty—
> Thy beauty that doth make me like thee well—

> Thou must be married to no man but me.
> For I am he am born to tame you, Kate,
> And bring you from a wild Kate to a Kate
> Conformable as other household Kates.
> Here comes your father. Never make denial;
> I must and will have Katharine to my wife.
>
> (2.1.269–77)

Exactly as he had done in his first verse paragraph after Katharina enters (lines 185–94), here Petruchio both frustrates and
praises her. When she first enters she asserts "They call me
Katharine that do talk of me" (line 184), and so Petruchio deliberately calls her "Kate" eleven times in ten lines; yet he also
extols her "mildness praised in every town," her virtues "spoke
of," and her "beauty sounded, / Yet not so deeply as to thee belongs" (2.1.191–93). Here Petruchio again infuriates her by calling her "Kate" five times and insisting that she will be
"conformable,"[32] but he also praises again her beauty, which
makes him "like her well." Petruchio's second mention of Katharina's physical beauty in this short scene[33] indicates his developing affection for her, which, as fitting the generally farcical
nature of the play, happens quickly. Yet even as he expresses his
romantic interest in Kate, whom he initially wished to marry
only because of her father's money, he simultaneously frustrates
her own selfish, uncompromising will. Throughout the play, Petruchio's manifest sexual interest in Katharina is evident in his
overtly farcical and often severe abuse, yet his tactics are intended to convince Kate of his love for her by making her see
herself as others have. Only when she realizes that her barriers
to romantic love are mainly self-created will she begin to appreciate Petruchio's actions.

In describing to Baptista, Gremio, and Tranio his first clash
with Katharina, Petruchio resorts to a fictional idealization, yet
this fiction embodies the romantic situation both of them desire:

> O, the kindest Kate!
> She hung about my neck, and kiss on kiss
> She vied so fast, protesting oath on oath,
> That in a twink she won me to her love.
> O, you are novices!
>
> (2.1.305–9)

Petruchio is exactly what Katharina says he is: a "half lunatic, /
A madcap ruffian and a swearing Jack, / That thinks with oaths

to face the matter out" (2.1.284–86). Yet by combining an imitation of Katharina's usual behavior with a suggestion of Petrarchan language and mannerisms, he elicits from her an emotional reaction that, judged by her weeping when he arrives (deliberately) late at the church, is sincere. Petruchio and Katharina have "'greed so well together" on only the volatility and independence of their characters, and the peaceful reconciliation of their wills is the business of the remainder of the play. For only when this reconciliation is achieved to their mutual satisfaction can Petruchio's fiction become reality.

For theater spectators, the most engaging feature of the play's first two acts is the ironic discrepancy between what they have *seen* between Petruchio and Katharina, and what they hear him *say* about what they have seen. The comic debacle in 2.1 is violent and centrifugal, implying that these two people could not survive together for long in one room, let alone cohabitate for a lifetime;[34] conversely, Petruchio's fiction, which "in plain terms" (2.1.266) summarily declares a sacramental union, is peaceful and centripedal. Petruchio's fictional account of his madcap encounter with Kate jolts spectators into an awareness of the comical irony they have just seen and heard, and this irony sustains spectators' interest in the only way through which Petruchio's fiction can become real: playing out the drama itself. It is as if those qualities in Katharina that Petruchio ironically conjures up in 2.1—her being "pleasant, gamesome, passing courteous, / But slow in speech, yet sweet as springtime flowers"; her inability to "frown," to "look askance"; her lack of pleasure in being "cross in talk"; and the "gentle conference, soft, and affable" with which she "entertain'st [her] wooers"—were themselves fictions that must become real if the marriage that Petruchio confidently predicts can ever succeed. Regardless of how well spectators know *The Shrew,* or Elizabethan viewers may have known the play's probable folk tale and narrative sources, in the theater they are unavoidably fascinated by the comical irony that Shakespeare has created by act 2 and simultaneously intrigued by the visual and verbal clash between Petruchio and Katharina that they realize is inevitable in the remainder of the play.

Petruchio's behavior at their wedding is consistent with his antics at his country house. Throughout acts 3 and 4 his own deliberate, hyperbolic shrewishness vividly mirrors Kate's. The farcical violence of these two acts, which one cannot appreciate when reading the play, creates "total theatre" for spectators as they see numerous visual images of Petruchio's self-confessed "game" that he plays with Katharina; however, that game itself and her reaction to it through 4.3 increase spectators' anxiety about just how these two people can possibly achieve marital peace. This anxiety is experienced and then resolved as dictated by the dramatic rhythm and structure of the play in performance. As Peter Saccio explains, *The Shrew* is not a "case history"; it is a *play* whose accelerating rhythms in acts 3 and 4 through farcical scenes of outrageous pretense and violence precipitate "a comic catharsis through which the characters come to a new recognition of their relationships."[35]

When the astonished Gremio asks, "Was ever match clapped up so suddenly?" (2.1.323) he speaks for the entire theater audience whose sense of the irony of this marriage is heightened by Shakespeare's placing it in the middle of the play only two short scenes after Petruchio's and Katharina's previous appearance on stage.[36] This sense of irony is intensified by Biondello's frantic report that Petruchio, who had asserted "We will have rings, and things, and fine array" (2.1.321) at the wedding, comes to the ceremony "a monster, a very monster / in apparel" (3.2.68–69). Petruchio's motley visually signals his disdain for ceremony and tradition and announces him as the enormously playful symbol and cause of the chaos that follows. Indeed, the very monstrosity of Petruchio's costume, which every production relishes, signals the hugely outrageous self-confidence of his scheme; his insatiable, spontaneous playfulness; and the farcical, hyperbolic antics he is about to employ. Kate's reaction to this self-centered yet shrewd folly is predictable: she responds indignantly to his order to leave immediately after the ceremony, reversing suddenly her crying after he failed to appear promptly:

> For me, I'll not be gone till I please myself.
> 'Tis like you'll prove a jolly, surly groom,
> That take it on you at the first so roundly.
>
> (3.2.212–14)

Katharina "will be angry," for she sees that "a woman may be made a fool / If she had not a spirit to resist" (3.2.216; 220–21). Her "spirit" is exactly what motivates Petruchio's desire to "tame" her; however, at this point her spirit succeeds only in eliciting from him an even stronger assertion of *his* determination to dominate her:

> Obey the bride, you that attend on her.

Go to the feast, revel and domineer,
Carouse full measure to her maidenhead,
Be mad and merry, or go hang yourselves.
But for my bonny Kate, she must with me.
Nay, look not big, nor stamp, nor stare, nor fret;
I will be master of what is mine own.

(3.2.223–29)

Petruchio is rude, irreverent, possessive, egocentric, and clever. The stage directions implicit in line 228 indicate that he has again, as in 2.1, thoroughly aroused Katharina's anger, which he then uses to justify his outrageous, yet sportive chauvinism. His "bonny Kate," not "Katharine," as she prefers, shall be what he says she is: his goods, his chattels, his house, his household stuff, his field, his barn, his horse, his ox, his ass, his "anything" (3.2.230–32). Petruchio's characteristically repetitive speech, and the escalating rhythm culminating in Kate as an "anything," parody the patriarchal attitudes[37] that Petruchio is gleefully smashing, just as he insanely and deliberately smashed the wedding ceremony itself.[38] As in 2.1, Petruchio again verbally dominates this hectic scene. The accelerating rhythm of his verbal abuse parallels the rising friction between, on the one hand, himself and Katharina and, on the other, himself and the entire wedding party. As the scene climaxes, so do Petruchio's histrionics: claiming that they are "beset with thieves" (3.2.236), he orders Grumio to draw forth his sword as they "rescue" Katharina from the astonished guests and from Baptista's thoroughly conventional ceremony. Reveling in his self-created role of "protector," Petruchio comically and deliberately magnifies the actual situation.[39] Petruchio's brandishing his sword may seem silly and unwarranted "in the library," but on the stage it exemplifies Styan's point that the eye and ear are inseparable in Shakespeare's stagecraft. Petruchio's sword "play" at this critical moment vividly heralds the hyperbolic "taming" he employs later and is also a comically monstrous phallic symbol that ironically indicates his wish to establish a mutually satisfying sexual relationship with Katharina. Like his verbal parody of patriarchy moments before, Petruchio's sword now monstrously mocks the sexual power with which men have traditionally subdued women. If Sly were still awake, he might approve what he thinks he is seeing and hearing; however, Shakespeare's caricature of male power in Petruchio's language and gestures alerts his Elizabethan spectators to the presence of a sustained, ironic, and deeply motivated critique of male sexual dominance.

Petruchio's antics after the wedding crown a dynamic scene that increases spectators' ironic insight into the play and also their anxiety about its main characters. Petruchio gladly acts out Katharina's view of him—a "half lunatic, / A madcap ruffian and a swearing Jack"—because doing so is part of his plan. Having been told in 2.1 that he intended to woo Kate with some "spirit," spectators know what Petruchio is doing; however, Katharina does not. Thus, spectators' emotions are pulled asunder: exhilaration at the sheer bravado and energy of Petruchio's performance; and sympathy, perhaps comically muted, for the victim of his improvised lunacy—his wife! Furthermore, despite their privileged knowledge of Petruchio's motives, the ironic discrepancy between how spectators of any era would expect newlyweds to interact and what they see and hear on the stage heightens the sense of the improbable and bizarre in this relationship. That both Petruchio and Katharina are, in Bianca's words, "madly mated," is far more evident in the theater than in the library, as is Petruchio's determination to show Kate the social consequences of her typical behavior. In the final moments of act 3, we note the beginning of a change in Katharina's attitudes as she realizes for the first time the effects on others of a will as strong and uncompromising as her own.[40]

The trek to Petruchio's estate is, by Grumio's account, terrifying; emphasizing both the sheer brutality of the journey and the obviously non-sequitur nature of Petruchio's actions, Grumio describes "how he left her / with the horse upon her, how he beat me because her / horse stumbled, how she waded through the dirt to / pluck him off me, how he swore, how she prayed that / never prayed before" (4.1.67–71). Although this narration suggests deliberate cruelty, it is also, like the actual wedding, kept off stage; like the wedding, it exemplifies Petruchio's deliberately irrational activity: Petruchio threw sops in the sexton's face because his beard grew "thin and hungerly," and he beats Grumio because Katharina's horse stumbles. The terrible journey plainly amplifies his frantic behavior at the wedding and anticipates the last stages of his severe but ultimately successful mimicry of Kate's obstinacy. If she will smash lutes over peoples' heads to please her own mad humor, so Petruchio, to fashion a mirror for her, will smash reason. In these ironic and self-conscious tactics we witness further evidence of Petruchio's personal interest in Katharina: if he did not strongly desire her as a compatible partner, he would not go to such extremes to elicit the secure bond evident between them in act 5.

His plan involves denying Katharina those basic necessities of life—food, clothes, and rest—for which, having been "Brought up as best becomes a gentlewoman" (1.2.86) she has never had to "entreat." His throwing about of the meal that, as Katharina admonishes him, "was well, if you were so contented" (4.1.157) is an obvious counterpart to Kate's smashing Hortensio's lute over his head, which Petruchio had seen in 2.1 and which had prompted him to exclaim "O, how I long to have some chat with her!"; Petruchio wishes Kate to see how unnecessary and ridiculous such activity is. Further, events that seem to a *reader* as unwarranted extensions of the couple's feud have just the opposite effect in the theater. Petruchio's actions at this late point in the play increasingly frustrate spectators' expectations of normal marital activity: the lack of a proper, solemn wedding ceremony; the couple's hasty, frenzied exit from the communal feast; their horrid journey; the lack of any clear signal from Petruchio that he wishes to consummate this marriage; and the sustained, noisy antagonism between them at his estate theatrically emphasize the constantly increasing distance and tension between the reality of this relationship and Petruchio's ironic, idealized, yet still unrealized version of it in 2.1.

Near the end of 4.1, Curtis tells us that off-stage Petruchio is in Katharina's chamber

> Making a sermon of continency to her,
> And rails, and swears, and rates, that she, poor soul,
> Knows not which way to stand, to look, to speak,
> And sits as one new risen from a dream.
>
> 4.1.171–74

John Bean remarks that these lines suggest Kate's immersion into a kind of bewilderment, or chaos, from which she will "awaken" liberated "from former rigidities,"[41] and although this immersion is only hinted in the play, to be developed in far greater depth in later, more obviously "romantic" comedies, this hint suggests a theatrical perspective from which to view the remainder of act 4; 4.1 concludes with Petruchio's second soliloquy, "Thus have I politicly begun my reign, / And 'tis my hope to end successfully." Petruchio addresses himself to theater spectators, thus involving them personally in his "plot" and soliciting their approval. This moment perhaps best reflects Bean's further insight into the unresolved tensions within *Shrew* between incipient romantic comedy and the play's fabliau and farcical sources and traditions.[42] Indeed, this tension is evident within the soliloquy itself. The first nine lines are the most notorious of the entire play, comparing Kate's "taming" to training a "haggard."[43] As he addresses these lines directly to the audience, strutting about, I would imagine, all sides of the large platform stage, one recognizes not only offensive imagery but also the same bravado Petruchio has exhibited since his entry in 1.2. Having ridiculed traditional marriage ceremonies and attire, and grotesquely parodied male sexual "authority" with his drawn sword, Petruchio sustains his theatrical energy and verbal mastery by trying to impress his listeners with an exaggerated, sportive description of his relationship with Katharina. Being in command of the stage, Petruchio can talk at will, using whatever imagery he chooses. His soliloquy emphasizes the deliberately exaggerated playfulness of his further actions:

> As with the meat, some undeserved fault
> I'll find about the making of the bed,
> And here I'll fling the pillow, there the bolster,
> This way the coverlet, another way the sheets.
>
> (4.1.187–90)

As Marianne Novy writes, Petruchio's falcon-taming "involves . . . hierarchy and coercion, but it also involves a wish for play and mutuality" (269). The overall playfulness of Petruchio's game, his catalog of undeserved faults, does not obliterate the animal imagery of the initial nine lines, nor the cruelty of his keeping her awake and denying her food. But the deliberate nonsense of the "undeserved faults" is clearly akin to his antics at the wedding ceremony and his spontaneous "rescuing" of her from the guests at her own wedding. Petruchio actually is doing all "in reverent care of her," killing her with an ironic and sometimes cruel kindness that only a woman of Katharina's temperament could appreciate. Thus, Petruchio's attitude toward Katharina has changed; the man who decided spontaneously to woo her "while the humor last[ed]"[44] has matured into a husband who truly cares for Katharina and wishes to establish a compatible relationship with her. Indeed, Petruchio's integrity is such that his "taming" has her interests in mind as well as his own. But Katharina must discern herself what Petruchio has told the spectators, and the change in her attitudes is evident only after she has scrutinized the bizarre mirror that Petruchio fashions for her and has fully understood his complex, playful, and sometimes cruel wooing.

The theatrical energy of the play intensifies and accelerates[45] with Katharina's opening speech in 4.3. Kate speaks three lines in 4.1; in 4.3, she speaks forty-five. She is initially, and justifiably, angry, feeling hungry and tired from Petruchio's denial of food and rest. Her exhausted appearance images the cruelty of Petruchio's intended actions in his soliloquy of 4.1. Her anger leads her to beat Grumio, as she momentarily hurls the play backward to her earlier violence against Bianca, Hortensio, and Petruchio himself ("Good Kate, I am a gentleman— / That I'll try. / I swear I'll cuff you if you strike again"[2.1.219–20]). She initially refuses to thank Petruchio for the meat he has (so he claims!) dressed himself specifically for her. As they and Hortensio sit to dine, a traditional stage image of community and an ironic replacement for their wedding banquet, Petruchio again resorts to a blend of farcical, rather cruel humor and spontaneous, but carefully contrived irony. Kate is very hungry, yet Petruchio urges Hortensio "if thou lovest me" to eat all the meat, while urging Kate to "eat apace." While Kate and Hortensio battle for the food, a visual image that spectators will probably see as funny, may justifiably see as cruel, and should certainly see as part of Petruchio's ongoing strategy, Petruchio hurries the scene forward; his business asketh haste. As he promised "rings and things" for their wedding in 2.1, so here he promises elaborate apparel for their return journey:

> And now, my honey love,
> Will we return unto thy father's house
> And revel it as bravely as the best,
> With silken coats and caps and golden rings,
> With ruffs, and cuffs, and farthingales, and things,
> With scarves, and fans, and double change of bravery,
> With amber bracelets, beads, and all this knavery.
> What, hast thou dined? The tailor stays thy leisure,
> To deck thy body with his ruffling treasure.
>
> (4.3.52–60)

Employing anaphora and obvious and elaborate repetition, his favorite rhetorical device, Petruchio envisions another grand, formal ceremony only so he can smash it. But this time, Petruchio's playfulness elevates the end of this scene far above traditional farce and typical shrew-taming narratives. As Kate attempts to eat, Petruchio rushes in the haberdasher and tailor, purveyors of the outward class distinctions so important in Elizabethan England. Petruchio damns the cap as a porridge bowl, and Katharina, again finding her voice, objects:

> Why, sir, I may have leave to speak,
> And speak I will. I am no child, no babe.
> Your betters have endured me say my mind,
> And if you cannot, best you stop your ears.
> My tongue will tell the anger of my heart,
> Or else my heart, concealing it, will break.
> And rather than it shall, I will be free
> Even to the uttermost, as I please, in words.
>
> (4.3.73–80)

As Petruchio ends his soliloquy in 2.1 "[A]nd now, Petruchio, speak," so here Katharina claims her freedom to speak—to the uttermost. Katharina claims a verbal power far more efficacious than the physical power she angrily employed earlier. Petruchio responds with three short lines that are probably unnoticed in the library but are positively wonderful in the theater:

> Why, thou sayst true. It is a paltry cap,
> A custard-coffin, a bauble, a silken pie.
> I love thee well in that thou lik'st it not.
>
> (4.3.81–83)

To what do his first four words refer? He apparently assents to her freedom to speak; "thou sayst true." But he may also, and simultaneously, and thus again with an amazingly spontaneous and ironic humor, claim that she is "right" in saying the cap is "paltry." But Kate said nothing of the kind; thus, as he apparently supports her claim for linguistic freedom, and thus assents to it, he also apparently usurps not only the freedom to speak he has apparently just defended but also her judgment. He may also be claiming that she cannot see well! The humor of this scene in the theater will depend partly on the condition of the actual "cap" used in performance, but surely the main theatrical point, which Shakespeare challenges his spectators to grasp, is that Petruchio is playing an elaborate word game with Katharina; and the rest of act 4, concluding with the scene on the road to Padua, continues this verbal wit contest that becomes increasingly humorous and ironic, and thus continually revelatory of Petruchio's and Katharina's developing compatibility.

Theater spectators would have to attend carefully the levels of wit and "play" that Shakespeare has built into this and their succeeding exchanges of acts 4 and 5. Sly, were he still present and awake, would probably not grasp what this play is trying to tell him about these two characters. Sly presumably would desire a "taming" as in *A Shrew;* within the limits of this impure mix of farce, fabliau, and nascent romantic comedy, Shakespeare is presenting his audience something different.

Katharina asserts "Love me or love me not, I like the cap, / And it I will have, or I will have none." Petruchio does not respond; instead, he immediately turns to the next stage of his play. He is knowingly and monstrously wrong about the gown; no doubt it was made, as the tailor asserts, "According to the fashion and the time." Katharina again speaks assertively:

> I never saw a better fashioned gown,
> More quaint, more pleasing, nor more commendable.
> Belike you mean to make a puppet of me.
>
> (4.3.101–3)

Katharina is right about the gown; the initial humor of this unit of the scene depends on the gown being exactly what Kate and the tailor insist it is. Katharina's suggesting that Petruchio intends to make a puppet of her, ironically recalling her previously limited range of responses,[46] leads him to create a marvelously spontaneous play within his larger play. Again, as in his fabricated rescue of Kate from the wedding guests, his comic devices are deliberate exaggeration and repetition. The tailor says that Kate claims that Petruchio means to make a puppet of her; Petruchio responds:

> O, monstrous arrogance! Thou liest, thou thread, thou thimble,
> Thou yard, three-quarters, half-yard, quarter, nail!
> Thou flea, thou nit, thou winter cricket, thou!
> Braved in mine own house with a skein of thread?
> Away, thou rag, thou quantity, thou remnant,
> Or I shall so be-mete thee with thy yard
> As thou shalt think on prating whilst thou liv'st!
> I tell thee, I, that thou hast marred her gown.
>
> (4.3.106–13)

"[M]y goods, my chattels; . . . my house, / My household stuff, my field, my barn, / My horse, my ox, my ass, my anything." It is the same spontaneous, exaggerated, ridiculous cataloging Petruchio blurted at the wedding, and it was just as obviously self-aggrandizing rhetoric there as it is here. Having exhausted his abusive diminution of the tailor, Petruchio resumes the game of "Who marred the gown?" Grumio sustains it with the tailor for forty-five lines, encouraged by Petruchio ("Read it"; "Proceed"; "Ay, there's the villainy"), until it collapses in Grumio's bawdy about taking up gowns for his master's use, which reminds spectators that this marriage is still unconsummated and that the grand purpose of this early modern Abbott and Costello routine is a mutually satisfying sexual and emotional relationship between Petruchio and Katharina. Kate stands apart, silent, probably to one side of the platform stage, while Petruchio and Grumio play their game with the bewildered tailor for its own mad sake. This "game" may seem completely unnecessary while reading the play, but theatrically it gives Katharina exactly the perspective she needs, for she sees in Petruchio and Grumio a self-conscious, spontaneous play that ridicules obstinacy and the refusal to acknowledge the validity of others' viewpoints. The gown was no doubt a "ruffling treasure," made all the more obvious by Petruchio's and Grumio's determined blindness. The tailor will be paid, for like Petruchio and Grumio, the poor man has played his part well.[47] "Tailor, I'll pay thee for thy gown tomorrow. / Take no unkindness of his hasty words" (4.3.162–63).

Petruchio immediately catapults the energy of this routine into a most unfarcical, unfabliau-like sentiment that both caps this part of his play and heralds his later farce on the road to Padua. What matters finally to Petruchio is the quality of one's mind, which clothing can neither reveal nor conceal:

> Well, come, my Kate. We will unto your father's
> Even in these honest, mean habiliments.
> Our purses shall be proud, our garments poor,
> For 'tis the mind that makes the body rich;
> And as the sun breaks through the darkest clouds,
> So honor peereth in the meanest habit.

(4.3.165–70)

Petruchio is rough and woos not like a babe. Acts 3 and 4 exhibit the accuracy of this self-characterization. But the deeper purpose of his actions, and his concern for the mind of the spirited woman heretofore hidden to every other man in the play because they saw and heard, or wished to see and hear, only her violence and her anger, is clear in these lines. Further, Petruchio's theatrical sense is brilliant; the sharp, sudden contrast between the nutty game about the gown and Petruchio's assertion of Katharina's spiritual and intellectual integrity, which occurs just as Katharina rediscovers her voice in 4.3, highlights his assertion and demands again active spectator participation in this play. The actual "rescuing" of Katharina from an emotionally stifling, conventional life that Dennis Huston sees Petruchio initiating after the wedding (see note 39) climaxes here, as Petruchio rescues Kate from all dependence on the trappings of class and status that best "become" a gentlewoman.[48] The regeneration hinted in Curtis's remark that Katharina sits "as one new risen from a dream" at the end of 4.1 climaxes with her husband's insisting that her mind, which no other man in Padua's convention-ridden patriarchy cared to know, shall enrich her.

But Petruchio cannot end a scene with high-flown sentiment. In one of the most theatrically effective contrasts in the play, he immediately resorts again to "playing," but this time his play is "pure," motivated solely by the desire for mutual, spontaneous playfulness, and the theatrical success of this scene and 4.5 depend completely on spectators' grasping what surely Katharina now sees. Petruchio absurdly asserts that time shall be as he says it is, or they shall not go forward. He even gives away his game because playing it now depends on Katharina's being part of the routine. Moments before she watched Petruchio and Grumio in their routine with the tailor, whereas now, having heard Petruchio praise her mind, Kate plays Abbott to Petruchio's Costello:

> *Petruchio.* Let's see, I *think* 'tis now some seven o'clock,
> And well we may come there by dinnertime.
> *Katharina.* I dare assure you, sir, 'tis almost two.
> And 'twill be suppertime ere you come there.
> *Petruchio.* It shall be seven ere I go to horse.
> Look what I speak, or do, or think to do,
> You are still crossing it.—Sirs, let it alone.
> I will not go today, and ere I do,
> It shall be what o'clock I say it is.
>                    (4.3.183–91; emphasis added)

Petruchio is now turning his verbal power, which he has hitherto exercised in deliberate histrionics and bawling about pillows, back on himself; for he is now the subject of his own mad play.

Katharina's understanding of Petruchio's sport is evident on their journey back to Padua. During their whimsical mock debate about the sun and moon, she accepts Petruchio's astrological decrees because she perceives in his fantastic insistence that he can control the heavens an image of irremediable lunacy, of a madcap game pursued entirely for its own sake. As Marianne Novy explains, this is a game composed entirely of language that "turns on redefining the external world, and perhaps this . . . focus for redefinition makes it possible for her to join in and begin creating a new world and a new society between the two of them" (271). The substance of Petruchio's remarks does not matter. Lest Petruchio rashly decree that they return to his madhouse, Katharina agrees with his nonsense:

> Forward, I pray, since we have come so far,
> And be it moon, or sun, or what you please;
> And if you please to call it a rush candle,
> Henceforth I vow it shall be so for me.

> (4.5.12–15)

Kate is now far more clever than Petruchio; certainly on the large Elizabethan stage she could point to the distance between them and the nearer door, and hilariously undercut, and thus mock, this distance, for they have actually come but a few paces. Further, like Petruchio earlier in the play, Katharina can subtly ridicule; were the heavenly body they "debate" a "rush candle," not even Petruchio with his apparently supernatural vision could see it. Indeed, the moon does change even as Petruchio's mind. Again, as at the end of 4.3, Petruchio is making his own whimsically inconstant mind the subject of his own game. As the sun and moon seemingly depend on Petruchio's decrees for their very appearance in the heavens,[49] so apparently do the age and sex of the most flabbergasted character in the play: Vincentio. The brief exchange among Vincentio, Petruchio, and Katharina anticipates the farcical, disguised identity of the false Vincentio who encounters his adversity in 5.1, and also signifies the final stage in Kate's appreciation of her husband's play. In addressing Vincentio as "Young budding virgin, fair, and fresh, and sweet," and concluding "Happier the man whom favorable stars / Allots thee for his lovely bedfellow!" (4.5.36, 39–40) Katharina is, according to Saccio, producing "a sustained outburst of inventiveness, elaborating the fantasy to a wonderfully ridiculous extreme."[50] Yes, Kate's inventiveness is wonderfully sustained, but her images are far more than invention. Surely the inside joke here, which she assumes Petruchio grasps, is that her fantastic description of the aged Vincentio simultaneously images her own fantastic transformation into a sexually desirable woman "fair, and fresh, and sweet." Kate's immediate sense in this moment of the opportunity for mutually appreciated verbal play and a projection of herself as a "lovely bedfellow" again exemplifies the quickness of her wit and the immensely liberating power of "play" in her relationship with Petruchio, while also anticipating their eventual sexual union. Shakespeare demands that spectators perceive the dual energy fields animating this scene, and note the significant difference between Grumio's narration of their previous journey and this return trip. During both journeys, Petruchio is deliberately capricious; however, the differences between his earlier beating Grumio because Kate's horse stumbled and his later making himself an utter lunatic merely to spark verbal play that both he and Kate enjoy mark the huge *emotional* distance this couple has traveled. This, surely, is why Shakespeare gives his characters two journeys. From the wedding through acts 3 and 4 Petruchio may have embodied Kate's fear of the typically violent and irrational husband, whereas he here subjects his formerly presumed authority to verbal ridicule.

The final scene of the play must be viewed in relation to the "controversy" of 5.1. Petruchio's "Prithee, Kate, let's stand aside and see the / end of this controversy," and Katharina's "Husband, let's follow, to see the end of / this ado" (5.1.57–58, 134–35) frame the unraveling of the "counterfeit supposes" in act 5. Thus, the theater audience sees this episode from the joint perspectives of Petruchio and Katharina, whose recently achieved peace implicitly comments on the deceptions of the Bianca plot. Equally significant *theatrically* is their kiss, which is the last bit of stage business just before the communal and today a hugely controversial final scene. Petruchio asks for the kiss, and when Katharina, now modest and alert to the privacy of affection, says she is "ashamed" to kiss, Petruchio reverts to his (by now) rather stale ploy: he shall go home lest she kiss him. Thus Katharina kisses him, and the "rich savor" of this stage moment climaxes their "vigorous confrontation,"[51] in its romantic simplicity visually contrasts with the contortions of the Bianca plot, and establishes for the audience a perspective from which to view Petruchio's and Katharina's final moments on stage. Further, the theatrical potency of the kiss itself, like that of Kate's final gesture in the play, is simply invisible in the library; the duration and intensity of the kiss, which the actor playing Katharina can control, may visually signal the perspective from which Katharina's final speech should be understood. Shakespeare's placing of Petruchio and Katharina as frames to the actions in 5.1, and his placing of the kiss at the very end of the scene, indicate a superb theatrical sense that can only be realized in performance.

The final moments of *Shrew* are its most intense, most potent theatrically. The communal gathering is the first in the play since 3.2, and it contrasts sharply with Petruchio's frenetic estate; at Lucentio's banquet, Petruchio says, there is nothing but "sit and sit, and eat and eat!" Lucentio hopes that "raging war is done" and "scapes and perils overblown"; however, Hortensio and his wife provoke one final battle. Petruchio claims that "Padua affords nothing but what is kind," and Hortensio responds "For both our sakes, I would that word were true" (5.2.14–15). Petruchio, who simply cannot shut up, immediately jests that Hortensio "fears his widow," and when the widow claims that she is not to be trusted if she be "afeard," the following dialogue occurs:

> *Petruchio.* You are very sensible, and yet you miss my sense:
> I mean Hortensio is afeard of you.
> *Widow.* He that is giddy thinks the world turns round.
> *Petruchio.* Roundly replied.
> *Katharina.* Mistress, how mean you that?
> *Widow.* Thus I conceive by him.
> *Petruchio.* Conceives by me! How likes Hortensio that?
> *Hortensio.* My widow says, thus she conceives her tale.
> *Petruchio.* Very well mended. Kiss him for that, good widow.
> *Katharina.* "He that is giddy thinks the world turns round":
> I pray you, tell me what you meant by that.
> *Widow.* Your husband, being troubled with a shrew,
> Measures my husband's sorrow by his woe.
> And now you know my meaning.
> *Katharina.* A very mean meaning.
> *Widow.*                    Right, I mean you.
> *Katharina.* And I am mean indeed, respecting you.
>
>                                        (5.2.18–32)

There are two vital points here. First, Katharina *twice* asks the widow about her enigmatic line, "He that is giddy thinks the world turns round." Katharina, not Petruchio, suspects the widow's meanness and her severe misjudgment about Katharina herself and her marriage to Petruchio. Second, when Katharina, along with the other women, exits at line 48, she is angry, for she has been caricatured and stereotyped by another woman who has assumed that Kate is a shrew who shall create nothing but "woe" for her husband. Further, after the women leave, Petruchio's relationship with Katharina is misjudged by the men just as Kate's with Petruchio was by the widow. After Petruchio, who is quite jovial, offers his second toast to his companions (lines 37 and 51), this dialogue occurs:

| | |
|---|---|
| *Tranio.* | 'Tis well, sir, that you hunted for yourself. |
| | 'Tis thought your deer does hold you at a bay. |
| *Baptista.* | O ho, Petruchio! Tranio hits you now. |
| *Lucentio.* | I thank thee for that gird, good Tranio. |
| *Hortensio.* | Confess, confess, hath he not hit you here? |
| *Petruchio.* | 'A has a little galled me, I confess; |
| | And as the jest did glance away from me, |
| | 'Tis ten to one it maimed you two outright. |
| *Baptista.* | Now, in good sadness, son Petruchio, |
| | I think thou hast the veriest shrew of all. |
| *Petruchio.* | Well, I say no. And therefore for assurance |
| | Let's each one send unto his wife; |
| | And he whose wife is most obedient |
| | To come at first when he doth send for her |
| | Shall win the wager which we will propose. |

(5.2.55–69)

Thus by 5.2.69 both Katharina and Petruchio have been angered, or at least piqued, by members of their own sex who have assumed that their marriage will be unpleasant because Kate is a "shrew" and Petruchio has been duped and will be "held at a bay," implying that Petruchio and Katharina are two animals, one the hunter and the other the hunted.[52] Petruchio's wager, which he makes when Katharina is off-stage, and which is understandably offensive to contemporary audiences, is partly another moment of bravado among his mates, whom he wishes to prove wrong. But it is also generated by his faith that Katharina's "Nay, I will give thee a kiss. Now, pray thee, love, stay" (5.1.140–41) expressed a sincere desire for mutual affection.

The climactic moment of the play grows out of this anger and this affection, for in the theater these twin emotions, which may be ignored when reading the play, increase spectators' sense that here at play's end Petruchio and Katharina are growing apart from their same-sex companions and closer to each other. Equally important *theatrically* in the final scene is realizing that here Petruchio and Katharina are continuing their play-within-a-play begun on the road back to Padua, and although their "outer play" of rigid sexual roles and stark obedience seems to imitate the wooden, tradition-bound society of the other wedding guests, their "inner play" actually signals their determination to explode traditional marital roles. Thus present on stage in this final scene are both centripedal and centrifugal dramatic energies: Kate and Petruchio mutually "act out" a mock, neo-Paduan patriarchal scene for the other guests who, as Kate and Petruchio knew they would, mistake their "play" as an acceptance of a traditional male-dominant marriage; and Kate and Petruchio's mutual "playing" further solidifies their reliance on each other as they ridicule the Paduan society they are determined to leave behind, as, indeed, they shortly do.

When Katharina comes at Petruchio's "command," he insists to Hortensio "Marry, peace it bodes, and love, and quiet life, / An awful rule, and right supremacy, / And, to be short, what not that's sweet and happy" (5.2.112–14). Katharina comes at "command" partly to show to the widow and Bianca that she is not a "shrew," whatever Katharina may think that word now means, and partly to show that her marriage is not and shall not be one of "woe." When she throws underfoot the "bauble" she is wearing, she is "obeying" her husband by continuing their private, now thoroughly playful disdain for clothing[53] and again showing here, at another wedding feast, their distinctly unconventional disregard for social trappings: "'tis the mind that makes the body rich." Finally, one should realize that Kate's final speech is initially directed at the widow, who has insulted and stereotyped Katharina during her sister's wedding banquet, hardly a time to question the integrity of another woman's marriage.

Katharina's last speech grows out of this dramatic situation, and cannot be separated from it. It is the longest, by far, in the play; it certainly would have been delivered downstage center on the platform stage; in it Katharina claims not only again and most forcefully the freedom to speak she has twice before asserted—"I see a woman may be made a fool / If she had not a spirit to resist"; "I will be free / Even to the uttermost, as I please, in words"—but also seizes this opportunity for a grand performance that suddenly reverses the rhythm of short, staccato dialogue present throughout 5.2 and establishes her as the linguistic master of the play, thus overturning completely the verbal dominance Petruchio has exerted since his initial "speech" with her in 2.1. Further, Katharina's speech demonstrates her ability to mimic Petruchio's favorite rhetorical device, repetition, while using that same device, combined with superb irony, to play with the patriarchal absolutes with which she simultaneously lectures Bianca and, especially, the widow. She begins:

> Fie, fie! Unknit that threatening, unkind brow,
> And dart not scornful glances from those eyes
> To wound thy lord, thy king, thy governor.
>
> (5.2.140–42)

She gets started on women's anger, turns to patriarchal imagery, and then returns to women's anger:

> It blots thy beauty as frosts do bite the meads,
> Confounds thy fame as whirlwinds shake fair buds,
> And in no sense is meet or amiable.
> A woman moved is like a fountain troubled,
> Muddy, ill-seeming, thick, bereft of beauty;
> And while it is so, none so dry or thirsty
> Will deign to sip or touch one drop of it.
> Thy husband is thy lord, thy life, thy keeper,
> Thy head, thy sovereign.
>
> (5.2.143–51)

As Marianne Novy explains, Petruchio's catalog of Katharina as his "goods . . . chattels . . . anything" (3.2.230–32) parodies patriarchal authority;[54] here, Kate simply uses the same rhetorical device to parody the patriarch. And who is this "sovereign"?

> one that cares for thee,
> And for thy maintenance commits his body
> To painful labor both by sea and land,
> To watch the night in storms, the day in cold,
> Whilst thou liest warm at home, secure and safe;
> And craves no other tribute at thy hands
> But love, fair looks, and true obedience—
> Too little payment for so great a debt.
>
> (5.2.151–58)

Petruchio? Being the son of Antonio, "A man well known throughout all Italy" and well known to Baptista (2.1.69–70); having "crowns" in his purse and "goods at home"; and having secured a hefty dowry from Baptista, how much time is Petruchio likely to invest in labor, by sea or land, watching storms? Would the Kate who speaks these enormously energetic and clever lines really be content only to lie warm at home, passive and waiting? Is that an image of the woman Petruchio has married? Further, only Petruchio, plus the theater audience, can grasp the irony of this picture of marriage compared with her "honeymoon" at Petruchio's house of horrors. That Katharina can now joke about that experience shows that their mutual friction and alienation have been replaced by a mutual respect for their verbal and hence personal independence.[55] Petruchio was initially interested in Katharina after she expressed her distaste for lute playing by breaking one over Hortensio's head. Petruchio is now hearing the final stage of the "chat" he then longed to have with her, and she is doing all the talking.

In the next section of her speech, as John Bean has demonstrated, Katharina uses images suggesting the Renaissance humanists' revisions of traditional, medieval views of matrimony, including their elevation of companionship as central to a marriage.[56] This background to Kate's speech is crucial and is the basis of Bean's remark that in Kate's speech, "Male tyranny, which characterizes earlier shrew-taming stories, gives way here to a nontyrannical hierarchy informed by mutual affection."[57] Katharina's image of a well-ordered kingdom, in which "Such duty as the subject owes the prince, / Even such a woman oweth to her husband" (lines 159–60), which she elaborates for another eight lines, is certainly intended as instruction for Bianca and the widow; as a model suggesting order and mutuality, what Katharina says is undoubtedly acceptable and desirable to her.[58] But the rhetorical flourish with which all this "doctrine" is delivered emphasizes what is evident in the theater because Kate's speech must be *heard*: the theatrical energy of Petruchio's and Katharina's riotous first encounter modulates from the bizarre wedding through their initial journey to the chaos of Petruchio's house to the word games on the road back to Padua to the explicitly tender, quiet moment of Kate's, "Now pray thee, love, stay"; and thence to a resurgence of their mutual verbal and very soon physical energy and improvisation, which, this time, Kate is inaugurating because it is her turn! As Novy brilliantly observes, connecting this moment to the rest of the *play*, "Indeed, the

series of games and game images that has led up to this speech
makes it possible to see her improvisation very much as a
game. . . . Since socialization is a process of learning roles, a
sharp distinction between play and social reality seems difficult
to maintain even offstage, and here we are dealing with the conclusion of a game within a play within a game within a play."[59]

The final portion of Kate's speech, lines 169–83, is rhetorically
dynamic. She begins with a rhetorical question, "Why are our
bodies soft, and weak, and smooth" that she elaborates for four
lines, including her first use of rhyme (hearts, parts), and that
she knows Petruchio understands is not a completely accurate
description of her. "Soft, smooth," perhaps—but weak? Katharina's "spirit" was first evident to Petruchio in her lute smashing,
an act suggesting her contempt for order as symbolized by music
itself. She then appears to denigrate female independence and
boldness:

> Come, come, you froward and unable worms!
> My mind hath been as big as one of yours,
> My heart as great, my reason haply more,
> To bandy word for word and frown for frown;
>
> (5.2.173–76)

Even as Kate apparently satirizes the "big" (i.e., "haughty" or
"proud") minds of "froward and unable ['i.e., poor feeble crea-
tures'; Bevington, 4th ed.] worms," she bandies word for word
with such force that she virtually silences everyone else on stage
and utterly smashes the cultural stereotype of the "silent
woman."[60] Her final seven lines, beginning with, "But now I see
our lances are but straws" conclude with a rush of three heroic
couplets ("Compare-are"; "boot-foot"; "please-ease") as her rhetoric climaxes in a "goodly speech" that plainly announces its own
artifice and is as calculated a performance as she recognized
Petruchio's was in 2.1.[61] This performance concludes with the
play's final, perhaps most important, gesture; her offer to place
her hand beneath Petruchio's boot creates an electric moment
that can be fully appreciated and exploited only in the theater.
Given the length of Kate's speech, and its rhetorical playfulness,
her apparent gesture of submission raises momentary anxiety
among spectators; does Kate suddenly place herself with Bianca
and the widow in the conventional marriage that the sheer energy of her "uttermost" speech would seem to have precluded?
How will Petruchio respond? Given his verbal power throughout

the play, will he attempt a response, a riposte? How long will Petruchio wait to respond to Kate's "if"? Certainly the longer she suspends her hand, and the longer he waits to respond (i.e., the longer they hold this silent tableau), the greater the communal tension in the theater. But Katharina's hand does not go beneath her husband's foot—much virtue in "if." With Petruchio's wonderfully playful, "Why, there's a wench! Come on, and kiss me, Kate," as Petruchio and Katharina kiss for the second time in public, Shakespeare suddenly and finally releases his spectators from the ironic tension of his play in an appropriately abrupt, unceremonious manner. J. L. Styan asserts that Shakespeare creates stage contrasts assuming that an audience will deduce meaning from them;[62] what spectators will deduce from the vivid theatrical contrast between Katharina's long speech and her sudden dash off the stage with Petruchio is that these two people are about to begin the normal but hitherto frustrated rhythm of marital love with a marvelous gusto. Petruchio's earlier fiction—"O, the kindest Kate! / She hung about my neck, and kiss on kiss / She vied so fast, protesting oath on oath, / That in a twink she won me to her love"—is about to become reality in a sexual embrace.

Petruchio asserts that Katharina won him to her love, thus making her the active lover; in Petruchio's own view, absolutely nothing about Kate is passive. Petruchio's fictional narrative, however, indicates an important truth about both these characters and Shakespeare's achievement in the play. Although *Shrew* never completely escapes the genre of farce, nonetheless its characterization is theatrically both sophisticated and compelling. In place of the unreflective, unfeeling figures generally present in farce and in the traditional shrew-taming story, Shakespeare substitutes "two intelligent people [who arrive] at a modus vivendi";[63] similarly, in place of the often physically brutal taming of a wife in numerous contemporary versions, he substitutes a theatrical process in which his characters achieve an active self-knowledge that permits the fulfillment of mutual desires. Through her educational trial with Petruchio, Katharina learns to abandon her rigid, fearful, and angry responses to other people, whereas Petruchio learns that a woman may be loved, not for her dowry, which he never mentions again after 2.1, but for her beauty, merits, and especially the richness of her mind. Katharina's and Petruchio's "interior metamorphoses" are thus the heart of this play because they develop out of the clash between the enormously energetic and fascinating characters that Shakespeare makes so vocally and visually compelling.[64]

Two final, important points follow. First, Lynda E. Boose has recently argued that "For feminist scholars, the irreplaceable value if not pleasure to be realized by an historicized confrontation with . . . *Shrew* lies in the unequivocality with which the play locates both women's abjected position in the social order of early modern England and the costs exacted for resistance."[65] Boose argues that "Kate does, literally, 'stoop' to her lure" in her final speech, and that "The [scold's] bridle is an artifact that exists in *Shrew's* offstage margins—along with the fist-in-the-face that Petruchio does not use and the rape he does not enact in the offstage bedroom we do not see."[66] I do not quarrel with Boose's significant historical research into the cruelties of controlling supposedly unruly women in Elizabethan England. I ask only about what happens on stage in performance of Shakespeare's *play*. Kate's "if" is crucial to the dynamics of this final scene; any performance that is sensitive to Kate's images and the sheer strength of her verbal performance will surely insist that Petruchio intercept this highly rhetorical offer of hand under foot. To miss this theatrical fact is to miss Kate's faith in her husband's desire for mutuality, not mastery. Further, Kate is hardly "bridled" in this play; she, indeed, seizes verbal freedom in the most rhetorically complex and sophisticated speech of the entire play. I cannot see how a woman who has just dominated the stage for forty-four lines can suddenly "stoop" to an imagined lure after such a theatrical tour de force. This argument would make utter nonsense out of Kate's performance *in the theater*. One can argue that virtually anything exists in the "offstage margins" of any play. I have considered in this essay what I believe are the proper subjects of performance criticism: those dramatic and theatrical features that contribute to a play's success on stage, as opposed to the scholarly reading, aided by dozens of volumes on early modern everything, one can leisurely pursue in the library. By claiming that *Shrew unequivocally* locates "women's abjected position in the social order" of Elizabethan England, Boose prescribes what every actual production of *Shrew* must do, and must have done, before its opening night, almost as if Charles Marowitz were the only legitimate director-interpreter of this play.[67] This type of criticism seems unjustifiable to me, as it denies to Shakespeare's scripts what is most obvious about them: their openness to interpretation in performance. To submit drama to dogma before the curtain rises is to turn drama into propaganda. *The Taming of the Shrew* is not propaganda; it is play.

Second, consider the probable "place" of Kate's and Petruchio's final "play" on the platform stage in relation to Robert Weimann's elucidation of the "Bifold Authority" of the Elizabethan stage. Weimann writes:

> [W]hat the Shakespearean text seems to project are two different (and potentially divisive) locations of authority: the represented *locus* of authority, *and* the process of authorization on the platform stage. Thus, in relation to Shakespeare, "authority" needs to be studied as both an object of, and an agency in, representation. Authority is, first, an *object* of Shakespearean representation. . . . Distinct from authority as mimetically so represented, authority is, second, an *agency* residing within the textual and theatrical activity itself. This type of authority is not *represented*; it must be viewed as *representing* (and, as such, as legitimating from within) the work, the space, the language of dramatic composition, and theatrical production itself. . . . [T]he *locus* was associated with the localizing capacities of the fictional role and tended to privilege the authority of what and who was *represented* in the dramatic world; the other, the *platea*, being associated instead with the actor and the neutral materiality of the platform stage, tended to privilege the authority of what and who was *representing* that world.[68]

Weimann adds that the "noteworthy thing about authority in the Globe was the way it resided in proximity to the actual process of theatrical production and communication. Authority in this theatre . . . needed to be validated by the audience and was unlikely to result without the cooperative effort of the audience's "'imaginary forces.'"[69] If one imagines Kate and Petruchio "producing" their final "play" on the downstage, unlocalized *platea*,[70] igniting spectators' cooperative insight into their ironic slam at the upstage *locus* of patriarchal authority, one imagines them creating *during performance* their own irresistible theatrical authority with which they condemn the patriarchal society and then immediately—and wisely—abandon *together,* possibly through the central doors behind the central arras of the Elizabethan theater.[71] This "theatrical authority" that evolves from within and then reacts against the represented social structure is the authority of play itself.

# 3

# Inner Plays and Mixed Responses in *Love's Labor's Lost* and *A Midsummer Night's Dream*

Aʟᴛʜᴏᴜɢʜ the dating of Shakespeare's early plays is notoriously difficult, most editors now agree that both *Love's Labor's Lost (LLL)* and *A Midsummer Night's Dream* date from ca. 1594 to 1596.[1] Both plays thus date from the earliest years of Shakespeare's long association with the Chamberlain's Men, and, given Richard Burbage's presence in the company, presumably from the company's return to steady playing at the Theatre after the plague in 1592–94. Both plays may thus be seen as experimental in several ways. The grouping and pairing of lovers in both plays recalls Lyly's highly patterned court comedies, and in both plays we see Shakespeare experimenting with Lylian episodic structure and balanced design.[2] The patterned and balanced structures of both plays may also suggest Shakespeare's experimenting with his newly formed company, creating plays that presumably could have relied on fairly familiar blocking designs and stage groupings as Shakespeare learned the skills of his actors. One may also surmise that in creating Berowne in *LLL* and (presumably) Theseus[3] in *A Midsummer Night's Dream,* Shakespeare was experimenting with the voice and talents of Burbage, who, Shakespeare must have recognized immediately, would become the company's leading actor. One also notes in both these plays Shakespeare's deliberate inclusion of metatheatrical episodes, including scenes of rehearsal in *Dream* and plays-within-plays in both works, as if with his new company and presumably their return to steady playing at one playhouse Shakespeare were using both comedies to explore with his spectators the phenomena of both performance itself and spectators' own responses. In this chapter I will examine this last phenomenon in both plays, for in each Shakespeare intentionally creates among his on-stage, "inner-play" audiences multiple responses similar to those he recognized were integral to spectators' theatrical experience in Elizabethan public theaters.

The Lylian patterning of scenes and balancing of groups of characters are evident throughout *LLL*. In 1.1 we move from the quartet of young men proclaiming their steadfast devotion to learning, questioned only by Berowne's self-indulgent and witty ridicule of their vows, to the equally self-indulgent and horribly pedantic expressions of that which will undermine the young scholars' "academy": human sexual desire, in this case for the dairymaid Jaquenetta. In 2.1, Shakespeare introduces the Princess and her attendant ladies, whose delineations of the young men balance the men's earlier debate about the wisdom of entering their academy. When the men enter at 2.1.88, the debate about payment of a "hundred thousand crowns" (2.1.129) by the Princess's father to Navarre merely frames, and introduces, the play's more important debates: love versus learning, society versus seclusion. Even as the political questions are settled, the young men are exchanging witty lines with the women and asking Boyet their names. One topic having been settled, the second is begun. Indeed, Shakespeare's ruse here is transparent; the debate about payment exists only to get the eight young people on the stage, presumably in the "park" outside Navarre, so they can meet and thus initiate the debate about the place of romantic "affections" in young people's lives.

The misdirected letters of 3.1, first Armado's fantastic missive to Jaquenetta—"Thus dost thou hear the Nemean lion roar" (4.1.88) remarks Boyet after reading it—and then Berowne's to Rosaline, the latter instrumental in Berowne's unmasking, impel the plot forward to its theatrically most significant scenes. For example, 4.3 demonstrates Shakespeare's imaginative use of the Theatre's large platform stage. The eavesdropping scene demands that each character have his own "space" after his actual or presumed soliloquy. The audience has been prepared for Berowne's apostasy by his soliloquy in 3.1.172–203, but not for the others' defection from their vows. As first Berowne and then the King, Longaville, and Dumaine enter with their love poems and letters, and then as each (except Dumaine) steps aside to another part of the stage, spectators' perspectives on the stage action shift constantly. Spectators are initially sympathetic to Berowne, as he confesses his love for Rosaline; and when the King enters, they become immediately Berowne's ally as he eavesdrops on his fellow victim. But spectators are also attend-

ant on the King's confession, so their attention is divided between two men in entirely different "places" on the stage and in
two entirely different moods, one desperately in love yet de-
pressed at admitting it—"Sweet leaves, shade folly" (4.3.40)—the
other having accepted his failed vow and gleefully enjoying a
fellow victim's fall to Cupid. Shakespeare repeats and compounds this pattern when Longaville and then Dumaine enter
equally in love and equally reluctant to admit their "perjury"
and "Sweet fellowship in shame" (4.3.45). As the King and then
Longaville speak, retreat to their "place," perhaps a separate corner of the stage, and then comment on the latest expression of
love, spectators hear and see testimonies to love's overwhelming
power and then experience severe criticism of that power's ability to create fools and hypocrites: "Dumaine transformed! Four
woodcocks in a dish!" (4.3.78). Given the fluidity of staging on
the large unlocalized platform, each character can merely step
aside to be "invisible" to the others,[4] and as each character moves
to his place on the platform, the spectators nearest that place
become his confidants, sympathetic first to his confession of the
same desires that afflict everyone else in the theater, and then
fellow spies on his (and thus their) fellow victims in love. If one
imagines Berowne, the King, and then Longaville retreating to
different parts of the thrust stage, perhaps one upstage and
downstage left and one upstage or downstage right, or perhaps,
though I think unlikely, Berowne in the gallery above the stage,
one then imagines a scene in which expressions of emotions
and increasingly sarcastic attacks on those emotions crisscross
the acting area.[5] The scene draws spectators into the young
men's tumbling emotions; given the likely staging of this scene,
with three men occupying different corners of the stage, theater
spectators participate in this self-conscious collapse of the silly
academy proposed in act 1. With spectators ranged on three sides
of the stage, it is as if each young man's confession and attempt
at self-exculpation—"O, but her / eye! By this light, but for her
eye I would not love her. / Yes, for her two eyes" (4.3.8–10)—and
then his retreat to a portion or corner of the stage appeals not
only to spectators as a whole but also especially to that portion
of them nearest his retreat. Styan writes that the young men
were probably "disposed about the edge of the acting area in full
view of the spectators,"[6] by which I presume he means near the
front of the platform. But I would argue that Shakespeare's design of the scene would have used the acting area more imaginatively and would have involved the spectators more directly if

the actors had moved to more isolated corners of the stage and, while still visible to the entire audience, had more intimately involved separate portions of the spectators as comrades in first their confessions and then their spiteful criticism of their fellows. During performance on the thrust stage of the Theatre this scene clearly would have stimulated *multiple and constantly changing* versions of what Marco De Marinis terms "the intrinsically active nature which makes up the spectator's reception of the performance."[7]

The scene refocuses viewers' perspectives immediately as first Longaville; then the King; and, finally, Berowne emerge from "hiding" to chastise each other's hypocrisy. If Berowne has "hidden" himself in the gallery above the stage, his "descent" as he steps forth "to whip hypocrisy" becomes all the more ironic, as later he too, only moments before a "demigod," is trapped by the arrival of Jaquenetta and the letter Berowne intended for Rosaline. Berowne's confession, "Guilty, my lord, guilty! I confess, I confess" (4.3.201) introduces first a witty exchange about Rosaline's beauty—"black as ebony" asserts the King—and then Berowne's suitably pompous and witty monologue justifying their being "Affection's men-at-arms" (line 286). The scene closes with Shakespeare having created several contrasting emotional reactions among spectators while simultaneously using imaginatively the Theatre's ample stage. Shakespeare designs the scene to draw spectators into not only the generalized turmoil of youthful passions but also the passions of individual characters, as three of them are positioned in different parts of the stage and thus closest to different portions of the audience whose reactions to the scene the individual characters mediate. Indeed, Dumaine is the unluckiest of the four; as he stands forth to deliver his dreadful love poem, probably downstage center, the *platea* where the others have confessed, he has no one's sympathy anywhere in the theater: he is given neither chance nor place to hide. The multiple emotional responses acted out by the four men, in turn, create similarly multiple perspectives on the stage action among spectators surrounding the stage. These multiple perspectives are further developed in act 5, especially in the pageant of the Nine Worthies, one of Shakespeare's earliest uses of the inner play.

The extensive patterning and balancing of the first two acts is repeated in 5.2, as first the Princess and her ladies display and ridicule their ridiculous gifts; like the men themselves, their initial vow, and their protestations of love, these gifts are ostentatious. Having learned of the Muscovite entertainment from the ever-vigilant Boyet, the ladies exchange their favors, the men enter in costume and, mismatched, they form pairs about the stage. The staging of this scene at the Theatre would have been especially revealing and ironic if the couples retreated to separate parts of the stage as in 4.3, perhaps with Berowne, the King, and Longaville going to that part of the stage (assuming Berowne did not ascend the gallery) where each stood during the others' confessions. After much witty dialogue and ironic confusion enjoyed by the ladies and shared with various parts of the audience, Rosaline declares "Not one word more, my maids. Break off, break off!" (5.2.263), and the dance-like movements cease. When first the men, and then the women, return in their proper dress, Shakespeare repeats the unmasking scene from 4.3, this time with no place to hide and in full view and "understanding" of the women. The young lords' merriment, which I suggest was "played" downstage where I shall argue the pageant was also "staged," is "dash [ed] like a Christmas comedy" (5.2.463), and the mood created at this stage moment dominates both the men and the women as this long scene modulates to its next, carefully structured section: the entertainment of the Nine Worthies. This inner play exemplifies Shakespeare's careful, imaginative use of the shape of the stage in the design and intended effect of this scene.

As the pageant of the Nine Worthies begins, a central theatrical concern, essential to performance of the scene in the Theatre, would be the location of the various characters on stage. Let us assume, first, that the "Worthies" play center stage, presumably in front of the canopy on the downstage *platea*. Then the placement of the lords and ladies, one assumes in pairs,[8] about the stage, perhaps sitting on royal "seats" or cushions, creates the on-stage audience. Several options would pertain here. The nine spectators (including Boyet) might sit far downstage center, grouped tightly together, or they might sit behind the center stage area, under the canopy. They might also sit in different parts, or corners, of the stage, perhaps each couple going to that part of the stage where the man in the couple tried to hide himself in 4.3. Certainly any of these possible arrangements could have been chosen, perhaps collaboratively, with little rehearsal, but my point is that the dramatic impact of this scene for spectators at the Theatre would partly depend on how this inner play is blocked (i.e., how in Shakespeare's imaginative conception of this scene he envisioned it conveying meaning for his spectators).

Given the presence of royalty in this scene, the King of Navarre and the Princess of France, let us assume first that they and their lords and ladies would have sat upstage under the Theatre's canopy, thus assuming a sense of royalty here in the *locus* of Navarre's park. When the pageant is played before them, its actors, Armado, Costard, Nathaniel, and Holofernes, would then have attempted their impersonations downstage center, in the unlocalized *platea,* closest to that portion of the Theatre's audience in the yard and directly facing the front of the stage. In this arrangement, the bumbling efforts of the four "actors" would have been clear to theater spectators and certainly would have provoked, as they do in any production, great laughter at the actors' pathetic attempts. This staging would also suggest a seminal dramatic point about the pageant: that as it is being "played" in the stage space where probably the four lords "played" their own puerile "pageant," they realize that as the Worthies parade before them they are watching images of their own Muscovite ineptitude. This realization by theater spectators of the pageant's mirroring effect on the four lords is crucial to the scene's *theatrical* meaning (i.e., its "Dramaturgy of the Spectator"[9] in an Elizabethan performance).

Consider now what transpires during the pageant and recall Emrys Jones's assertion (Introduction, 20) that in Shakespeare's symbolic mode of drama all details, both visual and aural, aspire toward meaning. The actors playing the Nine Worthies do not get very far into their entertainment; Costard appears as Pompey, Nathaniel as Alexander, Holofernes for Judas and Mote for Hercules, and then, about 80 lines after the pageant begins, Armado appears as Hector. At line 669, 126 lines after the pageant begins, Costard, as "Pompey," reveals that Jaquenetta is pregnant by "Hector": "The party is gone. Fellow Hector, she is gone! / She is two months on her way" (5.2.669–70). The pageant suddenly collapses as Armado challenges Costard and Dumaine sarcastically calls for "Room for the incensed Worthies!" (5.2.694). During this brief pageant, the baiting of the "actors" by the young men becomes rather cruel. Berowne, who had realized that Boyet had detected their Muscovite "entertainment" earlier and revealed it to the ladies, leading to the women being masked and thus completely frustrating the men's conciliatory and romantic intentions, now joins Boyet in mocking first Costard as Pompey and then Nathaniel as Alexander; he then interrupts Nathaniel by calling to Costard as Pompey and telling him to "Take away the conqueror. Take away Alisander" (5.2.569–70). Costard dismisses Nathaniel, and then remarks that while as Alexander Nathaniel is a "little o'erparted" (5.2.580–81), he is nonetheless a "marvelous good neighbor, faith, and a very good bowler" (5.2.578–79). When Holofernes enters as Judas and Mote for Hercules, the young lords engage in petty wordplay that becomes cynical, if not brutal:

| | |
|---|---|
| *Holofernes.* | I will not be put out of countenance. |
| *Berowne.* | Because thou hast no face. |
| *Holofernes.* | [pointing to his face] What is this? |
| *Boyet.* | A citternhead. |
| *Dumaine.* | The head of a bodkin. |
| *Berowne.* | A death's face in a ring. |
| *Longaville.* | The face of an old Roman coin, scarce seen. |
| *Boyet.* | The pommel of Caesar's falchion. |
| *Dumaine.* | The carved-bone face on a flask. |
| *Berowne.* | Saint George's half-cheek in a brooch. |
| *Dumaine.* | Ay, and in a brooch of lead. |
| *Berowne.* | Ay, and worn in the cap of a tooth drawer. And now forward, for we have put thee in countenance. |
| *Holofernes.* | You have put me out of countenance. |

(5.2.603–16).

After several more lines of this, Holofernes speaks the most poignant line of all the actors in this pathetic and humiliated pageant: "This is not generous, not gentle, not humble" (5.2.626). After Boyet mockingly calls for a light to help Judas off the stage, the Princess remarks: "Alas, poor Maccabaeus, how hath he been baited!" (5.2.628). Armado then enters as Hector, is also ridiculed by the men, and during his presentation seeks patience and understanding: "Sweet Lord Longaville, rein thy tongue"; "The sweet warman is dead and rotten. Sweet chucks, beat not the bones of the buried" (5.2.655, 659–60).

During performance spectators' reaction to this mocking may be far more complex than might appear from the script on the page. The Nine Worthies may be absolutely hysterical in production, and the lords' mocking may be underplayed and hardly heard. One might also conclude that this mocking is deserved; after all, these are ludicrous pedants and country simpletons trying to impersonate famous men. So what other reaction would one expect from literate courtiers, especially egotistical literate courtiers such as Berowne et al. who themselves have recently been utterly humiliated by their witless masking and laborious love games? Labors lost, indeed. So, revenge is sweet, and after all the men are trying to impress the ladies with their ingenuity, and, being young and foolish, they get carried away and stumble into a game of baiting as earlier they stumbled into a game of masking. That one did not work; let us try another. Observing the "place" of their own "play," they wish now to appear superior to a kind of playing in which earlier they failed miserably. One might also stage this scene less uproariously, so that the poignancy latent in Holofernes's and Armado's complaints against the lords is more noticeable.

Consider here John Russell Brown's insight into Shakespeare's theatrical use of the inner play:

> In his developed use of the play-within-the-play, Shakespeare seems to suggest that for dramatic illusion to be complete, the amateur actor must have the imagination to be convinced of the "truth" of his role, and the audience must have the imagination to amend his "shadow." In the comedies, he used the ideal amateur actor as an image of the ideal lover whose every action should perfectly express his imagination, should be a "true" response to his complex, irrational, and compelling vision of the beloved's beauty. And a man's ability to accept a dramatic illusion performed by others was used by Shakespeare to show the nature of the onlooker's imagination, to show the quality of his inward nature.[10]

We do not know, and cannot ever know, exactly how The Chamberlain's Men staged this scene; *LLL* is a script, and thus open, as all scripts are, to unlimited performance options. But one notices here that the women do not engage in the cruel mockery of the amateur actors and that, indeed, they try to mollify them. The Princess, at line 628, pities how Holofernes as Maccabaeus is baited, and after Armado pleads with the men not to mock the bones of the buried, she says, "Speak, brave Hector. We are much delighted" (5.2.664). Why this difference in attitudes between the men and women, and how important would these differences be to spectators' experience of this scene in the Theatre? What kind of theatrical meaning emerges if, as I suggested, Shakespeare's company places the royal party in the upstage *locus* and the amateur actors in the downstage *platea*? I would argue that this staging would have made more prominent, at least aurally, the actors' complaints about the men in their on-stage audience, whose imaginations appear sorely deficient in that capacity for wonder and amendment that the actors, however pathetic their efforts, realize is necessary for even the simplest level of dramatic illusion to occur.[11] In the Theatre spectators' experience of this pageant is thus mediated by on-stage viewers who sharply disagree on the theatrical value of what they see. The disparities among the masculine and feminine responses to the pageant, which emanate from within the stage itself and may, in turn, affect differently various portions of the Theatre's spectators, compound the spectators' different perspectives from various locations within the playhouse, emphasize the various possible effects of the pageant itself on spectators, and stress that both sympathy and ridicule are incomplete reactions to this scene. Sitting in the Theatre, spectators see and hear on the stage itself conflicting reactions to this pageant that mirror and echo their own mixed responses. Indeed, the incompleteness of any one mediated response to the pageant may have been even more emphasized by a second possible staging of this scene. If the actors are upstage, and the royal party downstage, perhaps ringing the outer edge of the platform, as Styan suggests for 4.3, then the reaction to the pageant of those spectators centrally placed in the Theatre is apt to be more influenced by what the men in the on-stage audience say about Armado and his "company." Further, depending on where Berowne and Boyet especially are placed, perhaps far downstage left and/or right, that portion of the audience closest to either or both of them may be more responsive to their jibes at the poor actors than other spectators more distant from them in other parts of the playhouse. But regardless of the Theatre spectators' locations, their reactions to the pageant are mediated by the on-stage audience; and, regardless of the extent of this mediation, theirs are equally incomplete reactions to the poor pageant played before them.

My argument then is that the script of this scene of *LLL* allows for significantly different stagings on the large thrust stage of the Theatre, and that these options would create generally different spectator reactions.[12] Although all scripts are always "open" to different interpretations and stagings, this inner play staged at the Theatre or later at the Globe could readily create among a large portion of its spectators, as part of its theatrical meaning *during performance,* Shakespeare's sense that generousness, gentleness, and humility among spectators, qualities that Holofernes says are lacking in the lords' criticism of the amateur

Worthies, are absolutely essential to theatrical enterprises. If this scene were staged with the Worthies acting downstage, and the royal party upstage, theater spectators could more readily judge for themselves both the sincerity of the bumbling actors' efforts and the maturity and quality of the young men's imagination as expressed in their harsh criticism of the actors and as later they desperately beg for the women's love after Marcade's sudden announcement of the French King's death. Brown's analysis of Shakespeare's use of the inner play as a measure of the quality of one's imagination, and thus of one's capacity and readiness for love, is astute; and it suggests that a staging of the Nine Worthies at the Theatre or the Globe that stressed this point seems highly plausible. Shakespeare's imaginative conception of this scene, which inculcates multiple perspectives, some gentle, many cruel, on the internal theatrical action of the pageant, would seem to demand a staging that would have maximized the relevance of the on-stage spectators' various reactions to those of the theater spectators themselves and also would have emphasized visually and aurally that no one set of responses to theatrical performance, neither sympathy nor mockery, is ever complete.

When Marcade suddenly usurps the merriment, the Princess responds immediately: "Boyet, prepare. I will away tonight" (5.2.723). The *locus* of the play, only a moment before an enchanted park for idle pastimes, is suddenly a place of death. The Princess grasps the urgency of her returning home, while the King can only utter more "taffeta phrases" about "the extreme parts of time," and Berowne's "honest plain words" become hyperbolic Petrarchan conceits about ladies' eyes even as he admits to the courtiers' having "neglected time" and played "foul" with their oaths.[13] The foolishness of the young men's vow to study exclusively and to neglect all emotional and physical needs is vastly compounded by the suddenness of their requests for affection; all has been received, the Princess insists, as "bombast and as lining to the time" (5.2.777), for "The latest minute of the hour" is a time "too short / To make a world-without-end bargain in" (5.2.784, 786–87). Certainly the women are justified in sending these capricious young men to places far removed both physically and emotionally from the court of Navarre, and part of their reasons originate in the men's puerile mockery of the Nine Worthies. A staging of this scene on the thrust stage that elicits some sympathy for the amateur actors and emphasizes the courtiers' blindness to their sincere efforts reinforces the women's sound judgment in sending their "wooers" to hospitals and hermitages where they must try to humor people, such as Costard, Mote, and Nathaniel, who have become the "pained impotent."

*LLL* ends in verbal and visual dichotomies. Standing downstage center on the *platea,* which formerly was a "place" of youthful and inept "playing," Armado's final words suddenly transcend the dramatic illusion and directly address the Theatre spectators. His lines introducing the "dialogue" of winter and spring, "This side is Hiems, Winter, this Ver, the Spring; the / one maintained by the owl, th' other by the cuckoo" (5.2.881–82), indicate two divided groups of performers on the stage, and the explicit seasonal differences of the two songs, "daisies pied and violets blue" versus "icicles [that] hang by the wall" emphasize the gap that divides the apparently innocent beginning of the men's initial vow and its unexpectedly harsh conclusion. The owl's winter message stresses cold and death, harsh inevitabilities that the men of Navarre must concede before they can appreciate that the time for love in one's life is far too precious for "Figures pedantical" (5.2.409) and silly games. Armado's dismissal of the play and its dual (on and off-stage) audiences, "The words of Mercury are harsh after the / songs of Apollo. You that way; we this way" (5.2.918–19) further divides all those in the Theatre. As the actors presenting spring and winter apparently leave through separate stage doors, thus symbolizing the significant seasonal differences, so also must all the actors and the spectators exit differently, the actors through the stage doors, the spectators back through the theater doors from whence they entered. In this drama, which "doth not end like an old play" (5.2.864), while the actors simply disappear behind the theater's facade, the spectators must reenter the actual dichotomies of summer's cuckoo, which mocks married men, and winter's cold, which freezes blood and milk, dual symbols of human vitality and growth.

As in *LLL,* so in *A Midsummer Night's Dream* Shakespeare creates several scenes of "multiple-centered interest."[14] The sequence from 3.2, opening with Oberon and Puck, then progressing through the four lovers and their threatening quarrels with their real and false lovers and their same-sex rivals; their conveniently falling asleep next to their true lovers; the entrance of Bottom and Titania; the Fairie Queen's protestations of love for the "translated" weaver; their sleep and then the entrance of Puck and, finally, Oberon to release his queen just before Theseus and his train enter the stage together create a scene of multiple, yet simultaneous levels of meaning in which "all the lovers are caught within the same magic."[15] Spectators must assimilate the analogies among these groups both visually and aurally, and as Styan shows in his hypothetical blocking for this scene,[16] on the thrust stage of the Theatre all segments of this "pattern" would have been visible, and the size of the stage would have facilitated the dramatizing of these thematically linked scenes to enable spectators to grasp the emotionally similar predicaments among the various groups of characters.

Philip C. McGuire has written eloquently about the "silences" of Hippolyta and Egeus in 1.1 and 4.1 of *Dream:* Hippolyta is silent during Theseus' stern invoking of the law and warning to Hermia about disobeying her father's marital wishes for her, and Egeus in 4.1 does not respond when Theseus suddenly overrules the law and grants Hermia her wish to marry Lysander.[17] I wish to examine here another silence in *Dream,* that of Hermia and Helena during all of act 5, especially during the inner play of Pyramus and Thisbe. The four lovers enter at line 27, and from that moment on the two women do not speak for the rest of the play. Why did Shakespeare choose to silence these young, and, as revealed by their hasty flight to the forest, feisty and determined women? Given their husbands' reactions to the inner play, this silence seems surprising; like the silence of the four women (except for the Princess's two short lines) during the pageant in 5.2 of *LLL,* Helena's and Hermia's silence here raises fascinating questions about theatrical meaning and its relation to staging of this scene at the Theatre/Globe.

I begin with a fundamental question about the grouping of characters, the on-stage audience and the mechanicals, on the thrust stage. Let us assume that here, as in the pageant of the Worthies in *LLL,* the inner play was staged on the downstage *platea,* that stage area that Weimann characterizes as "*representing* . . . the work, the space, the language of dramatic composition, and theatrical production itself."[18] Then presumably the court audience, Theseus and Hippolyta and the four lovers, all (apparently) like Oberon and Titania since 4.1.86 "new in amity," would be further upstage, presumably near or under the canopy that here might symbolize and localize Theseus's palace. In this arrangement one assumes that Theseus and Hippolyta would sit center stage, certainly together, and the two couples would be arranged perhaps on their left and right, in full view of the theater audience. A second choice would be to reverse this arrangement, with Theseus and his "court" arranged downstage[19] and the inner play then played further upstage. Although there might initially seem little difference between these two blocking arrangements, I suggest that a scrutiny of Shakespeare's script for 5.1, including the silences of Hermia and Helena, indicates that he has considered the shape of his stage in the design of this scene.

Theater spectators have seen a rehearsal of the "tedious brief scene" of Pyramus and Thisbe in the woods outside Athens, and so know that the actors are inept, and that despite Bottom and company's great enthusiasm when he tells them that their play is "preferred," the inner play will probably be desultory. Shakespeare's inclusion of this scene in a relatively early play suggests some of the rehearsal practices common among Elizabethan companies, including the learning of the actors' "parts," and the work of the "book man" who, like Peter Quince the carpenter, must "build" a performance by organizing rehearsals and insisting that actors learn their cues, entrances and exits, and wear appropriate apparel. Quince and his company are clearly inept, and their "production" chaotic and unconvincing; yet even by 1594–96, the probable dates of *Dream* and *LLL*, Shakespeare's plays were far too complex dramatically for us to assume that the rehearsal process in *Dream* is simply being mocked by Shakespeare's using such "rude mechanicals" as examples of the actor's craft.[20] Possibly already familiar by 1594–96 with several of Shakespeare's plays at the Theatre, spectators would not dismiss as irrelevant the "rehearsal" of an inner play; rather, they would expect what indeed we find, an inner play intricately related to the outer play's dramatic structure—and, I would add, to Hermia's and Helena's silence.

As in *LLL,* so in *Dream,* most comments about the inner play are made by the young men, and even more prominently than in *LLL,* the inner play in *Dream* evokes considerably different reactions, which is one of Shakespeare's major dramatic points in the Pyramus and Thisbe playlet. In this early play, like *LLL* probably written fairly soon after the formation of The Chamberlain's Men and a return to playing at the Theatre, Shakespeare dramatizes the inevitability of mixed, inconsistent responses to his plays. Although Puck's epilogue is assumed to be Shakespeare's effort to elicit a unified (and agreeable) response from his spectators, Puck's request for "pardon" suggests Shakespeare's realization that his plays, regardless of their setting and audience composition, may not universally please, and

thus the actors may indeed wish for "restoration" after a performance: "Give me your hands, *if* we be friends, / And Robin will
restore amends" (5.1.432–33; emphasis added).

The "tangled chain" of Peter Quince's "disordered" prologue
immediately initiates criticism. Lysander says Quince has "rid
his prologue like a rough colt," and Hippolyta says he "hath
played on his prologue like / a child on a recorder: a sound, but
not in government" (5.1.119, 122–23). After Quince completes
his prologue, Theseus wonders "if the lion be to speak," and
Demetrius answers "No wonder, my lord. One lion may, / when
many asses do" (lines 151–52). Demetrius says that Wall is "the
wittiest partition that ever I heard discourse" (line 166); after
Pyramus and Thisbe have exchanged their initial vows through
the "chink" in Wall, Demetrius remarks that Wall was "willful to
hear without warning" (line 208). Hippolyta then complains that
"This is the silliest stuff that ever I heard," and Theseus responds
with the most critical lines from the inner play's on-stage audience: "The best in this kind are but shadows; and the / worst are
no worse, if imagination amend them" (lines 209–11). Theseus
evokes the great power of the imagination to mend even the
most humble of human enterprises—even, it seems, men and
women themselves:

> *Hippolyta.*   It must be your imagination then, and not / theirs.
> *Theseus.*      If we imagine no worse of them than they of them-
>                 selves, they may pass for excellent men.
>
> (5.1.212–14)

As during the Nine Worthies pageant in *LLL,* Shakespeare here
again explicitly links the power of the onlooker's theatrical
imagination, his ability to accept charitably the illusion performed before him, with the "quality of his inward nature."[21]
Theseus's willingness, however temporarily, to suspend disbelief, to accept the inherently honest if wholly unconvincing effort of these patent amateurs to "labor in their minds," is an
index of the power of his imagination to accept and, if necessary
as the play demands, amend the effort and thus accept it for
what it is, even as one realizes that it can be no other than what
it now is. Analogically, love demands that one must accept the
nature of the beloved, imperfect as she or he always is. This
acceptance, this realization, is vital to the analogy Shakespeare
is developing here, as in *LLL,* with his portrayal of an on-stage
audience, and is especially so in *Dream* because it comes from

a man who has wooed and won his spouse with his sword, "doing [her] injuries."

The responses of the on-stage spectators vary, and as in *LLL,* they cannot refrain from commenting constantly on the inner play. After Lion and Moonshine enter, the men's own wittiness, again as in *LLL,* usurps their attention to the "play":

| | |
|---|---|
| *Theseus.* | A very gentle beast, and of a good conscience. |
| *Demetrius.* | The very best at a beast, my lord, that e'er I saw. |
| *Lysander.* | The lion is a very fox for his valor. |
| *Theseus.* | True; and a goose for his discretion. |
| *Demetrius.* | Not so, my lord, for his valor cannot carry / his discretion, and the fox carries the goose. |
| *Theseus.* | His discretion, I am sure, cannot carry his / valor; for the goose carries not the fox. It is well. Leave it to his discretion, and let us listen to the moon. |
| *Moon.* | This lanthorn doth the hornèd moon present— |
| *Demetrius.* | He should have worn the horns on his / head. |

(5.1.225–37)

Later in the inner play, as Bottom playing Pyramus finds the mantle of his "dainty duck" Thisbe "stained with blood," and dies repeatedly—"Thus die I, thus, thus, thus" (5.1.296), the men do not realize the potential relevance of Pyramus's admittedly hysterical mock death to what they have experienced the previous night in the Athenian woods:

| | |
|---|---|
| *Demetrius.* | No die, but an ace, for him; for he is / but one. |
| *Lysander.* | Less than an ace, man; for he is dead, he is / nothing. |
| *Theseus.* | With the help of a surgeon he might yet / recover, and yet prove an ass. |

(5.1.303–8)

Yet Theseus closes the "revels" by insisting that the play "needs no excuse," and that it was "very notably discharged" (5.1.351–52, 356). It was, after all, presented by men who never before labored, or "played" in such fashion, and they thus deserve commendation for their effort. The lovers await their own sexual festivities, and can perhaps be excused for thinking this "play" tiresome. But like their counterparts in *LLL,* Lysander and Demetrius fail to grant charity to the amateur entertainers, and as in *LLL,* this failure is dramatized in an explicitly theatrical metaphor: the imagination of the men is unable to amend, and thus to appreciate and accept for what it is, the theatrical enterprise they have just witnessed. Furthermore, the young men fail completely to "see" the relevance of this "tragic" love story to their own experiences in the Athenian woods (i.e., to their recent "dream" of love). There love was also fragile, frightening, potentially violent, and nearly deadly; within the dramatic structure of their "dream," love's power and its effects were also at times completely beyond their control. Like Pyramus and Thisbe, the four lovers also fled to a remote "place," and in an Elizabethan theater this place in the inner play, "Ninus' tomb," would also have been the woods outside Athens, the same "place" on the downstage *platea* where the lovers chaotically pursued their own psychologically disturbing and confusing passions. Demetrius and Lysander exhibit their unimaginative and unforgiving response to the "playing" of roles that love often requires, and blindly ignore in Pyramus and Thisbe farcical, shadowy analogues of their own anguished journey through Athens's scary forests.

I return now to the actual staging of this scene at the Theatre and to Hermia's and Helena's silence in 5.1. If, as I suggested initially, the inner play were acted on the downstage center *platea,* the "place" of the lovers' dream, with the on-stage spectators seated perhaps in a semicircle in the upstage *locus* of Theseus's court, then the playlet would be staged prominently in full view of the playhouse audience. In this staging, assuming, as happens in nearly all modern productions, that "Pyramus & Thisbe" were played for high comedy, the ludicrousness of the whole performance would be dramatically emphasized and its humor unequivocally clear to playhouse spectators. Equally unequivocal in this staging, however comical its presentation, would be the fact of death-in-love, which would certainly suggest to theater spectators the near violence among the four lovers in the woods and the death in childbirth of the changeling child's mother. Theater spectators would see downstage center a comic version of the proximity of death to human passion, which Demetrius and Lysander seem not to grasp.

And what of Hermia's and Helena's silence in 5.1? The convincingness of the two young couples' relationships is, in production, a director's (and perhaps actors') choice. Similar choices and options would have been open to, and decided by, Shakespeare's players; as we know from the title page of the 1600 Quarto, the play was "Sundry times publickely acted." As McGuire reminds us, "Hamlet's emphasis is on *playing,* on performing a play rather than writing one, and it is, he says, the process of playing that makes it possible for a play to illuminate the world within which it is performed."[22] Certainly when they awake from their "dreams" in 4.1, the men protest "amazedly" their love for their proper partners, and denounce, as Demetrius says, the "sickness" of their former, ill-directed passions.[23] But as best we understand them and this play demonstrates, dreams are by their nature complex and protean, and often impossibly intermingled with what we take to be "reality":

| | |
|---|---|
| *Demetrius.* | These things seem small and undistinguishable, Like far-off mountains turnèd into clouds. |
| *Hermia.* | Methinks I see these things with parted eye, When everything seems double. |
| *Helena.* | So methinks; And I have found Demetrius like a jewel, Mine own, and not mine own. |
| *Demetrius.* | Are you sure That we are awake? It seems to me That yet we sleep, we dream. Do not you think The Duke was here, and bid us follow him? |
| *Hermia.* | Yea, and my father. |
| *Helena.* | And Hippolyta. |
| *Lysander.* | And he did bid us follow to the temple. |
| *Demetrius.* | Why, then, we are awake. Let's follow him, And by the way let us recount our dreams. |

(4.1.186–98)

The extent of this "dissolving" of the lovers' past identities and the composition of their awakened selves are incompletely defined by the end of the play. As the contents and shapes of dreams remain, as Demetrius insists, undistinguishable, so the script of this midsummer night's dream remains open, to be completed only in its playing. In its playing, Hermia and Helena react differently to the comical-tragical "Pyramus and Thisbe" than Lysander and Demetrius do. The women's silence may signal their grasp of the strange parallels between their own vexing and dangerous journeys through the Athenian woods and the sequence of Pyramus's and Thisbe's fatal love. As the four lovers ventured forth in innocence and youthful passion only to encounter frightening confusions, so the "fearful lovers" Pyramus and Thisbe, who must "whisper often, very secretly" through the wall which "stand'st between her father's ground" and Pyramus, venture to "Ninus' tomb" to seek love and instead find violent death. Perhaps also, the women recall Egeus's "I beg the law, the law, upon his [Lysander's] head" (4.1.154) when with Theseus he spied the four lovers in the forest and still insisted that his daughter marry Demetrius. Only Theseus's overbearing of Egeus's will saves the lovers, and apparently this fact, and the near violence among the four in the woods, especially Lysander's sudden turning on Hermia and Demetrius's threat to Helena of sexual violence, have passed completely from the men's memories. The women's silence may poignantly question whether their husbands have learned anything about human fallibility and whether they possess the compassion and sympathy for others that love demands. The men's sensitivity and openness, a suspension of disbelief, about their recounted dreams in 4.1 before Theseus, is not heard in their responses to the earnest, if unconvincing, actors. As Theseus remarks, the less the mechanicals' skill, the more sympathy they deserve.

All the world is a stage. If played on the downstage *platea,* the dramatic prominence of this entire scene, including the inner play and the vastly different reactions of the on-stage spectators, stresses its relevance to not only the six lovers but also to theater spectators themselves who see reflected in the lovers and in Pyramus and Thisbe varying images of the chaos often latent in human passion. When Puck begins his epilogue, "If we shadows have offended, / Think but this, and all is mended, / That you have but slumbered here / While these visions did appear" (5.3.418–21), one suspects that Shakespeare acknowledges that the "offense" in his play may have been some of the frightening images of love and passion his actors have dramatized. All of *A Midsummer Night's Dream,* from its abusive, patriarchal law to its maddening dreams and magical blessings, is part of the totality that, depending on one's imaginative grasp of the full complexity of human love, one may indeed find somewhat or partially offensive. James Calderwood asserts that "A major kind of knowledge made available to its audience by *A Midsummer Night's Dream* is that of the inner forms and impulses of the human mind itself—the tricks and shaping fantasies of strong imagination and the forces directing it but also the range and limits of cool reason."[24] Shakespeare distances the final "tragedy" of Pyramus and Thisbe by its rough humor, just as the temporary madness and bewildering journeys of the four lovers are distanced somewhat by being so obviously the "play" of Oberon and Puck.[25] Although Puck's epilogue may invite one to dismiss the lovers' ordeals as mere dreams—or, if one prefers, night-mares—the theatrical image of on-stage spectators watching en-actments of love's potentially tragic obsessions and reacting so variously to them emphasizes the limits of "cool reason" to dis-miss these events as but such stuff as dreams are made on. Just as Lysander and Demetrius—and, indeed, all the lovers on stage—risk minimizing the unruly complexity of love's demands by ridiculing and dismissing the Pyramus and Thisbe story, so theater spectators risk minimizing the full complexity of their emotional lives by failing to integrate into their vision of love all of the "dream" they have seen in this play.

As with *LLL,* so here with *Dream* one can inquire about differ-ent stagings of 5.1. The other major choice would be, as with the Nine Worthies in *LLL,* to place the mechanicals' play further upstage and the on-stage audience more downstage, perhaps ar-ranged about the outer perimeter of the platform stage. Watkins and Lemmon, for example, envision the whole court sitting "in a ring around the perimeter of the Stage, with their backs to us."[26] In this staging, the remarks of the Pyramus and Thisbe on-stage audience, especially Lysander and Demetrius, might seem more prominent, and perhaps, as with the onstage audience in *LLL,* might be more apt to influence theater spectators' views of the relevance of the playlet to human love affairs. What might also be more prominent in this blocking would be theater spec-tators' awareness, as in a similar staging of *LLL,* of the young men's immature judgment of the amateur actors, and this stag-ing might also emphasize more clearly Brown's point about Shakespeare's using the on-stage spectators' inability to "amend" amateur actors as indicating their limited imaginative openness to love. This staging was certainly an option for Shakespeare's company and, indeed, on any one day may have been used. Be-cause of our limited knowledge of Elizabethan acting companies' actual day-to-day practice in their theaters, we can only specu-late about stagings and their possible theatrical effectiveness. What I perceive to be Shakespeare's intent in including the "tedi-ous brief scene" in 5.1 of *Dream* suggests to me that "Pyramus & Thisbe" would have played out their lamentable tragedy on the downstage *platea,* the "place" of the lovers' dream, thus em-phasizing the inner play's comic analogue to the lovers' romantic journeys and more openly inviting theater spectators to judge for themselves its possible relevance to their own romantic lives. This staging would also emphasize the prominent difference be-tween Lysander's and Demetrius's ridicule of the actors and the paradoxical silence with which Hermia and Helena view the brief playlet. With the lovers' backs to most of the Theatre's spectators, as Watkins and Lemmon propose, much of the boy actors' ability to communicate visually the women's enigmatic responses would be severely limited, as would be spectators' ability to see and thus judge these responses; the women's visual reactions, along with their unexplained silence, seem to me as important to theater spectators' grasp of the full complexity of this scene *during performance* as their hearing and seeing the young men's baiting of Peter Quince's company.

In both *LLL* and *A Midsummer Night's Dream,* Shakespeare creates on-stage spectators whose responses to an internal play vary significantly. He thus creates within his scripts internal, metatheatrical images of what he knew occurred among his public theater patrons. The "action" of these internal plays is slight and uncomplicated, and although certainly immensely entertaining, neither seriously taxes theater spectators' emotions or attention spans. However, Shakespeare has created moments in which spectators' responses to stage action is mediated by on-stage spectators whose varied reactions are instrumental in producing similarly varied responses among the theater audience. These complex dramatic moments rely, in part, on the actual shape of the playhouse stage and the intimacy between stage and spectators that the thrust stage created during performance. In *The Merchant of Venice,* written two to three years after *Dream,* Shakespeare deliberately focuses this potential for spectators' diverse and intimate reactions on the character of Shylock, especially in the trial scene of 4.1. In the dramatization of this scene at the Theatre, the shape of the stage and its potential as an element in the creation of complex dramatic meanings during performance become essential components of Shakespeare's *theatrical* art.

# 4

## Shylock, Antonio, and *The Merchant of Venice* in Performance

Norman Rabkin's challenge to Shakespeare criticism (cf. Introduction, p. 15) to "consider the play as a dynamic interaction between artist and audience, to learn to talk about the process of our involvement rather than our considered view after the aesthetic event"[1] is central to my discussion of *The Merchant of Venice*. Rabkin especially laments the attempt by Shakespeare scholars, many of whose essays he critiques, to reduce to "patterns" of meaning the many complexities of *The Merchant of Venice*. Indeed, Rabkin argues that the term "meaning" is itself suspect when applied to a play: "The eddying signals communicated by a play arouse a total and complex involvement of our intellect, our moral sensibility, our need to complete incomplete patterns and answer questions, our longing to judge, and that involvement is so incessantly in motion that to pin it down to a 'meaning' is to negate its very essence."[2] Rabkin believes that critical readings "of similar methodology and equal brilliance" so often produce radically different conclusions because critics have greatly overvalued "reductiveness": "We have been betrayed by a bias toward what can be set out in rational argument."[3] All "critical essays" about a play are the product of contemplative study, and are divorced from the actual live, spontaneous experience of the play in a theater. Even "performance criticism," a type of which I am trying to write in these essays, is essentially criticism written from performance perspectives, or with performance "in mind," while staring at words on a page. As Homer Swander asserts, the Shakespeare "industry" errs in perceiving Shakespeare because it errs in perceiving drama as literature.[4]

Given the difficulty of writing about the "aesthetic event" of a modern production of a Shakespearean play, any attempt to describe the "actual experience" of a play in a theater that no longer exists is immensely difficult—indeed, perhaps impossible. We cannot know with any certainty what kinds of audience reactions any one production of *Merchant* created on any one day at the Theatre. What one can do, however, as Stanley Cavell asserts, is recognize that the artist is someone who ultimately is responsible for what happens in his work, and that our responsibility as audiences and critics is to appreciate as fully as possible what the artist has given us.[5] A dramatist's art is mediated through the production that animates it, and in theaters today each staging of a play is subject to the "vision" of directors, actors, set designers, lighting directors, and costume makers. When considering production of a Shakespearean play from ca. 1598 to 1600, when a Quarto edition of *Merchant* appeared, stating that by then the play "hath beene diuers times acted by the Lord / Chamberlaine his Seruants,"[6] presumably at the Theatre/Globe, one must first imagine the play in its initial theatrical setting and from there attempt to imagine, however imperfectly, what kinds of effects it might have had on its contemporary audiences. Although one cannot know definitely what these effects were, in the study of Shakespeare's developing sense of his stage and theater as elements in creating dramatic meanings during performance the script of *The Merchant of Venice* becomes crucial.

In this chapter, I will focus on Shakespeare's structuring of the theatrical energies that develop from Shylock's and Antonio's characters and radically different social positions and show how these cumulative energies create dramatic meaning during the trial scene when staged on the Theatre's thrust stage. Modern critical insights into the play can assist us somewhat in this investigation but must not be confused with presumed sentiments about the play's "meaning" among Elizabethan spectators. Although one can never recover the play's actual reception at any one Elizabethan performance in any one playhouse, one can nonetheless examine the script to see Shakespeare's skill at maximizing the dramatic effects of the multiple perspectives his stage created in the public theaters. My point is not just that conflict is essential to all drama; what matters is the kind of conflict Shakespeare has built into this play for the stage of the Theatre (and soon the Globe) at this point in his play-writing career.

Patrick Stewart observes that "there is ambivalence in every corner of [*Merchant*]";[7] regarding Shylock, whom he played for the RSC in John Barton's 1978 production, Stewart writes:

Shylock and his kind are outsiders, strangers, feared and hated for being different. They belong to the world's minorities. They are, as the laws of Venice state, alien, stamped by that world to be always vulnerable and at risk; therefore survival is paramount. . . . Shylock . . . has found a way of merging with his surroundings, shabby and unmemorable, and, if he attracts attention at all, appearing as an eccentric and harmless clown. Only Antonio, his competitor in business whose senses are sharpened by commerce, smells the contempt that hides behind Shylock's jokes.[8]

When Shylock walked onto the stage of the Theatre in 1.3, speaking initially of money, "Three thousand ducats, well" (1.3.1), he would have been perceived by Elizabethan audiences as an "outsider," a "minority," for both ethnic and spiritual reasons, evoking "a spiritual condition characterized by lack of faith and love."[9] M. M. Mahood adds that Elizabethan spectators would have regarded Shylock's soul as "already forfeit in so far as he, like his forbearers, refused to acknowledge the Christian Messiah."[10] Yet in Renaissance Venice Jews were certainly tolerated and allowed to function as moneylenders for state business, and apparently enjoyed some limited prosperity as well as protection under its law.[11] Thus, if Shylock would have been initially perceived as an "outsider" for ethnic and spiritual reasons by Shakespeare's audience, he also would have been seen as enjoying some social, legal, and monetary status in Venice.

In the initial meeting between Antonio and Shylock, instigated by Bassanio's quest for financial backing for Antonio's "credit," Antonio's and Shylock's mutual hatred is clearly evident. Shylock's hatred is vicious and devouring:

> I hate him for he is a Christian,
> But more for that in low simplicity
> He lends out money gratis and brings down
> The rate of usance here with us in Venice.
> If I can catch him once upon the hip,
> I will feed fat the ancient grudge I bear him.
> He hates our sacred nation, and he rails,
> Even there where merchants most do congregate,
> On me, my bargains, and my well-worn thrift,
> Which he calls interest. Cursed be my tribe
> If I forgive him!

(1.3.38–49)

Shylock's claim that Antonio hates, not just himself, but all Jews, seems justified. After Shylock's defense of usury, using the biblical story of Jacob and Laban which Antonio rejects as entirely specious,[12] Antonio is the first in the play to associate Shylock with hypocrisy and "the devil": "Mark you this, Bassanio, / The devil can cite Scripture for his purpose. . . . O, what a goodly outside falsehood hath" (1.3.95–96, 100). Shylock then accuses Antonio of continual vocal and physical abuse:

> Signor Antonio, many a time and oft
> In the Rialto you have rated me
> About my moneys and my usances.
> Still have I borne it with a patient shrug,
> For sufferance is the badge of all our tribe.
> You call me misbeliever, cutthroat dog,
> And spit upon my Jewish gaberdine,
> And all for use of that which is mine own.
>
> (1.3.104–11)

There is obvious hypocrisy in Shylock's self-characterization of his "patient shrug"; as he speaks, he is and has been seeking to "feed fat" his ancient grudge, the fulfillment of which he apparently sees as mandated by his Hebrew tribal identity. As Lawrence Danson argues, there is also "acting" in Shylock's persona of the "harmless dodderer" and cringing bondman, who, for "courtesies" such as Shylock enumerates, will "bend low" and "lend you thus much moneys."[13] Any suspicion that Shylock's claims against Antonio are unfounded is immediately shattered; Antonio's response is crucial for the entire play:

> I am as like to call thee so again,
> To spit on thee again, to spurn thee too.
> If thou wilt lend this money, lend it not
> As to thy friends, for when did friendship take
> A breed for barren metal of his friend?
> But lend it rather to thine enemy,
> Who, if he break, thou mayst with better face
> Exact the penalty.
>
> (1.3.128–35)

Shylock despises Antonio, and his enactment of the suffering "cur" who nonetheless lends money to his abuser is a ploy, born not of ennobling patience but of seething hatred. But as the title character of the play, the "Merchant" whose money, ships, and friendships are central to its design, Antonio is also represented as a man of hate who, despite his high standing among Venetian noblemen, is not above cursing and spitting upon the man whom all the Christians of the play, with the exception of Old Gobbo, revile and curse as the "devil." Shakespeare simply presents Antonio's loathing for Shylock as a given; Antonio has no explanation for his hatred, as Shylock has for his of Antonio. Indeed, Antonio's speech at lines 128–35 seems to support Shylock's claim, suggested broadly here and emphatically later in 3.1, that he is hated solely for being a Jew, for being, as Patrick Stewart observes, "different." Learned, reflective examinations of Antonio's actions later in the play will not do here; what Antonio does later in the trial is still three acts away. One must imagine the absolute dichotomy into which Shakespeare has split the stage, and recognize that neither Christian nor Jew has denied his hatred for the other. At this point in the play at the Theatre in 1598 one can imagine that spectators, presumably watching Antonio and Shylock spar from opposite sides (let us assume Shylock's "place" as stage left and Antonio's as stage right) of the downstage *platea,* may have identified with Antonio in believing "the Jew" a devil, and thus have agreed that Antonio's hatred and abuse were justified. Certainly Shylock's loathing for Antonio, and his express desire to "feed fat" his ancient grudge, would seem to justify that reaction. But if one is going to argue that Antonio is morally superior to Shylock in this play, and that Shakespeare elevates the Christian values that his audience at least nominally upheld, one must still acknowledge that the stage picture Shakespeare creates in their first meeting seethes with hate, and that Antonio's is less well motivated or "justified" than Shylock's. Ruth Nevo remarks that *The Merchant* actualizes the human harm and suffering that comedy exists to circumvent,[14] and in this early scene Shakespeare dramatizes a stage divided by racial and religious hatreds so totally inimical to the spirit of comedy as to be impervious to its solutions.

Except for a brief appearance as a messenger bearing news of Bassanio's sudden departure for Belmont in 2.6, Antonio is absent for all of act 2; in his place (i.e., in Antonio's "place" on stage from 1.3), Shakespeare further dramatizes the Christian community's collective attitudes toward Shylock and channels this evidence toward the play's climactic scene. After Morocco's entrance in Belmont to hazard his choice among the caskets, Shakespeare introduces Lancelot and Old Gobbo. Lancelot's clowning psychomachia was certainly meant to be humorous on the stage and is the kind of delicious moment that one might imagine Will Kempe "overdoing" so as to prompt Shakespeare's (via Hamlet's) complaints about irrepressible clowns several years later. Indeed, during Lancelot's clowning, there is "some necessary question of the play" being considered: like his Venetian betters, Lancelot, echoing Antonio himself from 1.3.96 and probably standing downstage in Antonio's *platea* location from 1.3, also sees Shylock as a "devil":

> To be ruled by my / conscience, I should stay with the Jew my master, / who, God bless the mark, is a kind of devil; and to / run away from the Jew, I should be ruled by the fiend, who, saving your reverence, is the devil himself.
>
> (2.2.20–24).

Later in the scene, after his father asks the way to "master Jew's," and tells Lancelot that he has a present[15] for Shylock, Lancelot describes Shylock as a stereotypical "Jew": "My master's a very Jew. Give / him a present? Give him a halter!" (2.2.100–101). Lancelot complains that he is "famished" in Shylock's service, a direct contradiction of Shylock's claim later in 2.5 that Lancelot, though "kind enough," is a "huge feeder." Despite, or perhaps because of, Lancelot's clowning in this comic scene, the general attitude of this Venetian society toward Shylock is emphasized; he has now been called a "devil" by Venice's most and least prominent citizen. Like Antonio's statement in 1.3 that he and Shylock are "enemies," this attitude toward Shylock is a "given" of the play's first two acts; rationalizations about how Shylock is shown mercy in the trial scene, if one perceives mercy there, are irrelevant to the *process* of watching this play in a theater. What we know of Shylock at this moment in act 2 is that he is considered a "devil" by members of several social strata in Venice. Given that there were few Jews in Elizabethan England, and that they had been exiled from England since 1290, one may correctly assume that at this point in a production of *Merchant* at the Theatre in 1598–99, most spectators might have shared Antonio's and Lancelot's belief that Jews were "devilish," or at least of the Devil's party, for the Hebrews' role in the death of Christ. If so, then Shakespeare has implicated his spectators in one of the racial attitudes that comprise the emotional complexity of this play in performance.

From 2.3 to 2.6, events accelerate: Bassanio has his money; a feast and masque are planned; Lorenzo hastily "steals" his Jewish princess; then suddenly the wind "come[s] about," and Bassanio and company depart. Amid this haste, which exemplifies the youthful energy and passion of the romance plot, other characters reinforce Antonio's diabolical view of Shylock even as his bond begins its "three months" (1.3.2) progress to maturity. In 2.3, Jessica laments to the ubiquitous Lancelot that her house is "hell," employs him as a messenger to Lorenzo, and in effect buys his complicity in her plot to leave her father: "There is a ducat for thee." Just as Jessica initiates her stratagem, she also laments her dishonoring of her filial bond, while simultaneously asserting that becoming a "Christian" will end her "strife." If Jessica speaks these lines standing in Shylock's "place" from 1.3, her downstage position on the *platea* further divides, or fractures, a stage already divided by racial and religious hate in 1.3:

> Alack, what heinous sin is it in me
> To be ashamed to be my father's child!
> But though I am a daughter to his blood,
> I am not to his manners. O Lorenzo,
> If thou keep promise, I shall end this strife,
> Become a Christian and thy loving wife.
>
> (2.3.16–21)

In 2.4 Lorenzo, after receiving Jessica's letter from Lancelot, speaks blandly of the "gold and jewels [Jessica] is furnished with"; in Shylock's house is a lady richly left! In the same speech, Lorenzo repeats the traditional spiritual superiority Christians claim over Jews:

> If e'er the Jew her father come to heaven,
> It will be for his gentle daughter's sake;
> And never dare misfortune cross her foot,
> Unless she do it under this excuse,
> That she is issue to a faithless Jew.
>
> (2.4.33–37)

Shylock's house is hell, and thus a Christian, while claiming spiritual superiority, can steal from him not only his daughter but also his ducats. Again, one might argue here that most of Shakespeare's spectators in 1598–99 would have enjoyed this stealth, the fairy-tale stealing of a captive beauty from the infidel's prison. But evident also in these secret and hasty endeavors is a singular lack of ethical reflection among the Christians. "Mark you this, Bassanio, / The devil can cite Scripture for his

purpose"; "My master's a very Jew. Give / him a present? Give
him a halter!" Jessica's eagerness to enter this community,
which she believes will redeem her "spiritually," exacerbates
spectators' responses to the initial racial and religious hatred
evident in 1.3.

The denigration of Shylock spreads among the play's Christians even as Shakespeare intensifies anti-Semitic stereotypes.
Staging at the Theatre/Globe would emphasize how irreparably
divided the play's society has now become. If during his dialogue
with Jessica in 2.5 Shylock occupies the "place" he held during
his initial talk with Antonio in 1.3, and Jessica stands in Antonio's "place" from 1.3, spectators see Shylock being further victimized by his own daughter who assumes Antonio's and the
Venetians' anti-Semitic "place" from within Shylock's own
household. Shylock is hateful, devouring, and almost ridiculously fixated on money:

> I am bid forth to supper, Jessica.
> There are my keys. But wherefore should I go?
> I am not bid for love—they flatter me—
> But yet I'll go in hate, to feed upon
> The prodigal Christian. Jessica, my girl,
> Look to my house. I am right loath to go.
> There is some ill a-brewing towards my rest,
> For I did dream of moneybags tonight.
>
>                                          (2.5.12–19)

In 1.3, Shylock voices his wish to "feed fat" his ancient grudge
against Antonio; here, as in popular medieval anti-Semitic leg-
ends, he again speaks of "devouring" Christian flesh.[16] For Shylock, even sharing a meal, a traditional image of community, is
occasioned by hate. As there are masques, Shylock orders Jessica to seal his house (i.e., his money bags, jewels, and ducats),
against merriment: "Hear you me, Jessica: . . . Let not the sound
of shallow foppery enter / My sober house" (2.5.29, 36–37). Shylock has "no music in himself," as Lorenzo says in 5.1, and is
thus antithetical to the now frantic merriment of the young
lovers, heralded by Gratiano's lines about the haste and risks of
prodigality.[17] As Portia's riches are certainly part of Bassanio's
interest in her, so Jessica's are part of Lorenzo's in her. In this
carnival haste, the "rescue" of the captive princess from the
upstage "tower" of the upper balcony, the symbolic *locus* of Venice proper from which she hurls her father's riches, which she
believes will purchase freedom, is genuinely comedic. Shake-

speare's audience, probably familiar with this Plautine plot-line, undoubtedly relished Jessica's liberation, as modern audiences certainly do. The difference in this plot, however, is Shylock's ducats. Jessica, in disguise, as if hiding what she is doing from herself, speaks of being "ashamed" twice (2.6.36, 42) and of wishing she were "obscured"; yet she willingly "gild[s]" herself with additional ducats, as if turning herself, her body, into gold. This is simply theft, albeit in comic guise, and Jessica's divided self symbolizes exactly the increasingly fragmented society and family now imaged in the stage action. If Shylock is but a "Jew," a miser, who dreams of money bags and hates Christians, then his ducats are there to steal for festive use. But even as Shakespeare concludes this romantic episode, he simultaneously prepares spectators for far greater ambiguity regarding Shylock. We do not know with what glee this scene was played by the Chamberlain's Men; we do not know how "stereotypically" Shylock was played on stage. But we do know, Mahood remarks, that because of the "faintly discordant elements" of Jessica's elopement "we never quite board the merry-go-round of festive comedy. . . . Instead, the lovers slip off into the night to be married"[18] and, as we soon hear, to buy monkeys. Even as he dramatizes the lovers' amorous flight from emotional and sexual repression, Shakespeare sustains before spectators the dual images of Shylock as a rapacious, sinister Jew who hates Christians partly because they are Christians; and as a man hated and bedeviled because of who, and what, he is—a Jew—who therefore deserves halters. He has made Jessica's life hellish in his house, and in response, Jessica and her lover take the means by which he lives. "O Lorenzo, / If thou keep promise, I shall end this strife, / Become a Christian and thy loving wife" (2.3.19–21). Jessica's initial act as member of this Christian community—indeed, the means *by which* she becomes a member of it—is stealing. The increasingly divided and fractured "space" of the Theatre/Globe stage from 2.3 to 2.6 superbly illustrates Rabkin's seminal point about the complexity of audience response to the *process* of attending this play.

2.8 ends this rush of activity. Salerio and Solanio speak of both Shylock and Antonio, thus keeping their parallel fates before the audience. One must not assume that they are absolutely reliable reporters, nor must we allow them to speak for all of Venice in their remarks about either Antonio or Shylock. Although they cruelly ridicule Shylock in 3.1, one must not assume that they are automatically more anti-Semitic than anyone else in Venice, nor that their affection for Antonio is necessarily misplaced or exaggerated.[19] Their function in 2.8 is clear: to emphasize the huge differences between Antonio and Shylock at this point in the play. Standing downstage, in the space used by both Antonio in 1.3 and Jessica in 2.6, Solanio recalls, perhaps cruelly mocking Shylock's voice or "stage accent" that the actor may have used, Shylock's "confused" passion about the loss of his daughter and his ducats. No earlier moment in the play crystallizes so fiercely Shylock's terrible ambiguity, and to "hear" this scene as only comic ridicule is to minimize its theatrical significance. Having Solanio report this scene, rather than having Shylock himself rant hysterically before spectators, emphasizes that at least one other person in Venice realizes that his passion is "strange, outrageous, and so variable" because he is an egregiously injured human being. Whatever failings Shakespeare has given Shylock, he has also given him the ability to feel pain, and this pain causes hideous confusion within Shylock about what he values. His daughter has fled with a Christian, with one from among those who call him, as Solanio does here, "the dog Jew," and even now his ducats have become "Christian!" Shylock cries, ironically, on "Justice! The law" as his only recourse, thus anticipating that which he thinks will satisfy him. One may argue that Solanio here is only parodying Shylock; indeed, Salerio's response suggests that for all the boys in Venice, the old man's despair is but a source of extemporaneous ridicule. (Apparently Jew baiting extends to the very young.) But I am convinced that we are to assume that Shylock is terribly distraught by the loss of *both* his daughter and his ducats, and that in the theater this narration of Shylock's intense pain from the stage place where Antonio cursed him and Jessica denounced him is meant to influence considerably spectators' reactions to him, especially during the trial of act 4.

Solanio and Salerio next speak of the wreck of a Venetian merchant ship in the English Channel, which may be Antonio's, and of his parting with Bassanio. Solanio urges Salerio not to tell Antonio of this reported shipwreck immediately, for "it may grieve him" (2.8.34). Salerio then speaks of Antonio's farewell to Bassanio:

> A kinder gentleman treads not the earth.
> I saw Bassanio and Antonio part.
> Bassanio told him he would make some speed
> Of his return; he answered, "Do not so.

> Slubber not business for my sake, Bassanio,
> But stay the very riping of the time;
> And for the Jew's bond which he hath of me,
> Let it not enter in your mind of love."
>
> (2.8.35–42)

This short speech superbly illustrates Shakespeare's ability to stimulate audience response at a crucial moment. Salerio claims Antonio is immensely kind; however, if Antonio is so kind, why does he bait Shylock, call him "dog," spit on him, and say he will do so again? Salerio's statement illustrates Rabkin's cogent argument about the impossibility of reducing this play to a "pattern" of meaning without ignoring so much of what happens to spectators during performance. The only spectators who could miss the hypocrisy of Salerio's praise of Antonio are those who, like Salerio, do not believe that cursing and spitting on Jews does not disqualify one as being "kind." Kindness in this Christian community is continually defined from within its own ranks, and, despite Christ's commandment to "love thy Neighbor," as well as thy "enemy," kindness and acceptance are shared selectively. Here at the end of the Venice portion of act 2, Shakespeare encapsulates in these Venetian commentators opposite attitudes toward Shylock and Antonio that lead directly to the trial scene. Shylock's human loss is ridiculed, and his very humanity is questioned; Antonio is praised as being extremely kind, yet he shares with many in Venice a socially sanctioned, virile hatred toward the alien Shylock.

One must appreciate 3.1 as what it is: a prelude to the trial, and especially here one must avoid the temptation to reflect back on the "meaning" of the scene from the perspectives of innumerable modern commentaries on Shylock's actions, especially his notorious plea, "Hath not a Jew eyes?" Rather, one must focus on the scene's structure and its theatrical effects in performance. Virtually every element of 3.1 breaks into nearly equal parts. The scene (in Bevington's 4th ed.) is 123 lines long. Antonio's man enters at line 69, and Tubal at line 72, so their twin entrances divide the total scene into nearly equal halves. In the first half of the scene, with Salerio and Solanio, Shylock is baited about his daughter's blood relation to himself and about what he could do with a pound of Antonio's flesh; in the second half, with Tubal, Shylock is violently torn between his daughter and his ducats. In performance on the thrust stage at the Theatre, the scene's divided structure and its severe emo-

tional dichotomies, designed precisely to create disparate spectator reactions, superbly anticipate the far greater emotional,
psychological, and theatrical dichotomies of the trial scene.

Shylock's entrance into 3.1 is heralded by Solanio as "the devil
... in the likeness of a Jew." This diabolic label is by now common in the play, but the absolute evil it attributes to Shylock is
shaken immediately by the ensuing dialogue. Solanio first asserts that Shylock and Jessica are not blood relatives. Standing
downstage left where he quarreled with Antonio in 1.3 and
where he stood while ordering his deceiving daughter to lock
up his house in 2.5, Shylock confronts men who here assume
Antonio's and Jessica's stage places while viciously denying to
him what every theater spectator would recognize as the most
sacred of human bonds: that of parent and child. "There is more
difference between thy flesh and / hers than between jet and
ivory, more between your / bloods than there is between red
wine and Rhenish" (3.1.36–38). Having been denied his child,
whom Shylock claims despite her rebellious flight to the Christians, Shylock is immediately asked if he has heard of Antonio's
possible losses, thus establishing the dialectical pattern for the
entire scene. Shylock's "Let him look to his bond," thrice repeated within four lines (3.1.44–47), leads to Salerio's question
about the value of a pound of a man's flesh, and then to Shylock's
famous speech. Its first and last images are of revenge, and while
Shylock initially recounts Antonio's abuse of him, evidence of
which spectators have seen in the play and which Antonio has
predicted they may see again (1.3.128–29), the second half of
the speech reaches far beyond physical and psychic abuse to
the core of Shakespeare's dramaturgy in this play. Although the
*critical* debate about whether Shylock's speech "Hath not a Jew
eyes" is anti-Semitic[20] or whether his appeal to "common humanity" deserves genuine sympathy[21] is endless, the *theatrical*
point is that in performance creating this immense dubiety is
the scene's primary dramatic function. For Shylock's speech generates virtually irreconcilable reactions among spectators that
will severely complicate their theatrical experience of the ensuing trial. A seminal point about Shylock's attempt at justifying
revenge, regardless of whether or not one believes that the Venetians' actions justify Shylock's claim that he has learned revenge
from them, is that his claim for a "common humanity" incorporates the audience:

> To say that this speech gives dignity to Shylock is not to say that it
> amounts to a genuine defense or provides a real excuse for him. . . .

The speech provides a brief summary of the state of fallen man, who feels "The penalty of Adam, / The seasons' difference." He is subject to pain, injury, and disease. Most important, his passions are unruly and not controlled by reason. When he is wronged, he wants revenge. Shylock, in seeking revenge against Antonio, is not justified. He is merely acting as fallen human beings tend to act. Therefore, in this speech, he does not so much justify himself, though he believes he does, as implicate others.[22]

In the Theatre, these "others" are all around Shylock. To the extent that this speech implicates all humans' desire for revenge, whether through violence or trials, the "difference" between Shylock's flesh and that of all spectators in the playhouse suddenly collapses.[23] Although modern critics may assert that few spectators today would be fooled by Shylock's macabre "defense" of revenge, nonetheless a compelling performance of this speech certainly creates more emotional bonds between Shylock's humanity and that of his spectators' than reductive "readings" of the play, replete with numerous "after-thoughts," readily acknowledge. Further complicating spectators' reactions to Shylock's speech is their realization of the sheer impossibility of his task; however deceptive his rhetoric, Shylock pleads his humanity and "justifies" his revenge before two of Venice's worst bigots who callously deny his fatherhood and ignore his agony. Understood as an intense dramatic moment related only to what has occurred so far in the play, not to what spectators who could not have read it or had not seen it before do not know is coming (i.e., the trial of 4.1), and rather than as a speech analyzed independently of its dramatic context, Shylock's taunting threats and sudden strength initiate an audience involvement with him that Shakespeare expands during the trial: in such circumstances, who among the spectators would not seek revenge? On the thrust stage of the Theatre, those spectators nearest downstage left, where I imagine Shylock appearing in this and earlier scenes since 1.3, recognize perhaps more immediately than spectators in other parts of the playhouse the cumulative effects of the abuse Shylock has incurred since Antonio's initial curses in 1.3. This intensifying of the dramatic experience of part of the theater audience, those closest to Shylock's stage position throughout, heightens spectators' awareness of the racial and religious dichotomies searing the stage as *The Merchant* builds toward its climactic scene.

But Shakespeare does not allow spectators to indulge this visceral involvement with Shylock. Certainly attentive spectators at any performance of the play, Elizabethan or modern, will note the specious logic of his further argument. "If you / prick us, do we not bleed? If you tickle us, do we not / laugh? If you poison us, do we not die? And if you / wrong us, shall we not revenge?" (3.1.60–64). Shylock would have us believe that just because all humans bleed when pricked and laugh when tickled, all revenge is justified.[24] The contradictions in Shylock's claim that Christian example justifies his revenge are obvious, but spectators have heard him called dog, and cur, and devil, and have heard Antonio say he will spit on Shylock again. He has been denied his only child. In the play so far, considered as what Rabkin reminds us it is, a *process of involvement,* spectators have witnessed enough abuse from the Christians to sense the great depth of Shylock's anger and how it could twist his thinking as it has. To claim, as D. M. Cohen does, that Shylock's argument about revenge is specious because he receives mercy from Antonio at the trial[25] is to miss entirely Rabkin's point that during performance the *play Merchant of Venice* is experienced *sequentially,* and during Shylock's ravings in 3.1 the trial has not yet occurred and thus cannot be part of spectators' involvement with or judgment about his actions here. The significant theatrical elements of this scene are Shylock's history of abuse and the distorted hatred that it partially causes, for these are the dramatic forces that will collide violently in the trial scene.

The few remaining moments of 3.1 are remarkably compressed. A "man from Antonio," who says his master (how that term must enrage Shylock!) seeks Salerio and Solanio, clears the stage, leaving in Shylock's mind the image of the man whom he hates ordering others about. Tubal then enters, and he, like Shylock moments before, is greeted as devilish: "Here comes another of the tribe. A third / cannot be matched, unless the devil himself turn Jew" (3.1.73–74). This exit line exists only to reemphasize the Venetian Christians' relentless racial prejudice; Tubal is diabolic simply because he is a Jew, for he has no bond with Antonio for a pound of his flesh. In the second half of this scene, Tubal's manipulation of Shylock is, in Holderness's phrase, "almost comically mechanistic."[26] It is also horribly frightening. Spectators now witness the utter collapse of Shylock's claim to sharing a common humanity. The "passion so confused" merely reported by Solanio in 2.8 now lacerates the stage:

Why, there, there, there, there! A diamond
gone, cost me two thousand ducats in Frankfort! The
curse never fell upon our nation till now; I never felt it
till now. Two thousand ducats in that, and other
precious, precious jewels. I would my daughter were
dead at my foot, and the jewels in her ear! Would she
were hearsed at my foot, and the ducats in her coffin!

(3.1.79–85)

All men may bleed if pricked and laugh if tickled; however, all
men do not wish their only daughter dead at their feet. Certainly
spectators recoil from Shylock's grotesque inhumanity here, for
his "confusion" is such that his daughter is no longer equated
with the human dignity Shylock moments earlier claimed for
himself, much less with his own "flesh and blood" as he asserted
to Salerio and Solanio, but rather with an amount of ducats
spent in seeking her. Yet to focus here on only Shylock's hideous,
demented ravings is to miss the connections within Shylock that
Tubal's litany of Antonio's and Shylock's "loss upon loss" is designed to elicit among spectators. Antonio is fresh in Shylock's
mind, his man servant having just left the stage. When Tubal
tells Shylock of Antonio's reputed loss, Shylock's history of per-
secution from Antonio, his loss of his daughter to a "Christian
husband," their using Leah's ring in Genoa to buy a monkey,[27]
and his desire for revenge convulse to create perhaps the most
frightening (and most anti-Semitic) moment in the play:

Go, Tubal,
fee me an officer; bespeak him a fortnight before. I will
have the heart of him if he forfeit, for were he out of
Venice I can make what merchandise I will. Go, Tubal,
and meet me at our synagogue. Go, good Tubal; at our
synagogue, Tubal.

(3.1.118–23)

Cohen asserts that for an Elizabethan audience these lines "convey the notion that Shylock is repairing to his place of worship
immediately after learning that he can now legally murder the
good Antonio. Bloodletting and religious worship are brought
into a very ugly and insidious conjunction."[28] This conjunction
is, indeed, insidious, and viciously anti-Semitic; however, one
must see it as exploding from the increasingly terrifying "confusion" within Shylock compounded of his passionate hatred for
Antonio, his thirst for revenge, and the irreparable loss of his

only child to a thieving Christian husband. No reductive reasoning process divorced from the increasingly violent energy of Shylock's pain can accommodate the complex spectator reactions this pain generates during performance. These reactions are the material from which Shakespeare builds what was to be the most theatrically sophisticated scene he had yet created: the trial of 4.1. In this scene, the actual shape of the stage at the Theatre becomes an essential component of dramatic meaning.

In 3.3 Antonio and Shylock meet briefly before the trial. Shylock rejects Antonio's pleas and insists six times within fourteen lines on having his bond, whereas Antonio tells Solanio that "The Duke cannot deny the course of law" because to deny it "Will much impeach the justice of the state" (3.3.26, 29). No one mentions mercy; spectators anticipate a strictly legal procedure, with Antonio and Shylock diametrically opposed in the trial.

As Anthony Brennan demonstrates, Shakespeare divides the trial scene, by far the longest in the play, into three phases, each with three balanced sections.[29] I would argue here that the careful construction of the scene demands careful staging, and I would argue also, as I will in subsequent essays on different plays, that the trial scene in *Merchant* would have been carefully rehearsed and staged so as to elicit maximum dramatic meaning on the Theatre's thrust stage. One cannot know exactly how the Chamberlain's Men would have staged the trial scene, nor can we know certainly how much rehearsal they would have devoted to it. However, one can examine the scene focusing on the myriad subtexts of Shylock's relations with the Christians and envision an Elizabethan staging that maximizes the complex tensions of the script. One can examine, that is, how the trial scene would have enhanced for its spectators what the process of the play to this point has created.

In this crowded scene, the location of characters is important.[30] One imagines the Duke and his train, as embodiments of formal Venetian authority, probably seated in the upstage *locus* to preside over the trial itself. Antonio enters, speaks briefly, and then steps aside, let us assume stage right, where I imagine him standing in his initial meeting with Shylock in 1.3. Bassanio, Salerio, and Gratiano are also on stage, and, as they support Antonio, would be on his side of the stage. Shylock enters, and speaks for twenty-seven lines, probably before the centrally placed Duke. After this speech, in which he warns the Duke of abjuring Venice's reliance on the law and "explains" that he pursues his bond because of a "lodged hate and a certain loathing /

I bear Antonio" (4.1.60–61), he must also take his stage position for the actual trial. If, as seems probable, Shylock steps to the opposite side of the stage from Antonio (i.e., stage left) as in 1.3, one now imagines a stage again divided by their mutual hatred. When one considers this scene on the thrust stage of the Theatre, one realizes that whereas Antonio and Shylock are probably equally distant from spectators facing center stage, each is also closer to one portion of the audience than to the other: Antonio to those nearer stage right, Shylock to those nearer stage left. Thus, given the placement of the main characters and their different physical relationships with spectators on three sides of the stage, and presuming Shylock and Antonio remain in these generally similar stage positions during most of the trial, the multiple perspectives from which spectators view the trial compound the scripted complexities of the scene itself. Spectators sitting nearest Antonio's stage position will share more directly his experience of the trial, whereas those nearest Shylock will more directly share his. The crucial point for this scene played at the Theatre is that the trial and its results are simply not the same experience theatrically for all of its spectators. One is tempted to see this stage picture as merely divided camps, like those of Richard and Richmond in act 5 of *Richard III.* But the stage image is far more complex, for during performance this play relentlessly refuses to divide itself into neatly separated categories, or stage positions, that can be labeled "good" and "evil."

Shylock's "lodged hate" for Antonio prompts Antonio's response to Bassanio's reasoning with Shylock about love and hate: "You may as well do anything most hard / As seek to soften that—than which what's harder?— / His Jewish heart" (4.1.78–80). Yet this apparently simple dichotomy between Jewish hate and Christian love immediately collapses in Shylock's accusation, directed from the downstage-left *platea* against "official" Venice seated in the Duke's chair in the upstage *locus,* about the Venetians' having "many a purchased slave," which they use "in abject and in slavish parts, / Because you bought them" (4.1.90, 92–93). Thinking perhaps of Jessica's flight with a Christian, Shylock taunts the court: "Shall I say to you, / 'Let them be free, marry them to your heirs!'" (4.1.93–94). As the Venetians will not do so because the slaves are theirs to use as they will, so Shylock reasons that "The pound of flesh which I demand of him / is dearly bought, is mine, and I will have it" (4.1.99–100). Shylock's "reasoning" here, as in his argument justifying revenge from "Christian example" in 3.1, is specious, and seems to justify Antonio's characterization of his hard "Jewish heart." But equally important for the remainder of the trial is that Shylock's accusation of the Venetians' wholly unchristian yet legal practice of slavery goes unanswered in the court.[31] Indeed, the Venetians' inability to respond to Shylock's just accusation seriously weakens whatever moral authority the "Court" may believe it possesses. Shakespeare simply refuses to allow this trial and its participants a simple dichotomy; Antonio is, according to Salerio, the kindest man to walk the earth, yet he and his society of wealthy Venetians buy and use slaves. In this trial these slaveholding Venetians are the ones who shall dispense justice to the Jew, another they consider an alien.

Between Shylock's accusations about purchased slaves and the reading of Bellario's letter and then Portia's entrance as Balthasar, Shakespeare inserts both Bassanio's claim that he will willingly die for Antonio and Gratiano's abusive tirade about Shylock's soul having transmigrated from a wolf "hanged for human slaughter" into his "unhallowed dam" (4.1.134, 136). As those spectators nearest Shylock watch him maliciously whet his knife, those nearest Antonio hear Gratiano, who is *never* silenced during the trial, employ the animal imagery first used against Shylock by Antonio in 1.3 and then repeated throughout the play. From different parts of the Theatre's thrust stage visual and aural images of savage enmity ricochet and collide, creating enormous tension, drawing spectators into the venom engulfing the stage, and dissolving the distinctions between cause and effect, victim and victimizer that Shakespeare's script repeatedly refuses to sustain. Regardless of the degree of anti-Semitism among Shakespeare's audiences (i.e., regardless of how most Elizabethan spectators may have viewed Shylock in his visual response to Gratiano's verbal abuse), these few stage moments immediately before Portia's entrance hardly suggest that spectators are about to witness an impartial trial.

Portia's entrance alleviates temporarily the tension present on stage. She takes her "place," as ordered by the Duke, presumably center stage between Antonio and Shylock, who "stand forth," presumably now somewhat closer to center stage, though, one imagines, still clearly separated. Spectators know of Portia's plans from 3.4, and from Jessica's remarks about her father and Antonio in 3.2.284–90 they also know that Portia understands Shylock's murderous intentions.[32] Knowing the law, and how she must use it to free Antonio, Portia presumably wishes to avoid such scrupulous tactics; hence, her appeal to Christian mercy, enunciated downstage center between the enraged Shylock and his equally hateful Christians accusers: "Therefore, Jew, / Though justice be thy plea, consider this, / That in the course of justice none of us / Should see salvation" (4.1.196–99). Yet as Holderness argues, this appeal is certainly disingenuous: Shylock, as a Jew, cannot expect Christian salvation, being, as he (and his daughter at 3.5.9–10) is constantly reminded in this play, an alien Jew outside the Christian dispensation.[33] Shylock is thus, in his mind, pursuing the justice that he believes is his, and that, as revenge, he claims he has learned from "Christian example." Further, Portia's "us" implicitly includes the Venetians presiding over this case, who keep and use slaves, as well as the Theatre's audience; all are complicit in the imperfections of humankind, such as their pursuit of revenge. Paramount among humans' imperfections is their limited capacity to judge: "Judge not, that ye be not judged."[34]

Yet judgment is precisely what this scene demands and what its Theatre performance renders nearly impossible. Ruth Nevo argues that Jessica's report to Portia in Belmont that her father has long wished for Antonio's death is different from his actual decision to seek Antonio's death.[35] Spectators' inability to be certain about what explicitly prompts Shylock's decision to seek Antonio's flesh increases the ambiguity of their response to Shylock at the trial: just how evil is he, and is his wish for revenge, stated in 1.3, only activated by Jessica's flight? If the latter is true, Shylock's motivations at the trial are far more frighteningly complex than mere revenge on Antonio for his financial losses caused by Antonio's lending money gratis. As the dominant stage figure standing forth downstage on the *platea,* Shylock accuses these Venetians who judge from the upstage *locus* of secure power not only of racism and slavery but also, as a desperately wronged father, of complicity in the gilded abduction of his only daughter. Thus, at the Theatre the trial divides the stage, and its onstage spectators, into intersecting, venomous antipathies that even Portia cannot fully grasp: as Antonio and Shylock on opposite sides of the downstage *platea* split the stage into their mutual loathing, so Shylock's intense anger at the whole of Venetian society represented by the Duke and his authoritarian chair upstage rives the *platea* and *locus* into yet another enmity the depth and pain of which only Shylock can feel.[36]

Bassanio offers, with Portia's money, "twice the sum" of Shylock's bond: "If that will not suffice, / I will be bound to pay it

ten times o'er / On forfeit of my hands, my head, my heart"
(4.1.208–10). This will not do; in his and Portia's presence in
3.2, Jessica has said no amount of money will placate her father.
So Bassanio asks the impossible, wresting once the law to Balthasar's authority, and so introduces the strictness of the law which
is both kind and cruel, merciful and hypocritical. With Portia's
"I pray you, let me look upon the bond" the entire scene pivots.
Portia initially assures Shylock that the law supports him and
that the bond is forfeit; she again urges mercy, Shylock refuses
and she orders Antonio to prepare his bosom for Shylock's knife.
Portia urges Shylock "for charity" to have a surgeon by, but as
this is not "nominated in the bond," Shylock refuses and is not
challenged again by Portia. Portia's strict interpretation of the
law thus increases tension on the polarized stage among the increasingly fragmented participants in this trial and among the
spectators surrounding the stage in the Theatre, while simultaneously anticipating exactly the legal strategy that she will use
to eviscerate Shylock's bond.

Shakespeare further delays the climax of the trial with Antonio's morbid farewell to Bassanio, and Bassanio's and Gratiano's
comic denial of their marriage vows, two actions probably acted
out on Antonio's downstage right portion of the *platea*. Yet note
that even here both Bassanio and Gratiano continue to label
Shylock, still standing downstage left opposite the Christians, a
"devil" and "currish Jew" as Venetians have throughout the play;
racial hatred continues to blur distinctions between simplistic
ideas of good and evil, innocent and guilty, and even infects these
Christian husbands' vows of marital fidelity. As he was possibly
driven to plot Antonio's death by the news from Tubal in 3.1 of
his daughter's flight and marriage, so here, cursing these "Christian husbands" and hearing Balthasar say that a pound of Antonio's flesh is his, Shylock approaches Antonio, presumably
crossing the stage to Antonio's "place" and visually crossing and
thus violating Portia's neutral space between the scene's lethal
antagonists. As he does so, Shylock's well-sharpened knife suddenly embodies the image of "feeding fat" his ancient grudge
that he has uttered earlier;[37] Shylock ritualistically bears to Antonio's side of the stage a hatred as visceral as the Christians'
with which he hopes to destroy Venice's most prominent merchant, this "most kind" pillar of the Venetian state. But Shylock
is defeated by exactly that which he had thought his ally; Venetian law is applied with a maddening precision[38] to Shylock's
bond, and then is revealed to be not his ally but rather that

which perpetuates the alien status he has borne throughout the play.[39]

As Shylock is stripped of his goods, presumably dropping or abjectly surrendering to one of the Venetians near him the knife that had visually symbolized his threat throughout the trial (how terribly ironic should he perhaps relinquish this image of hatred and revenge to Gratiano, the trial's worst bigot), and slowly returning to his formerly powerful "place" downstage left, his rapid demise on stage focuses sharply the intense ambiguities of audience response that *Merchant* sustains in performance. Portia labels Shylock an alien, pronounces judgment on him, and then, gesturing toward the Duke, the *locus* of Venice's theatrical authority, Portia concludes the trial with two orders to Shylock: "Down therefore, and beg mercy of the Duke" (4.1.361). Expecting mercy, because the brilliantly scrupulous lawyer who gutted Shylock's bond has just demanded it, Shakespeare's Christian audience instead is jolted by a stunning visual/aural contrast. As Shylock kneels, now perhaps turned upstage toward the Duke, his visual submission is shattered by Gratiano's revived bigotry: "Beg that thou mayst have leave to hang thyself!" Gratiano maligns Shylock because suddenly the Jew is destitute: "And yet, thy wealth being forfeit to the state, / Thou hast not left the value of a cord; / Therefore thou must be hanged at the state's charge" (4.1.362, 363–65). The Duke acts mercifully in sparing Shylock's life, dividing his wealth between the "state" (i.e., the upstage *locus* of Venetian authority) and Antonio. Shylock's agonized plea, not for life, but for death—"You take my life / When you do take the means whereby I live" (4.1.374–75)—prompts Portia's question to Antonio about mercy, which is again answered by Gratiano's lethal hatred: "A halter gratis! Nothing else, for God's sake" (4.1.377). Antonio, speaking from his downstage right position, or perhaps now moving upstage toward the Duke—"So please my lord the Duke and all the court"—then asks the court to condone his own judgment, which remits a fine for one half of Shylock's goods and asks that the other half go to the gentleman "That lately stole his daughter" (4.1.383). Antonio countenances and then rewards with yet more ducats Lorenzo's escape with Jessica, a lady now even more "richly left." By invoking the court's approval, Antonio symbolically combines the downstage *platea,* moments before utterly divided by his and Shylock's mutual wrath, with the upstage *locus* of Venetian authority to condone stealing daughters and ducats and Shylock's forced conversion.

Yet in performance at the Theatre this image of apparent stage unity yields just the opposite effect. Antonio spares Shylock's life, and this is mercy beyond what Shylock could imagine practicing and had any right to expect; indeed, the cultural gap between Jew and Christian, which Shylock's "I am a Jew" in 3.1 ironically asserts, is most evident in his insisting on the "law" in the trial and rejecting any compulsion to practice mercy.[40] But Shakespeare entangles the stage Christians' practice of mercy, and thus his presumably Christian spectators' judgment of the trial, by their forced conversion of Shylock to a culture that purchases and uses slaves, defines aliens as they wish, denies them legal protection, and then uses that legal system to defeat them. Rabkin correctly asserts that "The issue is not how Elizabethans felt about the relative advantages of dying in or outside the church, but how Shakespeare forces his audience to respond to this particular conversion in its context."[41] The theatrical context of this conversion in 1598–99 was the play's performance in a theater in which a likely staging of this scene as I described would have its spectators perceiving its action from different perspectives, yielding different immediate responses: those closer to Antonio watch Shylock crumble at what Antonio and his fellow Christians consider not only justice but also mercy; whereas others, closer to Shylock as he leaves the stage walking upstage left, see him decimated by Christians who show absolutely no awareness of their hypocrisy or the circularity of their hatred: Shylock is a Jew, and therefore an alien, an inhuman dog, a cur, and even his daughter is not his own flesh and blood; therefore, he can be destroyed with impunity, since he is an alien anyway, a dog, a cur.[42]

Shylock is cursed off the stage by Gratiano: "In christening shalt thou have two godfathers. / Had I been judge, thou shouldst have had ten more, / To bring thee to the gallows, not the font" (4.1.396–98). From where on the stage does Gratiano sling these words? How do the Christians react? Do they approve of him? Laugh at his jibe? One can argue that Gratiano does not represent the general attitude of the Venetians toward Shylock, or Jewishness, in the play. However, if one imagines him now standing downstage center of the *platea*, perhaps in the place Portia occupied as Balthasar, one hears Gratiano's curse as the Christian community's final, *authoritarian* dismissal of Shylock uttered from the central place of judgment used by Balthasar as she freed Antonio and the Christians from Shylock's bond. Gratiano's curse comes just eleven lines after Antonio's urging that Shylock "presently become a Christian" (4.1.385). Again, Shakespeare refuses to allow any one impression to dominate the stage. As he has done throughout the play, and especially during the trial itself, Shakespeare relentlessly compounds his spectators' responses. Theater spectators have to wonder how "accepted" Shylock will be in this Christian community that refuses to silence its loudest bigot at precisely that moment in the play when Christians ought to be most willing to extend that charity that Christ urged on all his followers. This irony is most disturbing when one realizes that Shylock is now, or will soon be, a "fellow" Christian.[43]

As a coda to the trial itself, Portia's "ring episode" recapitulates in comic form the very means by which she has defeated Shylock. The Duke and his court having left (s.d., line 405), Portia, now the sole reigning authority on stage, takes full advantage of her position. Her acquisition of her husband's ring is clever but deceitful; acted out on the *platea* where her scrupulous reading of the law saved Antonio from Shylock's knife, Portia's manipulation of Bassanio images again the ruthlessness with which people in this play, even its comic heroines wishing to teach their rash, immature husbands a lesson about fidelity, can pursue and exercise power. Even as this play swings back toward the moonlit romance of Belmont, its Venetian *platea,* where Antonio and Shylock first quarreled in 1.3, remains an enigmatic "place."

I close with two salient points about act 5 in performance. First, Jessica's brief appearance and especially her final line raise significant questions about the extent of "community" present either on stage or among spectators during act 5. Ejner Jensen argues that as the worlds of Shakespeare's comedies "correspond more fully to societies in which men and women must work and live, and . . . seem to be judged appropriately by standards of psychological credibility—the reductionism of . . . teleological criticism seems less and less valid."[44] For all the moonlit romanticism of Jessica's and Lorenzo's duet, they speak of unfaithful and tragic lovers: Cressid, Thisbe, Dido, Medea; their remarks about themselves are, at minimum, ambiguous and ironic, if not callous:

> *Lorenzo.*                              In such a night
> Did Jessica steal from the wealthy Jew
> And with an unthrift love did run from Venice
> As far as Belmont.
> *Jessica.*                              In such a night

> Did young Lorenzo swear he loved her well,
> Stealing her soul with many vows of faith,
> And n'er a true one.
>
> *Lorenzo.*                              In such a night
> Did pretty Jessica, like a little shrew,
> Slander her love, and he forgave it her.
>
> (5.1.14–22)

The patterning of their exchange may create in the audience a comic detachment from these tragic emotions,[45] but even this distancing is temporary. Lorenzo's observation about the immeasurable gap between the "harmony [that] is in immortal souls" (5.1.63), and human imperfection imaged by the "muddy vesture of decay" that "grossly" closes in our own inattentive souls is immediately evident even as the play seeks to fulfill its comic form. Jessica's final line, "I am never merry when I hear sweet music" recalls the merry-making of the maskers as they "stole" Jessica and embarked on their magical flight to Belmont, and also Shylock's fierce objection to all such merriment:

> Hear you me, Jessica:
> Lock up my doors, and when you hear the drum
> And the vile squealing of the wry-necked fife,
> Clamber not you up to the casements then,
> Nor thrust your head into the public street
> To gaze on Christian fools with varnished faces.
>
> (2.5.29–34)

The dramatic point is not just Shylock's absence from act 5; it is that Jessica's line emphasizes her own significant ambiguity now in this play. Where is she at this moment on stage? This seems one of those small moments that an immensely professional company, as Shakespeare's had surely become by 1598, would have staged with maximum theatrical impact in mind. For if, as she says this line, Jessica occupies the stage space that her father occupied during the trial, downstage left on the open *platea,* her line assumes an immense visual meaning that complements its verbal poignancy, especially for those spectators nearest her stage position who recognize it as her father's moments before. Jessica is now the outsider; reductive, or what Jensen calls teleological arguments for harmony at the end of this play, cannot ignore another potent silence in the theater: Jessica does not speak again in act 5. Indeed, as Ralph Berry notes, no one even speaks *to* her again for the final 238 lines in act 5.[46] Although modern productions often cast Antonio in act 5 as the play's "outsider" among the returning of rings and bawdy vows of fidelity, images that certainly recall for spectators Portia's manipulation of Bassanio's emotions after the trial, Jessica's silent presence during the final 238 lines again divides the audience, for those spectators nearest to where she stands for the rest of the scene will be more conscious than spectators in other parts of the theater of her immense, long silence and the internal pain that silence may symbolize. When Portia presents Shylock's deed of his goods unto Lorenzo and Jessica, perhaps again occupying the "place" she assumed during the trial, she speaks only to Lorenzo, and Nerissa apparently gives the actual deed to Lorenzo:

| | |
|---|---|
| *Portia.* | How now, Lorenzo? |
| | My clerk hath some good comforts too for you. |
| *Nerissa.* | Ay, and I'll give them him without a fee. |
| | There I do give to you and Jessica, |
| | From the rich Jew, a special deed of gift, |
| | After his death, of all he dies possessed of. |
| *Lorenzo.* | Fair ladies, you drop manna in the way |
| | Of starvèd people. |

(5.1.288–95)

The deed comes, not from Shylock, but again, as so often, from the Jew, the (formerly) rich Jew, Jessica's father; and Lorenzo's use of "manna" here seems among the cruelest ironies of the play. The food from heaven, actual as well as spiritual, that miraculously saved the Jews during their wandering in the desert is here reduced to ducats which further gild Lorenzo's seizing of Jessica from her father's house. Jessica says nothing; on the large platform stage, is Jessica beside Lorenzo as he accepts the deed? Or, as I would suggest, is she alone in that portion of the stage her father occupied during the trial, never merry when she hears the Christian music that will now fill her married life? Jessica's silence makes all the more ironic her remark to Lancelot in 3.5: "I shall be saved by my husband. He hath made me a Christian" (lines 17–18).

My second point concerns Portia's brief conversation with Nerissa on returning to Belmont. Their dialogue is prompted by Portia's remark about the light she sees in her hall, and its brightness relative to the moon. They then hear music, presumably that which Jessica says will never make her merry. Portia then says, "Nothing, I see, is good without respect" (5.1.99). Editors agree that the phrase suggests that the meaning of any event is in its context and that nothing human is absolutely good.[47] Portia expands this idea by paraphrasing *Ecclesiastes*: "How many things by season seasoned are / To their right praise and true perfection!" (5.1.107–8). Certainly Portia's lines reflect her awareness of the nature of her deeds during the trial. Yes, Antonio was spared and Shylock defeated. Portia recognizes the desirability of both these consequences, which may, in time, be "seasoned" to greater good. But *during performance* (not later in the library) the turbulent, conflicting emotional reactions generated by the trial obliterate any consensus about its absolute goodness. As the play concludes, spectators are reminded by Portia's lines, and by her likely stage position where she manipulated Shylock and the law, of the sharp dichotomies of the just completed trial; as they sense Jessica's silence and isolation, they realize that not one of the characters now standing on stage, including Antonio and Portia, can unequivocally praise either what Portia had to do to save Antonio or what this Christian "community" has done to Shylock. Jessica provides mute testimony to that complete impossibility, and her silence extends that impossibility to the spectators of this play.

# 5

## Falstaff and the Theater of Subversion: The Audience as Thieves In *I Henry IV*

> This house is turned upside down since Robin Hostler died.
> —Shakespeare, *I Henry IV*

THE preference of academic scholars for literary overviews of Shakespeare's plays, such as one finds in the "Introductions" to modern editions, has been especially damaging to appreciations of *I* and *II Henry IV* as distinct *plays*. For example, in his influential essay "*Henry IV*: The Structural Problem Revisited" Sherman Hawkins argues that Shakespeare initially planned the two parts of *Henry IV* and that together the two plays constitute, like Spenser's *The Faerie Queene,* an "epic of princely education."[1] In Hawkins's view, Hal's returning to Falstaff and the Boar's Head Tavern in part 2 is not a flaw in Shakespeare's design, but rather the final, necessary stage in Hal's education. Speaking of Hal's relationship to Falstaff, Hawkins writes: "[I]n Part 1, whose theme is valor, it is the old reprobate's cowardice that is exposed, while in Part 2, whose theme is justice, it is his slanderous misjudgment of the prince."[2] Part 1 then is "completed" by part 2 and is best understood in relation to its successor, which Shakespeare wrote shortly after completing part 1 "partly, no doubt, to capitalize on the enormous theatrical success of Falstaff and partly to finish the story of Falstaff's rejection."[3]

This literary "overview" of the two plays, indeed of the four-play "Henriad," has led to the modern preference for staging Shakespeare's history plays as cycles; for example, audiences at English and American Shakespeare festivals are treated to both parts of *Henry IV* in a single day: part 1 in the afternoon and part 2 in the evening. However, as Scott McMillin reminds us, in Shakespeare's time such productions in "cycles" probably did not occur: "Shakespeare's own acting company probably did not stage anything like a cycle. Even two-part plays, of which there were many in the Elizabethan period, were not always performed on successive days. . . . Whatever we claim about the intentions of the author, it is unlikely that Shakespeare's company ever gave him a first or second tetralogy in successive performances."[4] In considering a production of *I Henry IV* then at the Theatre, one should think of it as a separate, self-contained artifact, regardless of how "unified" scholars may believe parts 1 and 2 are, regardless of what we believe Shakespeare's "intentions" may have been in writing part 2, and regardless of how accustomed we are to seeing *I* and *II Henry IV* performed either in tandem or as parts of a larger "cycle" of history plays. This is the approach I wish to take here. I want to examine *I Henry IV* as what it is: a separate play designed to be played separately at the Theatre, probably in late 1596–97,[5] starring the fattest; most eloquent; most infamous; and, therefore, I shall argue, most subversive thief of the Elizabethan stage. My argument focuses only on part 1, ignoring Falstaff's banishment in part 2 simply because it does not occur in part 1. Further, I ask that we recall that Will Kempe, the company's by then (i.e., 1596–97) famous clown, like his predecessor Dick Tarlton a brilliant improviser, probably played Falstaff for the Chamberlain's Men;[6] and also that we remember that the Theatre, like other Elizabethan playhouses, thrived in a heterogeneous society utterly divided about the public theatres: although some factions of that society sustained and defended them, others hated and strenuously tried to destroy them. As an enormously vigorous and immensely hilarious character, Falstaff delighted; however, as a selfish reprobate who misuses the King's press when the crown is threatened by rebels as self-righteous as himself, Falstaff is dangerous. On stage Falstaff exploits, manipulates, and ridicules with irresistible humor and wit the very powers that consigned his theatrical existence to the outskirts of London. In so doing, I shall argue, Falstaff encouraged his spectators in his own "house," the playhouse called the Theatre, to a similarly invigorating and subversive thievery.

London's public theatres existed in the "margins" or "Liberties" of Elizabethan society, outside the city walls and its jurisdiction. Steven Mullaney maintains that awareness of this "place" of the stage is crucial to our appreciation of its cultural significance. Regardless of how central we think popular drama may be to our knowledge of Elizabethan culture, we must recall that this drama "situated itself neither at the heart of the community nor even within it. Born of the contradiction between Court license and city prohibition, popular drama in England emerged as a cultural institution only by materially embodying that contradiction, dislocating itself from the strict confines of the existing social order and taking up a place on the margins of society."[7] London's reigning hierarchies viewed the popular stage as an "eccentric phenomenon, an extravagant and incontinent form of recreation," and its audience as "an imminent and unruly threat to the health of the body politic."[8] Mullaney quotes John Stockwood, who in a sermon at Paul's Cross in 1578, complains of "Houses of purpose built . . . and that without the Liberties, as who woulde say, 'There, let them saye what they will say, we wil play.'"[9] This determination to "play" survived numerous attempts by civic authorities to close the theatres, including a petition from the Lord Mayor and the Aldermen to the Privy Council 28 July 1597, the year *I Henry IV* was probably first played at the Theatre, earnestly requesting the "present staie & fynall suppressinge of the saide Stage playes, aswell at the Theatre, Curten, and banckside, as in all other places in and abowt the Citie," for such plays contain "nothinge but prophane fables, lascivious matters, cozeninge devises, & scurrilus beehaviours, which are so set forth as that they move wholie to imitation & not to the auoydinge of those faults & vices which they represent." Further, the Lord Mayor and Aldermen complain, among the "inconueniences that grow by Stage playes" are that the theaters are

> the ordinary places for vagrant persons, Maisterles men, thieves, horse stealers, whoremongers, Coozeners, Conycatchers, contrivers of treason, and other idele and daungerous persons to meet together & to make theire matches to the great displeasure of Almightie God & the hurt & annoyance of her Maiesties people, which cannot be prevented nor discovered by the Gouernours of the Citie for that they are owt of the Citiees iurisdiction.[10]

In this single petition one finds summarized decades of civic and religious (i.e., Puritan) opposition to the public stages: the playhouses, their plays, and their players subvert civic and religious order, hierarchy, and authority.[11]

Michael Bristol contends that Elizabethan debates about the public theaters were fundamentally about the possibility that such theaters "might actually be a form of diabolical mis-

education, capable of substantive disruption in the prevailing
organization of social life."[12] The controversy about public theater focused on "the structure and the allocation of authority."[13]
The public theaters are attacked by men such as John North-
brooke and Philip Stubbes because on stage they combine and,
therefore, belittle differences in social class, dress, and language;
Bristol writes that these attacks must be seen as part of a larger
attack on popular or plebeian culture, with its "pervasive and
tacit sanction of misrule in all the patterns of everyday life."[14]
Public theater imitated plebeian culture in exalting laughter,
which "discloses the relative weakness of a social structure and
the impunity with which its constraints may be violated. . . . In
the laughter of popular festive form, the community gets away
with a refusal to conform to the social system or to accept its
ideological and cosmological claims."[15] Plebeian culture acknowledges the "arbitrary, ramshackle structure of authority
and political power" and "the relative incapacity of that power
substantively to alter the objective and material conditions of
life."[16] Further, the clowns and devils in popular drama, sources
of great humor, "double as characters and as critical interpreters
of a play's crude and immediate contingency with the wider
world of public and collective life. Their presence within the
theater, and their intrusion or capture by a dramatic narrative,
are an active discouragement to projects of unity and of
closure."[17]

Bristol argues that contemporary scholars should not dismiss
as the work of a few unappreciative cranks the civic and religious
attacks on popular theater. As an institution existing on the margins of Elizabethan society—and, therefore, on the margins of
that society's political power—popular theater was correctly
seen by the authorities as an institution that by its mere existence, yet alone its huge popularity, threatened the social and
political hegemony of those who attempted to govern the very
people who daily thronged to the "theatre district" to make Richard Burbage and Will Kempe among the most famous of London's citizens, and Shakespeare a wealthy man when he retired.
When one approaches *I Henry IV* and especially Falstaff, an
accomplished thief, from these perspectives, one sees a play that
energizes successfully, and thus dangerously, complete disregard
for every conceivable form of political authority and social hierarchy. As a history play, *I Henry IV* simply explodes at its end,
for in Falstaff's gigantic "resurrection" the actual performing of
the play brilliantly images the Theatre's carnivalesque glorifica-

tion of acting and its refusal to submit to normative order and power.

The King's opening words, spoken from the upstage *locus* of royal power, indicate the very instability of rule that haunts this play:

> So shaken as we are, so wan with care,
> Find we a time for frighted peace to pant,
> And breathe short-winded accents of new broils
> To be commenced in strands afar remote.
>
> (1.1.1–4)

Bolingbroke desires a campaign to the Holy Land to divert his kingdom's attention from the "intestine shock / And furious close of civil butchery" (1.1.13–14). His plans change immediately upon Westmorland's news of the "noble Mortimer's" capture by Glendower; images of slaughter continue:

> A thousand of his people butcherèd—
> Upon whose dead corpse there was much misuse,
> Such beastly shameless transformation,
> By those Welshwomen done as may not be
> Without much shame retold or spoken of.
>
> (1.1.42–46)

The King's news from Sir Walter Blunt links Hotspur's initially welcome victory with similarly horrid images of bloodshed:

> The Earl of Douglas is discomfited;
> Ten thousand bold Scots, two and twenty knights,
> Balked in their own blood, did Sir Walter see
> On Holmedon's plains.
>
> (1.1.67–70)

Hotspur's victory and his many prisoners are "an honorable spoil," a "gallant prize," and lead the King to praise Hotspur as "A son who is the theme of honor's tongue" and make him thus more desirable as a son than his own "young Harry" (1.1.80, 85). But the succession of images associated with such victories, with the "civil butchery" of Bolingbroke's attempts to repress several revolts and maintain his stolen crown with the Percies' aid,[18] immediately link such victories and the resulting "honor" with the grotesque slaughter of medieval warfare. This slaughter, which history and the chivalric code demand of soldiers, Falstaff will denounce and ridicule when, at Shrewsbury, he will argue for "life" as opposed to the horrible deaths reiterated in the play's opening scene.

Directly contrasting Bolingbroke "shaken and wan with care," Falstaff is, by Hal's own words, fattened by consumption—of everything: old sack, capons, bawds, even time. Falstaff, the quintessential carnival figure, is on perpetual holiday, "sleeping upon benches after noon," and generally disregarding the proper "time" for proper duties, as indeed London authorities complained their citizenry did at plays: "They maintaine idlenes in such persons as haue no vocation & draw apprentices and other seruantes from theire ordinary workes."[19] Standing, or perhaps like Bolingbroke sitting on or lying prone upon (is he just awakening?) a mock throne upstage in Bolingbroke's "place" (i.e., *locus*) as he will in 2.4, Falstaff pleads that stealing, the profession he shares with Bolingbroke, be judged the work of gentlemen:

> Let us be Diana's foresters, gentlemen of the shade,
> minions of the moon; and let men say we be men of
> good government, being governed, as the sea is, by our
> noble and chaste mistress the moon, under whose
> countenance we steal.
>
> (1.2.25–29)

As the King is a thief, and thus an "actor" in his role, yet wishes to be considered a man of "good government," and tries desperately to achieve that image in the play, so Falstaff wishes to gain royal protection for his "profession." If spectators in 1596–97 knowing their history could accept nonetheless Bolingbroke's efforts within the play to appear credible as king, then why not accept Falstaff's efforts to appear credible as a thief? Falstaff, after all, is an agent of the world that Richard and Bolingbroke cooperated to create; Richard represented legitimacy, but destroyed the sanctions and continuities of royal authority, and Bolingbroke stole the scraps of kingship: "Here, cousin, seize the crown." Insecurity reigns; "wisdom cries out in the / street, and no man regards it" (1.2.87–88). As official, royal power in this play has been legitimized by stealing, why not, analogically, its carnivalesque inversion—especially because throughout the play both occupy and pontificate from virtually the same "place" (i.e., are in performance literally interchangeable) on stage?

Hal, the son of one thief, companion of another, and legendary ale-house roister,[20] attempts to convince Falstaff to take time more seriously, thinking of his inevitably becoming king of England and how this historically necessary time will affect Falstaff: "a purse of gold" snatched on Monday night and spent on Tuesday morning leads "by and by in as high a flow as the ridge of the gallows" (1.2.37–38). In the witty riposte that follows about buff jerkins, paying one's "part" with "my hostess of the tavern," the existence of gallows when Hal is king, and whether Falstaff as a "rare hangman" shall hang a thief or himself be hanged as one, Falstaff's spontaneous, evasive, and self-protective wit is brilliantly effective. Falstaff has no intention of "giving over" his life, as his immediate response to Hal's question, "Where shall we take a purse tomorrow, Jack?" clearly indicates: "Zounds, where thou wilt, lad, I'll make one. An I do not, call me villain and baffle me" (1.2.97–99). Thus, one assumes he genuinely wants to know if gallows shall stand when Hal is king. Falstaff's request, "Do not thou, when thou art king, hang a thief," elicits Hal's response "No, thou shalt" (1.2.59–61). Falstaff's line asks that Hal as king not hang thieves, a profession to which Falstaff is thoroughly dedicated; however, it also urges Hal himself not to hang as a thief when he is king, a possibility given that Hal is the son of a thieving monarch, suggesting thereby that Hal shall not change on becoming king (i.e., that history shall have no compelling claim on him). Falstaff's elusive wit is his most potent weapon in a campaign of carnival laughter aimed squarely at those forces that would hang thieves had they the legitimacy to do so.

Falstaff wishes he knew "where a commodity of good names were to be bought" (1.2.81–82). In this kingdom, good names are for sale, and apparently both Falstaff and the Prince need one: "There's neither honesty, manhood, nor good fellowship in thee, nor thou cam'st not of the blood royal, if thou darest not stand for ten shillings" (1.2.136–38). As the son of a thief, Hal is a traitor to his chosen fellows, and failing in his princely training for the Crown,[21] if he will not steal, especially as it is so easy; Poins boasts: "I have bespoke supper tomorrow night in Eastcheap. We may do it as secure as sleep" (1.2.127–28). Like the rebels later in 3.1, who on a map will divide up a kingdom they have not yet won, Poins and his rebels have spent at a tavern money they have not yet robbed. But then thievery is, indeed, easy in this kingdom, on this stage, in these "liberties" outside London's walls so feared and loathed by the city's authorities. With immense rhetorical dexterity Falstaff blithely, confidently sermonizes his way across the platform stage, across the boards of this kingdom and the "place" of corrupted royal power, using carefully balanced phrasing and biblical imagery[22] as he urges Poins to persuade the Prince to pursue his "true," inherited vocation:

> Well, God give thee the spirit of persuasion and him
> the ears of profiting, that what thou speakest may
> move and what he hears may be believed, that the
> true prince may, for recreation's sake, prove a false
> thief, for the poor abuses of the time want countenance.
>
> (1.2.148–52)

Theater as recreation, as re-creation, as carnival demands that the true prince prove a false thief—that is, Falstaff prays that the theater may show the prince as he truly is, a false thief, and thus a true son of another false thief who wears the crown in this kingdom, on this stage, where theft is secure as sleep, even at places "notorious for robberies" that would have been recognized as such by an Elizabethan audience.[23] Hal has robbed before—"As, for proof, now: a purse of gold most resolutely snatched on Monday night and most dissolutely spent on Tuesday morning, got with swearing 'Lay by' and spent with crying 'Bring in'" (1.2.33–36)—and Falstaff asks only that the prince prove true to his vocation, and thus true to his heritage.[24] Falstaff prays that theater as "recreation" recreate the crime that identifies the theater's image of royal authority in this play. Usurping Bolingbroke's "place" on stage, the upstage *locus* of royal power in 1.1, Falstaff with equal "authority" plots a crime that shall imitate the King's and, he believes, be endorsed by the Prince of Wales. The poor abuses of the time do indeed lack countenance, such as only royalty can provide.

Immediately before Hal's soliloquy, spectators see him planning to rob the robbers: "The virtue of this jest will be the incomprehensible lies that this same fat rogue will tell us when we meet at supper" (1.2.180–82). Poins and Hal shall be "in disguise," yet not so; the true prince will still be himself, a thief, robbing the King's money and thus, to theater spectators, laboring in his father's vocation: robbing a king. As Poins predicts, it shall be as secure as sleep. In restealing the pilgrims' crowns, Hal is not only imitating comically his father's seizing of the Crown but also imitating Falstaff's vein in the pursuit of a jest for its own humorous sake. Even as Hal imitates both his "fathers,"[25] his and Poins's plan kindles spectators' anticipation of

Falstaff's return to the stage, thus instigating the theatrical rhythm that is central to Falstaff's enormous audience appeal.

Of Hal's notorious soliloquy, "I know you all, and will awhile uphold / The unyoked humor of your idleness" (1.2.189–211), one can say as Alan Dessen does of the "Shylock problem": there will be no final solution to it.[26] Although I do not propose a "solution" to this problematic speech, and would suggest rather that it is dramatically valuable precisely because it is so problematic, at this moment we must recall that Hal's soliloquy is a moment in a play, a "script" designed to be experienced sequentially in an Elizabethan playhouse, rather than a detachable speech in a "text" to be issued (and later reissued "with corrections") in a scholarly "critical" edition. Elizabethan spectators, perhaps knowing of Hal's legendary antics and eventual reformation from chronicles and *The Famous Victories,* would surely recognize historical inevitability in Hal's soliloquy: as the King's elder son, Hal must in time become King. Standing downstage center, Hal proclaims to the Theatre's audience that he is like the sun, which "doth permit the base contagious clouds / To smother up his beauty from the world" (1.2.192–93). Hal shall, like the sun, "when he please again to be himself," break "through the foul and ugly mists / Of vapors that did seem to strangle him" (lines 194, 196–97). Hal deliberately speaks metaphorically; why? Who/what are these "base contagious clouds," "foul and ugly mists?" On the Elizabethan stage, Falstaff, i.e., Will Kempe. Hal is unwilling to name Falstaff; i.e., Burbage is unwilling to name Kempe. Rather than mention specifically[27] the character (i.e., actor) who embodies the holiday attitude that the Theatre itself enacts, both by its very presence in the "Liberties" and the actual performance of this play (i.e., the actors' "playing holiday"), Hal expresses his eventual reformation in terms of absolute and calculating power: as the sun that shall in its own chosen time burn away the contagious clouds and ugly mists. Within the *process* of the play, Hal's speech is a challenge to Falstaff and to the huge carnival energy he embodies. It is also an expression of raw power, of royal prerogative to deal how and when it wishes with carnival and its proponents. It is, finally, a challenge to the Theatre and its audience who insist on playing holiday every day of the week to the rage of civic and Puritan authorities.

Hal insists that "If all the year were playing holidays, / To sport would be as tedious as to work" (lines 198–99). According to the Lord Mayor and Aldermen of London, the public theaters were a threat to the economic health of the commonwealth because the plays "draw apprentices and other seruantes from their ordinary workes."[28] Already obvious in 1.2, in the brief dialogue about the hanging of thieves when Hal shall be king, is the extemporaneous genius of Falstaff's wit. Like Tarlton's and Kempe's improvising on the stage, Falstaff's wit is "out of time"; as Falstaff deliberately misconstrues what Hal is trying to tell him about hanging thieves, so Tarlton's and Kempe's legendary improvising in their parts was out of the ordinary, the predictable—the "holiday" of improvisation as opposed to the "everyday" of scripted performance. Hal's labeling as "contagious" and "ugly" these theatrical forces creates the dramatic and metatheatrical tension within this play: Hal proclaims that Falstaff must be, at some future unspecified time, discarded; Burbage, playing Hal in a history play, the embodiment of eventual royal power, challenges Kempe, the Chamberlain's improvising comic genius, to a theatrical combat. Hal and Falstaff, and Burbage and Kempe, are to battle for control of genre. Thus, this soliloquy, like Hal's and Poins's planned "jest" with Falstaff on Gad's Hill, furthers spectators' anticipation of Falstaff's return to the stage.

Hal continues: "So when this loose behavior I throw off / And pay the debt I never promisèd, / By how much better than my word I am, / By so much shall I falsify men's hopes" (1.2.202–5). As James Winny shows in his extensive analysis of the psychological tension between Hal's relations to Bolingbroke and Falstaff, the calculating nature of Hal's soliloquy and his "biting moral awareness" of his father's moral lassitude are most evident in these lines.[29] Both Bolingbroke and Falstaff are thieves, and as in the inner play in 2.4, Hal can displace criticism of his father onto Falstaff and thus temper his disgrace at his father's errors. But to see the soliloquy only, or even primarily this way, is to argue a critical overview and to deny in Hal during the play the lure of Falstaff's vitality that the audience experiences.[30] To argue that Hal is immune to Falstaff is to argue that Hal is less susceptible to carnival than the Theatre's spectators. It is to argue that Burbage is immune to Kempe. The remainder of the play indicates far otherwise.[31]

Shakespeare returns to history in 1.3, the second longest scene in the play after 2.4. Thus, Shakespeare maximizes audience anticipation for Falstaff's return by interposing the long and acrimonious debate about prisoners, the remains from the bloody slaughter described in 1.1, and Hotspur's singular pursuit of honor. The attempted parley immediately dissolves;

Worcester is dismissed, and Hotspur launches into his long defense of his conduct in battle, especially regarding the "certain
lord, neat and trimly dressed" who asks for his prisoners. Bolingbroke's refusal to ransom "revolted Mortimer" certainly recalled
for his spectators the King's illegitimate, and tenuous, grasp of
the throne. The King accuses Hotspur of lying about Mortimer's
encounter with Glendower, and after Bolingbroke leaves, the
rebels lay their plot against the King, a thief and an impostor, a
deadly serious version of the comical plot laid by Hal and Poins
against Falstaff, another thief and impostor. After encouraging
his father and uncle to clear their names from having helped
to the throne "this thorn, this canker, Bolingbroke" (1.3.176),
Hotspur proclaims his view of honor:

> By heaven, methinks it were an easy leap
> To pluck bright honor from the pale-faced moon,
> Or dive into the bottom of the deep,
> Where fathom line could never touch the ground,
> And pluck up drownèd honor by the locks,
> So he that doth redeem her thence might wear
> Without corrival all her dignities;
> But out upon this half-faced fellowship!
>
> (1.3.201–8)

Hotspur seems not to realize the fanatical, self-destructive nature of his pursuit. His grossly exaggerated images befit his ego
and his temper; neither his father nor his uncle can restrain
his tongue:

> Why, look you, I am whipped and scourged with rods,
> Nettled and stung with pismires, when I hear
> Of this vile politician, Bolingbroke.
> In Richard's time—what do you call the place?—
> A plague upon it, it is in Gloucestershire;
> 'Twas where the madcap duke his uncle kept,
> His uncle York; where I first bowed my knee
> Unto this king of smiles, this Bolingbroke—
> 'Sblood, when you and he came back from Ravenspurgh.
>
> (1.3.238–46)

Speaking from the same "place" on stage as Hal and Falstaff
earlier, and thus providing from the *platea* yet another perspective of this diseased kingdom, Hotspur's broken syntax contrasts
sharply not only with Hal's far more controlled syntax in his

earlier soliloquy, but also with Falstaff's assured prose and spontaneous wit. Hotspur's inspired chivalry in defense of the kingdom helped produce the "Ten thousand bold Scots, two-and-twenty knights, / Balked in their own blood" (1.1.68–69) at Holmedon, which immediately prompts Bolingbroke's wish that Northumberland's son were his own. Thus despite the images of slaughter from act 1, the chivalric values fanatically represented and narrated[32] by Hotspur become the perfect foil for Falstaff, whose own version of "honor" spectators hear later in the play. Though he too would be a thief, Hotspur's code of honor allows no "space" for wasted time; pots of ale; carnivalesque reversion of values; improvised speech; theater; and, finally, acting.

In 2.1 the second carrier complains that "This house is turned upside down since Robin Hostler died" (lines 10–11). "House" signifies of course the supposed location of the scene, "An innyard on the London-Canterbury Road" ("2.1. Location"; Bevington, 4th ed., 773). This inn is overrun with fleas, carriers are poorly housed, the horses' food is rank, the hostler is late, and disorder is everywhere. But "house" here has several other meanings, all germane to the play. On the bare platform stage, on the upstage *locus,* the "location" of this scene, an innyard, is situated symbolically in the same "place" as other locations in the play: the King's court in 1.1, 1.3, and 3.2; and Hal's meeting with Falstaff in 1.2, presumably the Prince's London quarters. This *locus* will also be the "place" of the tavern scenes as well as the rebels' various meeting places and the Shrewsbury battle scene. This fluidity of the Elizabethan stage makes all "places" essentially identical and thus heightens the symbolic resonances of stage pictures among a play's multiple scenes. The "house" that is upside down is symbolically the realm of England itself because a thief is on the throne; as the inn is chaotic since Robin Hostler died, so England is chaotic under a counterfeit king. Further, spectators have seen and heard two sets of thieves plotting to rob the kingdom of its monarch and its money. The inn itself, where the King's subjects work, is infested not only with fleas, perhaps suggesting the spread of the plague, but also with thieves and spies, who, as Gadshill says, "pray continually to their saint, the commonwealth, or rather not pray to her but prey on her, for they ride up and down on her and make her their boots" (2.1.80–83). Furthermore, insists Gadshill, robbery in this commonwealth truly is "as secure as sleep": "Justice hath liquored her. We steal as in a castle, cocksure. We have the receipt of fern seed; we walk invisible" (2.1.86–88). The commonwealth is an inn with no security where the employees (i.e., subjects) are themselves thieves who steal with impunity because justice itself has "liquored" (i.e., literally and metaphorically "sacked") authority.

In this scene, "house" has another crucial symbolic meaning for this play, for the "house" that is "turned upside down" is also the "playhouse," the Theatre; *at this moment in performance,* symbolic resonances abound within this house of play. The playhouse itself is "upside down," an image of misrule and antirule thriving in the margins or "liberties" of Elizabethan society, exasperating civic and religious authorities who considered its trade in playing holiday diabolical. By their very attendance at such performances, spectators approve the Theatre's flagrant, persistent abuse of contemporary authority ("as who woulde say . . . we wil play"). Further, the calculated mockery of authority and social conventions native to Falstaff's spontaneous, disruptive, consumptive, and irresistible humor boldly ridicules the traditional, historically sanctioned power and chivalry that Bolingbroke, Hal, and especially Hotspur continually try to enact. The kingdom is the battlefield is the court is the inn is the tavern, and all are "this house," the Theatre; thieves are everywhere, for *I Henry IV* boldly features them within its script as the Theatre openly contains them within its walls. The Elizabethan theater is, as well as contains, carnival; although *I Henry IV* has many "places" within its script, the Elizabethan theater reduces all of these places to one *locus* that metatheatrically stages a struggle for generic legitimacy between the sanctioned authority of Hal's history and Falstaff's carnival antithesis.

The two robberies of 2.2 occur in the same "place" on the highway near Gad's Hill—that is, on the bare stage, in the center of another thief's kingdom, in the "place" of his court meeting with the rebels in 1.3, and "in place of" his court, as if these twin robberies, one involving the heir apparent, were interchangeable with royal proceedings. These thieves literally "ride up and down" on the commonwealth. In a kingdom as unruly as a playhouse, in a kingdom that *is* a playhouse, each "turned upside down," Shakespeare secures spectators' approval of comic versions of official royal behavior by making robbery immensely funny. Why not? Is not laughter in the face of thwarted authority appropriate response for a social institution that thrives on such thwarting?[33]

Besides being unruly, when "brawling" about his missing

horse might alert the thieves' intended victims, Falstaff is "be-witched" with affection for Poins:

> I am accursed to rob in that thief's company. The rascal hath re-moved my horse and tied him I know not where.... I have forsworn his company hourly any time this two-and-twenty years, and yet I am bewitched with the rogue's company. If the rascal have not given me medicines to make me love him, I'll be hanged; it could not be else—I have drunk medicines.... Eight yards of uneven ground is three-score-and-ten miles afoot with me, and the stony-hearted vil-lains know it well enough. A plague upon it when thieves cannot be true to one another!
>
> (2.2.10, 15–19, 24–27)

A. C. Bradley remarks that Falstaff "has affection in him ... which he cannot jest out of existence."[34] Later in 3.3, Falstaff will insist to Hal "Thy love is worth a million; thou owest me thy love" (lines 136–37). Shakespeare insists on Falstaff's capac-ity for human affection and warmth even as Falstaff laments the lack of loyalty that plagues not only these thieves, but also the entire kingdom; as Bolingbroke quarrels with the noblemen who helped him to the throne, so now his son shows in his plot against Falstaff not only that he is indeed of the "blood royal" but also his capacity for "play" in a kingdom in which his father "plays" at being king. Uttered from the *locus* of a robbery at Gad's Hill that is the stage place from which the royal thief who stole a crown opened the play, Falstaff's pervasive humor ridicules the King's authority by carnivalizing his occupation, stealing:

> *Prince.* Lay thine ear close to the ground and list if thou canst hear the tread of travelers.
> *Falstaff.* Have you any levers to lift me up again, being down?
> . . . . . . . . . . . . . . . . . . . . . . .
> *Prince.* Out, ye rogue! Shall I be your hostler?
> *Falstaff.* Go hang thyself in thine own heir-apparent garters! If I be ta'en, I'll peach for this. An I have not ballads made on you all and sung to filthy tunes, let a cup of sack be my poison. When a jest is so forward, and afoot too! I hate it.
> . . . . . . . . . . . . . . . . . . . . . . .
> *Falstaff.* There's no more valor in that Poins than in a wild duck.
>
> (2.2.31–34, 41–46, 99–100)

But even as Falstaff elicits laughter he speaks more truly of this kingdom—and this "house"—than perhaps even he realizes. When Gadshill tells him there are "eight or ten" riders, Falstaff cries, "Zounds, will they not rob us?" (2.2.64). Thieves are everywhere; in the kingdom in (and symbolized by) this playhouse, every sizable group of people is to be feared as thieves. (Theaters are "the ordinary places for vagrant persons, Maisterles men, thieves, horse stealers."[35]) Falstaff insists, in the presence of this threat, that he is no coward. His running away moments later flatly contradicts this last claim,[36] again creating audience expectation of his return and the "incomprehensible lies that this same fat rogue will tell us when we meet at supper—how thirty at least he fought with, what wards, what blows, what extremities he endured" that Poins predicted in 1.2. But the very predictability of Falstaff's action creates the opportunity for his complete thrashing of not only their expectations, but also of order and authority in the tavern scene of 2.4.

Hotspur, the "mad-headed ape," refuses to believe the anonymous letter from a "pagan rascal" that warns that "the friends you have named [are] uncertain, the time itself unsorted, and your whole plot too light for the counterpoise of so great an opposition" (2.3.11–13). This scene, which prepares the audience for the disintegration of Hotspur's plot beginning in 4.1, is also the perfect foil for both Hal and Falstaff in 2.4. Here, as in 2.2, thieves cannot be true to one another, though Hotspur refuses to believe the warning, and from this refusal comes the rebels' defeat at Shrewsbury. Hotspur is utterly inflexible and secretive: "That roan shall be my throne. / Well, I will back him straight"; "But hark you, Kate, / I must not have you henceforth question me / Whither I go, nor reason whereabout" (2.3.70–71,102–4). Both Hal and Falstaff in 2.4 will be verbally and emotionally far more open and expansive; indeed, the playing of "roles" by both Hal and Falstaff is the essence of the tavern scene. Hotspur's choleric dedication to his cause and to "honor" will be ridiculed by Hal in 2.4 as an obsession for which he is not yet ready; perhaps more significantly for the carnival essence of this play, Hotspur is gradually emerging as the principal threat, not so much to Hal as to Falstaff. Hotspur would not tolerate Falstaff for an instant; though himself a rebel and aspiring thief, Hotspur would turn upright this upside down house, this kingdom and playhouse, this plebeian burlesque of history and authority that the play *I Henry IV* continues pretending is its theme. Thus Hotspur's myopic fanaticism, as he rides off alone into the night, must be clear to spectators just before Falstaff's explosion of the traps and constraints that history and authority would impose on him.

Shakespeare's organization of act 2 stresses the theatrical importance of scene 4. Act 2, scene 1 is 98 lines; 2.2 is 110; and 2.3 is 117. By contrast, 2.4 is 545 lines, five times the average length of the previous three scenes. Thus, 2.4 explodes onto the stage, as the play's "history" and "carnival" collide. Mark Rose has brilliantly demonstrated that the tavern scene is a carefully structured diptych built around two major themes, language and time, with two major segments: "Falstaff ascendant," from Hal and Poins baiting Francis to their baiting of Falstaff about the robbery; and "Falstaff descendant," including the messengers from the court and the sheriff and the inner play involving Falstaff and Hal. The search through Falstaff's pockets Rose terms the scene's coda of 22 lines.[37]

Hal has told spectators in his soliloquy in 1.2 that at an unspecified future time he will throw off his loose behavior and pay a debt he "never promised." The essential ambiguity of this assertion—that he will pay a debt not necessarily because he wants to, but because history insists that he must—dominates his actions in the whole tavern sequence. His opening request to Poins is that he "lend me thy hand to laugh a little" (2.4.2), and he asks Poins to aid in his mocking game with poor Francis "to drive away the time till Falstaff come" (lines 27–28). Hal seems almost lost without Falstaff, not knowing what to do with himself. He ridicules the drawers' and underskinkers' sparse language, and of his learning the tinkers' whole language in "one quarter of an hour" he says to Poins: "Ned, thou hast lost much honor that thou wert not with me in this action" (lines 19–20). Is this jesting, or ridicule? Perhaps both, as well as a sly, subtextual attack on Hotspur's defining word, honor, to whom Hal will refer shortly. His game with Francis, including his apparent surprise at Francis's five-year indenture for the "clinking of pewter," and his question whether Francis will rob his master and flee,[38] seems unnecessarily cruel. Rose argues that although Hal seems here a "snide bully," the principal thrust of the episode is emblematic: "in Francis Shakespeare expects us to recognize a comic image for the prince himself, called simultaneously in two directions, the tavern and the court."[39] This interpretation is suggested by Hal's questions about Francis's servitude and Hal's projecting into an indefinite future his payment of a promised debt: "No Francis; but tomorrow, Francis, or, Francis, o' Thursday" (lines 65–66). But however emblematic this episode may be, it is nonetheless bound to be unsettling in a public theater that contains, among its socially heterogeneous audience, apprentices such as those the Lord Mayor and Aldermen of London complained were drawn to plays from "theire ordinary workes."

Rose observes that Hal's dwelling on Francis's verbal poverty is psychologically linked to his sudden ridicule of the "intellectual poverty"[40] of Hotspur, who, as this scene unfolds at "the pupil age of this present twelve o'clock at midnight" (lines 94–95), is "offstage" galloping alone toward his collision with honor. The verbal and intellectual poverty of Francis and Hotspur are dramatically perfect foils for Falstaff, whose dexterous wit and copious vocabulary create whole battle skirmishes supposedly lasting for hours. Rose asserts: "Our response as we watch Falstaff at his vocation can perhaps best be described in vitalist terms: after the narrow, mechanical, constrained world of Francis and Hotspur in the first episode, we find ourselves in the presence of something organic and alive, and the effect is of release into sudden freedom."[41] Falstaff's role at Gad's Hill reproduces itself spontaneously—not even his ballooning of his adversaries can match the sheer audacity of his nerve in simply telling (i.e., acting) this story. Although Hal and Poins allow Falstaff's chivalric fantasy to erupt, one assumes that either Falstaff is continually inventing more adversaries to make himself seem more heroic because he thinks Hal believes him, or that at some point before Hal tells him the "plain tale" of what actually happened Falstaff realizes Hal's purpose, and he continues the comic mushrooming of men and valor to create an even more spectacular escape for himself to further entertain the Prince; or both.[42] Regardless of the option one selects here (perhaps on studious reflection in the library), the effect *in the theater* among disparate spectators viewing this astonishingly witty acting in the "place" of the phony king's throne is an overwhelming sense that all of the preceding is happening simultaneously. Further, because all of the invention, the acting, is Falstaff's—spectators saw what actually happened in 2.2 (i.e., its "history")—his preposterous, immensely funny, wholly carnival performance threatens to obliterate *theatrically* the history of the Gad's Hill robbery and by extension the possibility of any verifiable history as a subject of this play.

Because spectators are hearing from Falstaff exactly what Poins predicted in 1.2, the utter theatricality of his performance, its improvised playfulness and sheer bravado, are all the more entertaining. He insists that he is one of the three "good men unhanged in England" (lines 128–29) and accuses Hal of not being of "blood royal" because he did not assist in their initial robbery; Hal is thus an "untrue" thief. After calling both Poins and Hal cowards, he flatly denies doing so when Poins threatens to stab him, and wishes simply he could run as fast as Poins, presumably to aid his fleeing when Hal and Poins attacked him. Having been viciously attacked by a dozen "two hours together," he has "scaped by miracle." To accept Falstaff's outlandish fantasy, to be carried along as spectators are by the increasing expectation of an imminent collapse[43] of his denial of a history that spectators have seen, is to accept that his escape was indeed miraculous, especially given what follows.

> *Prince.*  What, fought you with them all?
> *Falstaff.*  All? I know not what you call all, but if I
> fought not with fifty of them, I am a bunch of radish.
> (2.4.182–84)

Spectators know he did not fight with fifty of them; thus, by Falstaff's own logic, he must be a bunch of radish. Yet, he is not.

> *Falstaff.*  But, as the devil would have it, three misbegotten
> knaves in Kendall green came at my back and let drive
> at me; for it was so dark, Hal, that thou couldst not see
> thy hand.
> (2.2.219–22)

Falstaff has, apparently, trapped himself; accused by Hal of lying, he screams: "What, art thou mad? Art thou mad? Is not the truth the truth?" (lines 227–28). In this verbal battle, a kind of "one-upsmanship" between history and holiday, between Burbage and Kempe, the one trying to enact a history play in which fat, unruly knights are serious threats to order, the other committed only to his own carnival existence and contemptuous of authority and the very idea of history, Hal's version of the "truth" of Gad's Hill can be summarily denied; nothing is but what is not, or at least as Falstaff says it is. When Hal insists that Falstaff explain how he could see Kendall green in the dark, Falstaff refuses to explain "upon compulsion." At this moment, his wit totally dominates Hal; his refusal to speak upon compulsion evades Hal's question, to which their dialogue never returns. Falstaff prolongs the ensuing name calling that Hal initiates presumably to give himself time to create his most hilarious, and therefore most convincing, escape. When challenged to find a "starting hole" to evade Hal's true history of Gad's Hill, Falstaff simply outwits the Prince: "By the Lord, I knew ye as well as he that made ye. Why, hear you my masters, was it for me to kill the heir apparent?" (2.4.264–66). ("He that made" Hal is, of course, Bolingbroke, another thief; Falstaff thus claims that the "heir apparent" was/is recognizable in and by the act of stealing.)

I stress Falstaff's dexterous wit here because in the remainder of 2.4 and throughout the play, Falstaff employs this wit to avoid, if not eviscerate, history's and authority's claims upon him. Hal does not press Falstaff further, nor challenge his valiant lion theory. Hal can ridicule Francis, and can fetch from Bardolph and Peto a "true account" of what happened at Gad's Hill. But Hal is no match for Falstaff when the fat rogue is on stage. Thus, even before the inner play Falstaff's carnival contempt for authority and history, which are embodied in Hal's debt that he never promised and his frequent references to time, not only threatens the political history that this play struggles to enact but also obliterates the "history" at Gad's Hill that spectators themselves have seen. The play's huge Falstafflan energy is directed squarely at the twin presumptions that history is a verifiable construct about whose content and meaning people can agree and that the structures of authority that history requires can even exist. Consider again Harry Berger Jr.'s remark (Introduction, 16) that Elizabethan theater established "the primacy of imaginary space time" by marking off an area and walling out the rest of the world.[44] The very existence of the physical structure itself, its renowned and popular "place" in the Liberties, flaunted London authorities who sought vainly to marginalize and thus eviscerate it; within its walls, within the "play" of imaginary space and time, thieves "prey on" the commonwealth, "rid[ing] up and down on her and mak[ing] her their boots" as they strut across the place, the *locus*, of kings, turning the throne into a tavern with absolute impunity and thereby winning approval from spectators by the sheer subversive power of their acting.

"What doth Gravity out of his bed at midnight?" (line 291). We hear of midnight twice in the first half of this scene: once from Hal, who says he is "of all humors" since Adam to "this present twelve o'clock at midnight" (lines 92, 94); and here from Falstaff as he attends the "nobleman of the court at door." This upside-down scene, where "history" becomes verbal improvisation, suggests an atemporal realm of eternal carnival twixt night and morning in which fat knights "scape by miracle" and moral authority[45] has no place. This is the dramatic environment in which the inner play about English kingship must be understood.

The impetus for the play, for acting within acting, is Falstaff's, not Hal's: "Well, thou wilt be horribly chid tomorrow when thou comest to thy father. If thou love me, practice an answer" (2.4.369–71). Thus, underlying the "play" of Hal's reunion with his father is the question of Hal's love for Falstaff, which Falstaff continually asserts ought to be Hal's main concern when he comes to court. The comic and symbolic appropriateness of this "court" (i.e., a tavern) as a testing of that love immediately becomes apparent as does the struggle between Hal and Falstaff for control of this "play":

> *Prince.*   Do thou stand for my father, and examine me upon the particulars of my life.
>
> *Falstaff.*   Shall I? Content. This chair shall be my state, this dagger my scepter, and this cushion my crown.
>
> *Prince.*   Thy state is taken for a joint stool, thy golden scepter for a leaden dagger, and thy precious rich crown for a pitiful bald crown.
>
> (2.4.372–78)

The initial symbolism of this setting is clear: the tavern is the court, and Falstaff is king; Hal's "test" is his response to this "king's" command to "keep with" him, as heir to this "kingdom" (i.e. the tavern), its "goodly portly . . . cheerful" carnival leader, as Falstaff wistfully describes himself. The setting and dialogue also extend directly into the larger play's history. Hal recognizes the comic relevance of Falstaff's "state" to his father's; as James Calderwood asks, "If Bolingbroke is a false king, a lie, and Falstaff is a burlesque king, a metaphor, where does true kingship reside?"[46] In the Theatre, this scene presumably would have been played under the canopy, upstage center, in the *locus* where Bolingbroke's "court" was staged in 1.3. This "court" is now simultaneously counterfeited by and reduced to a joint stool, as is the royal crown counterfeited by and reduced to a ragged cushion. Yet these "counterfeits" are also perfectly accurate *theater* images of court and crown. On stage court and crown are seen as, *in performance* actually *are*, carnival; royal power thus assumes an accurate image of its pretensions to authority under the thief Bolingbroke. In the Theatre, the play gives its spectators two versions of "authority," but in each the "acting" ruler is a thief, and in each the ruler refuses to admit his own erroneous self-image. Bolingbroke is no less a "player king" than Falstaff, yet ironically only Falstaff realizes that as a thief, Hal is, both within and without their play, the image of his father:

> If then thou be son to me, here lies the point: why, being son to me, art thou so pointed at? . . . Shall the son of England prove a thief and take purses? A question to be asked. (2.4.402–04,406–07)

As Hal's father is, like Falstaff, a thief, and Hal is thus truly of the "blood royal," then Hal is "pointed at" for reasons Falstaff playing Bolingbroke knows well: because all three—Hal and his two "fathers"—are thieves and thus images of corrupted authority. The audience has seen the "son of England" take purses at Gad's Hill. In the same "place" on stage, the *locus* of stage authority, spectators have also seen a player king plagued by thieves who cannot be true to one another and the fat pretender to the "throne" extemporaneously and effortlessly demolish the history of Gad's Hill and with it the dramatic genre this "history play" is supposedly enacting. These facts being so, on what basis in this "play" is Bolingbroke to be preferred to Falstaff as king? The royal court to this roguish court? These questions are especially pertinent as at this moment in a production at the Theatre the king's crowns stolen at Gad's Hill are in this "house": "Then did we two set on you four, and, with a word, outfaced you from your prize, and have it, yea, and can show you it here in the house" (2.4.253–56). This "house," the Elizabethan playhouse, which brought spectators "into a theatrical enclosure for the express purpose of seeing a play"[47] brings spectators of *I Henry IV* into a play, into acting, which ridicules the very authority that sought to marginalize and thus control it. This "house" also shelters thieves, among them Hal, and the spectators know the money is here; thus, if Falstaff can "play" at king here (i.e., within this inner play) and be accepted as such, why cannot Bolingbroke also be king here? Is not one equal in "authority" to the other? If all the realm is ruled by a thief who only plays at being king, then is not the Theatre at this moment in this "inner play," as well as in the playing of the "history" play *I Henry IV,* the image of the kingdom—indeed, the kingdom itself? If the kingdom and its authority in the outer play are corrupt, no more than the dramatized image in this inner play, a joint stool and a leaden dagger, on what historical basis then does Tudor authority claim in 1597 to condemn its citizens for attending theater?[48]

The instability of order, history, and authority that *I Henry IV* dramatizes is most striking in the second half of the playlet. Here, as Hal and Falstaff switch places and "roles," Shakespeare dramatizes the utter fictitiousness of rule in Bolingbroke's England. Hal complains about Falstaff's "rule":

> *Prince.*     Dost thou speak like a king? Do thou stand for me, and I'll play my father.
>
> *Falstaff.*   Depose me? If thou dost it half so gravely, so majestically, both in word and matter, hang me up by the heels for a rabbit-sucker or a poulter's hare.
>
> (2.4.428–32; note again Falstaff's speaking of "hanging")

In this inner play there is no orderly succession to the throne, no proper assuming of royal power; a "king" is as easily deposed by his "son" as thieves take purses: "We steal as in a castle, cocksure." Thus the inner play comically depicts Bolingbroke's deposing of Richard II. The tavern's carnival reduction of royal authority thus ironically reinforces the lack of succession and proper passing of authority that has produced an England where a thief is king, and all other thieves worry that any band of men met on the road may themselves be thieves: "Zounds, will they not rob us?" As Bolingbroke stole the crown from Richard, so here Hal, the young thief, who has the "real" King's money here "in the house," has stolen the "pitiful bald crown" of the inner play's reigning monarch, and become himself a carnival ruler with a cushion on his head and thus now an apt image of his royal father. Again, the tavern *is* the kingdom. Hal symbolically steps into history only to mock it, to turn it and its authority into this "excellent sport." Further, the actual playing of this scene at the Theatre would emphasize this instability. Recall the sight lines created by the thrust stage of the Theatre and, later, the Globe that J. L. Styan describes.[49] Spectators sitting generally to one side of the thrust stage first see Falstaff facing them as king, and then as Hal; those on the other side first see Hal facing them as Hal, and then as king. Who is the king? Who is his son? Who is Falstaff? Who is Hal? In the Theatre there is for spectators no dominant, singular perspective on kingship, authority, or identity in this entertaining and mischievous "play"; rather than political stability, spectators see images of severe instability, of constantly shifting authority in which ale-house kings rule for but a moment of slapstick midnight revelry. Kings here have neither power nor history. Further, given its symbolically mimetic relationship to the larger play *I Henry IV,* and to the England whose history the play continually struggles to enact, Hal's and Falstaff's own instability as rulers satirizes and reduces to carnival, to "harlotry players," pretentious kings (and queens?) who assume power is theirs to inherit and exploit.

In their remaining speeches, Hal, as king, condemns Falstaff as Hal for carousing with the "reverend Vice," the "abominable misleader of youth" whom J. Dover Wilson identifies as the traditional Vice figure of morality plays;[50] and Falstaff as Hal defends himself. Falstaff's encomium, with its balanced, Lylian phrases and crescendo rhythm,[51] is the most affective, humorous, pernicious, and theatrical lie of the entire play:

> *Falstaff.* ... but for sweet Jack Falstaff, kind Jack Falstaff, true Jack Falstaff, valiant Jack Falstaff, and therefore more valiant being as he is old Jack Falstaff, banish not him thy Harry's company, banish not him thy Harry's company—banish plump Jack, and banish all the world.
>
> (2.4.470–75)

Falstaff as king, and Falstaff as Hal, both praise Falstaff as Falstaff. (Note that Falstaff escapes "playing" himself; that would demand an accounting he is not yet ready for, and would also be too easy.) Hal's celebrated response to Falstaff's claim that to banish plump Jack is to banish all the world—"I do, I will"—ends their present fiction, their harlotry playing, and heralds Hal's future deed in the history that he is supposedly enacting. Hal's first "banishment," his only actual attempt at authority within the inner play, fails completely: he cannot banish Falstaff's prodigious carnival energy, which reasserts itself right through to Shrewsbury and there resurrects itself. His prophecy of banishment, presumably to occur when he, sun-like, breaks through the "foul and ugly mists" of his Eastcheap riots, does not happen *in this play.* Hal, sitting on a joint stool wearing the regalia of the tavern throne, is neither kingly nor authoritarian;[52] yet, and therefore, he is an accurate image of this king, his father, whom theater boldly, playfully mocks.

The second intrusion on the tavern, this time the sheriff, abruptly ends the inner play. "The sheriff and all the watch are at the door. They are come to search the house. Shall I let them

in?" (2.4.484–85). Bardolph insists the watch is "most monstrous"; many constables are certainly at the door, and they are
"monstrous" also in their audacious intrusion into plebeian
laughter and midnight revels. In this superbly metatheatric moment, Elizabethan authority, the law, has come to search the
house, the playhouse, which houses thieves and the king's
money, not only that from the fictional robbery at Gad's Hill but
also that of Londoners who have paid to attend this play much
against the authorities' wishes. In this house, that authority is
being roundly mocked. Gravity is out of its bed again, and this
time demands a reckoning. Falstaff places his fate squarely in
Hal's hands: "If you will deny the sheriff, so; if not, let him enter.
If I become not a cart as well as another man, a plague on my
bringing up!" (2.4.490–92). (Does Falstaff mean this? Is this
proof of his "valor"? Does he know what Hal will do?) One may
argue, as Sherman Hawkins does from a literary overview, that
Shakespeare's carefully crafted structure of the two *Henry IV*
plays accounts for Hal's protecting Falstaff here; however, I think
the more convincing argument originates *from within the
script during performance*: Falstaff's theatrical energy—his insistence on acting, on playing—is too colossal, too prominent,
to be carted out by mere authority. The Theatre, and its spectators, will not permit this, and in having Hal "protect" Falstaff,
Shakespeare boldly asserts the irrepressible vitality of theatrical
carnival which by its very nature, at this moment in this play
in an Elizabethan production, warrants royal protection even as
the law seeks to arrest it.[53]

Hal calls for a "true face and good conscience" as he prepares
to face the sheriff, to which Falstaff responds: "Both which I
have had, but their date is out, and therefore I'll hide me"
(2.4.498–99). Thomas McFarland asserts that Falstaff is "on the
one hand a deviant who refuses to accept the binding social
force of honor . . . [and] on the other, the frustrated idealist who,
by implication, finds society itself giving mere lip service to
honor."[54] Because the King is a thief, Falstaff sees authority as a
sham; why succumb to a hangman's cart when the king's son is
willing to protect him? Falstaff is again doing what he does so
well: creating a self-image he (apparently) pretends to believe—
"if I fought not with fifty of them, I am a bunch of radish"—but
what is most remarkable here is his absolute refusal to bow to
any, or any one's, code of behavior he deems inimical to his

livelihood. As Bradley discerns, Falstaff's essential characteristic is his "refusal to take anything seriously."[55]

"A hue and cry / Hath followed certain men unto this house" (2.4.502–3). Among those "men" are patrons of the Theatre, and certain players, including Will Kempe. Hal insists that Falstaff is not here: "For I myself at this time have employed him" (line 508). Hal promises that Falstaff shall be answerable to the law, and with the sheriff's "Indeed, my lord, I think it be two o'clock" (line 520), the Eastcheap revels have slipped past the protective charm of midnight into the morning of history. Hal must to the court. His last act in the tavern, this house of thieves, is to order Peto to search Falstaff's pockets; Hal is indeed of the "blood royal." Falstaff's last act is to fall asleep, utterly disdainful of authority beyond the Theatre; the "place" on stage of the false king's throne is now that of the fat king's slumber. Falstaff shall sleep when and where he pleases, including "upon benches after noon," obedient only to his own improvised rhythms. Richard Burbage has employed Will Kempe, perhaps unwittingly and to the detriment of his own history play, in the maintenance of carnival.[56]

After the "monstrous" hiatus of 2.4, the history play earnestly resumes in act 3. Shakespeare establishes a distinctive pattern for the remainder of the play: as the rebels become more divided, so the King's forces become more united. In 3.1 Glendower's pretensions to an almost supernatural birth enrage Hotspur, who ridicules Glendower's claims and then begins an argument about land he has not yet won. Hotspur's remark that he would "rather live / With cheese and garlic in a windmill, far, / Than feed on cates and have him [Glendower] talk to me / In any summer house in Christendom" (3.1.157–60) signals again his impetuousness while symbolizing the discord which eventually dooms the rebels' plans. When Lady Percy refuses to sing, and so to prolong this brief, almost pastoral interval before war,[57] Hotspur immediately calls for the "indentures" to be drawn, and hurls the play back into time: "I'll away within these two hours; and so, come in when ye will" (3.1.258–59).

Hal's reunion with his father in 3.2 is the structural center of the play. From this point on, matters of "history" dominate the action.[58] Bolingbroke is severely critical of the carnival atmosphere of 2.4, and, speaking throughout the scene from the *locus* so thoroughly trashed by Falstaff's kingly carnival, sees Hal's deviousness as perhaps a punishment for his "mistreadings":

> Tell me else,
> Could such inordinate and low desires,
> Such poor, such bare, such lewd, such mean attempts,
> Such barren pleasures, rude society,
> As thou art matched withal and grafted to,
> Accompany the greatness of thy blood
> And hold their level with thy princely heart?
>
> (3.2.11–17)

Yet in rebuking his son, the King seems not to recognize in Hal the crafty politician Bolingbroke admits is part of his own political history. Bolingbroke admits his calculated progress to the crown, avoiding "vulgar company" so that "being seldom seen, I could not stir / But like a comet I was wondered at" (3.2.46–47). He admits to a kind of "theft":

> And then I stole all courtesy from heaven,
> And dressed myself in such humility
> That I did pluck allegiance from men's hearts,
> Loud shouts and salutations from their mouths,
> Even in the presence of the crownèd King.
> Thus did I keep my person fresh and new,
> My presence, like a robe pontifical,
> Ne'er seen but wondered at; and so my state,
> Seldom but sumptuous, showed like a feast
> And won by rareness such solemnity.
>
> (3.2.50–59)

Bolingbroke's own imagery suggests a deceptive royalty.[59] Like Macbeth, also guilty of regicide, and like Falstaff, whom Bolingbroke is now "playing" in the same stage place the other, fatter thief claimed as his equally illegitimate, and therefore equally legitimate, throne, Bolingbroke has dressed himself in borrowed robes, in a show of humility, and his kingly presence is merely outward, a "robe pontifical." Yet Bolingbroke insists on his "sunlike majesty," not realizing the discrepancy between his self-description moments earlier and this grandiose metaphor of royal power. When the King insists that Hal is his "nearest and dearest enemy," who may fight against him "under Percy's pay," Hal speaks directly of the "debt he never promised" in 1.2:

> For every honor sitting on his helm,
> Would they were multitudes, and on my head
> My shames redoubled! For the time will come
> That I shall make this northern youth exchange

His glorious deeds for my indignities.
Percy is but my factor, good my lord,
To engross up glorious deeds on my behalf;
And I will call him to so strict account
That he shall render every glory up,
Yea, even the slightest worship of his time,
Or I will tear the reckoning from his heart.

(3.2.142–52)

Percy, in his fanatical pursuit of "honor," is but Hal's "factor," a kind of "set up" in Hal's calculated scheme to gain his own honor and regain royal favor. Hal is thus as calculating and scheming as his father, and Shakespeare structures act 3 so as to present in scenes 1 and 2 the twin forces heading for their historical collision at Shrewsbury. Thieves against thieves; royalty and rebels equally scheming and calculating; using and abusing others as their purposes warrant; one faction headed by a king who has killed a king, the other by a "mad-headed ape" who wishes to repeat that crime.

These are the moral postures of the warring sides with which Falstaffian carnival must now contend. After 2.4 the number and duration of Falstaff's appearances diminish. However, the very cogency of Hawkins's arguments about Shakespeare's deliberate planning of *Henry IV* as a two-part play, and his creation of several "unhistorical" events for part 1, indicate just how carefully Shakespeare has devised Falstaff's role. For the remainder of this chapter, I wish to concentrate on how the structure of the second half of the play directs Falstaff's theatrical energy toward the play's final tension between history and carnival.

Like Hal in 3.2, Falstaff in 3.3 is aware of time; the equipoise of the tavern scene is gone, and time has brought change: "Bardolph, am I not fallen away vilely since this last action. Do I not bate? Do I not dwindle? Why, my skin hangs about me like an old lady's loose gown; I am withered like an old applejohn" (3.3.1–4). Like Hal, Falstaff claims he will repent: "Well, I'll repent, and that suddenly, while I am in some liking. I shall be out of heart shortly, and then I shall have no strength to repent" (3.3.4–7). As he claimed in 2.4 that he was one of but three good men unhanged in England, so he now claims that "Company, villainous company" has spoiled him. He recalls an earlier time when he was "as virtuously given as a gentleman need to be, virtuous enough," but now admits he lives "out of all order, out of all compass" (3.3.14–15, 20). Yet this immense "disorder," symbolized by his great belly, remains immensely vital. In the midst of his quarrel with Bardolph ("Do thou amend thy face, and I'll amend my life."), he metamorphisizes Bardolph's face into a lantern: "O, thou art a perpetual triumph, an everlasting bonfire light! Thou hast saved me a thousand marks in links and torches, walking with thee in the night betwixt tavern and tavern" (3.3.40–44); and the dozen shirts Hostess Quickly has bought him are reduced to "Dowlas, filthy dowlas. I have given them away to bakers' wives; they have made bolters of them" (3.3.69–71). When Hal, and presumably Peto, enter "marching," bringing military discipline with them, Falstaff immediately turns the demands of history into play: s.d.: "Falstaff meets him playing upon his truncheon like a fife"; "How now, lad, is the wind in that door, i'faith? Must we all march?"

The ensuing debate about the "picking" of Falstaff's pocket and its contents reminds spectators again that this "house" keeps thieves, Falstaff included; again, the court is the tavern, and both are the Theatre. As in 3.2 Bolingbroke and Hal attempt reconciliation, so in 3.3 Hal attempts reconciliation with Falstaff. Hal's exact motives here are enigmatic; arguing that Hal's gradual reformation was part of Shakespeare's intended two-play structure, Hawkins contends that despite "his virtuous resolution for the future, Hal is not ready to abandon Falstaff yet. And if he is not, then the turning point in their relation is still to come."[60] This argument makes critical sense as an overview of Shakespeare's probable grasp of his material and his artistic intentions. But to Elizabethan spectators, not privy to scholarly overviews nor used to experiencing the *Henry IV* plays sequentially in a "festival" (and even if they had seen the anonymous *Famous Victories),* 3.3 is not part of some grand, epic two-part design but rather a second tavern scene into which Hal attempts to bring the demands of history. Within the play, Burbage, as Hal, having come from the court, brings history "marching" into the tavern, the once and future place of royal and roguish "authority," and Kempe as Falstaff uses this "intrusion" into his realm to further embellish his allegiance with his audience.

Falstaff lies about what was in his pockets, as he did about the men in buckram at Gad's Hill. He is terribly nasty to Mistress Quickly, to whom he owes money and shirts; he is also, in his nastiness, terribly witty: "There's no more faith in thee than in a stewed prune, nor no more truth in thee than in a drawn fox. . . . She's neither fish nor flesh; a man knows not where to have her" (3.3.113–14, 128–29). He also flatly asserts another of

Hal's debts: "A thousand pound, Hal? A million. Thy love is worth a million; thou owest me thy love" (3.3.136–37). When Hal insists that Falstaff's ring is copper, and challenges him to his word, Falstaff is again superbly evasive:

*Falstaff.* Why, Hal, thou knowest, as thou art but man, I dare;
but as thou art prince, I fear thee as I fear the roaring
of the lion's whelp.

*Prince.* And why not as the lion?

*Falstaff.* The King himself is to be feared as the lion.
Dost thou think I'll fear thee as I fear thy father?
Nay, an I do, I pray God my girdle break.

(3.3.146–52)

But surely Falstaff fears not this king, a fellow thief. Besides, these are the "days of villainy," when one may steal "as secure as sleep." What matter that one's pockets are full of "tavern reckonings, [and] memorandums of bawdy houses"? By his own conniving logic Falstaff's huge gut is not only an emblem of the times but also, and therefore, an excuse for his gross errors:

Dost thou hear, Hal? Thou knowest in the
state of innocency Adam fell; and what should poor
Jack Falstaff do in the days of villainy? Thou seest I
have more flesh than another man, and therefore
more frailty. You confess then you picked my pocket.

(3.3.165–69)

Having obtained Hal's confession for this robbery, Falstaff again reigns in his kingdom: he orders Mistress Quickly to prepare breakfast, love her husband, look to her servants and guests, and then leave, as if she were a mere servant in his court. Further, Falstaff's thieving is exonerated, if not blessed: "O my sweet beef, I must still be good angel to thee. The money is paid back again" (3.3.177–78). Hal is now "good friends" with his father, and may do anything; his first act after this reconciliation, here in the tavern that is the court, is to absolve Falstaff's (and analogically and symbolically, his father's) "profession." No fear of hangmen here. Rather than robbing the exchequer, as Falstaff requests, Hal provides him with a legitimate, actually more secure means of robbery: a "charge of foot." Because misuse of the King's press was well known,[61] Hal and the spectators certainly know what Falstaff will do with his commission. Given the coming war between bands of thieves, Falstaff's complaint that he is "heinously unprovided" is perfectly logical. A "fine thief," nimble and young, would, indeed, make the best soldier in such a war.

To see this scene only in relation to a larger historical narrative, as Hawkins does, is to minimize its significance in an Elizabethan performance. The King's son admits again to being a thief, to being of the blood royal; he then not only excuses Falstaff's theft but also legitimizes his entry into history by giving him a responsibility within that history from which he will profit by infecting the war effort. What Falstaff makes of war ought not be unexpected; what matters *theatrically* is the subversive effect of his rendition of it. As spectators heard in 1.1, war cannibalizes; now, they will see it carnivalized.[62]

At the end of 3.3, Hal grants Falstaff a "role" at Shrewsbury; he is to have a charge of foot and "money and order for their furniture." Then immediately after in 4.1 Hotspur, whom Douglas terms the "king of honor," learns that his army is disintegrating; his father is "grievous sick," and Glendower "cannot draw his power this fourteen days" (4.1.16,126). Hotspur is yet determined to pursue the war; indeed despite Worcester's opinion that "The quality and hair of our attempt / Brooks no division," Hotspur makes his father's and Glendower's absence a virtue: "I rather of his absence make this use: / It lends a luster and more great opinion, / A larger dare to our great enterprise, / Than if the earl were here"; "My father and Glendower being both away, / The powers of us may serve so great a day" (4.1. 61–62, 76–78, 131–32). Hotspur idealizes combat, mythologizing its grandeur: the King's forces "come like sacrifices in their trim, / And to the fire-eyed maid of smokey war / All hot and bleeding will we offer them. / The mailèd Mars shall on his altar sit / Up to the ears in blood" (4.1.113–17). He urges all to "muster speedily," and embraces doom: "Doomsday is near; die all, die merrily" (4.1.l.134). This is the slaughter of medieval warfare heard in act 1: "Ten thousand bold Scots, two and twenty knights, / Balked in their own blood, did Sir Walter see / On Holmedon's plains" (1.1.68–70).

Having been invited into the war, Falstaff brings the tavern; his first command sends Bardolph to Coventry for sack. Hotspur ennobles combat, whereas Falstaff is "ashamed of [his] soldiers." They are "a commodity of warm slaves ... ragged as Lazarus"; "revolted tapsters, and hostlers trade-fallen ... ten times more dishonorable-ragged than an old feazed ancient"; "tattered prodigals" and "scarecrows ... most of them out of prison." McFarland declares that Falstaff's comic diminution of heroic idealism is a protest against "society's irresponsibility in destroying human life in the cause of a murderous and usurping ruler";[63] it is also supreme disregard for rule and authority. If the King is a thief, why waste good men in his defense? If the inevitable result of war is dead bodies in a pit, why not employ "slaves as ragged as Lazarus" and "the most of them out of prison"? On the Elizabethan stage, Falstaff ridicules not only his assigned role in these English wars (given him, recall, by the heir apparent) but also the very means used by English monarchy to maintain its power. The actual maintenance of the state becomes a subject of sinister derision.

From 4.3 to the end of 5.1, Falstaff's second soliloquy, Shakespeare recapitulates the history behind his play. In 4.3 Vernon, Hotspur and Douglas debate their "honor" and whether to fight "tonight," or wait until morning when all men and horses shall be fresh. Walter Blunt enters as Bolingbroke's emissary and hears from Hotspur a long recitation of the King's wrongs to his former allies. Archbishop York's letters to friends in 4.4 anticipate the later rebellion of part 2, and inform the audience that Glendower, "o'erruled by prophecies," will not be at Shrewsbury. During Worcester's long debate in 5.1 with Bolingbroke about the King's "violation of all faith and troth / Sworn to us in your younger enterprise" (5.1.70–71), Falstaff is on stage; and the theatrical purpose of his presence, perhaps in grotesquely unmilitary garb, is clear: the corpulent carnival figure visually embodies a radically different view of the stage action. Hal's challenge to Hotspur of single combat is honorable but will lead to one of them paying a debt he owes to death. Just as Falstaff's first soliloquy at the end of 4.1 undercuts Hotspur's gallant call to arms and glory in battle, so here his second, his "catechism" on honor, which begins with a characteristic refusal to pay a debt,[64] undercuts not only the scene's long debate about the meaning of past historical events but also the heroic code by which Hal hopes to redeem his past "on Percy's head." The question-and-answer format of Falstaff's catechism is a dialogue with his spectators and his concluding arguments have ample warrant in the play:

What is "honor"? A word. What is in that word
"honor"? What is that "honor"? Air. A trim reckoning!
Who hath it? He that died o' Wednesday. Doth he feel
it? No. Doth he hear it? No. 'Tis insensible, then? Yea,
to the dead. But will it not live with the living? No. Why?

> Detraction will not suffer it. Therefore I'll none of it. Honor
> is a mere scutcheon. And so ends my catechism.
>
> (5.1.133–40)

Falstaff's rigorous analysis of his "questions" yields a conclusion assailable only if one is willing to die for a word, for "air." Bolingbroke's "honor" has not survived long; detraction has slandered it, as have the Percies. Why then die, even honorably, for such a King? For such a kingdom? At the Theatre ca. 1597 Falstaff poses questions to his spectators that, as in 4.2, reduce to "air" principles like honor, allegiance, and obedience on which the state maintains its authority and hence its power. Falstaff thus mocks that power itself, including its attempts to close the public theaters. Lumbering about the entire stage, so mammoth that he cannot see his own knee, transgressing the *locus* of both court and tavern as he lectures spectators from the stage of his theatrical security, which lately shielded him from the sheriff and a monstrous "watch," Falstaff enunciates in his irresistibly logical and energetic catechism those principles of faith that affirm his gigantic resistance to historical necessity, including the necessity that men shall die in war. With the cooperation of the spectators to whom he speaks, Falstaff privately subverts the history into which he has been invited. Ironically, the final target of this subversion will be the one who invited him into this history—Hal—and who seeks precisely that which Falstaff scorns—honor.[65]

Shakespeare's manipulation of audience response in the final scenes of act 5 maximizes the tension between history and carnival. As at Gad's Hill, so at Shrewsbury, England is beset by thieves who cannot be true to one another. Worcester will not trust Bolingbroke's "offer of our grace" from 5.1: "It is not possible, it cannot be, / The King should keep his word in loving us; / He will suspect us still and find a time / To punish this offense in other faults" (5.2.4–7). Worcester says that Bolingbroke "mended" his "oath breaking" by "now forswearing that he is forsworn" (5.2.1.38). There is even deception within the rebels' camp; Worcester insists that Hotspur must not know of Bolingbroke's offer, for while "harebrained" Hotspur's offenses may be forgotten, Worcester fears he and Northumberland will not be forgiven: "We did train him on, / And, his corruption being ta'en from us, / We as the spring of all shall pay for all" (5.2.21–23). By contrast, Hal's praise of Hotspur in 5.1.85–92, where he termed

Hotspur the bravest man alive, elicits from Vernon unequivocal praise:

> But let me tell the world,
> If he outlive the envy of this day,
> England did never owe so sweet a hope,
> So much misconstrued in his wantonness.
>
> (5.2.65–68)

As the battle begins in 5.3, Hal's pursuit of honor, and the admi-
ration he has won from the rebels, contrasts sharply with the
continuing image of Bolingbroke as a deceitful king whose word
means nothing, and with Falstaff's credo that "honor" is but a
word for which it is not worth dying.

"The King hath many marching in his coats," Hotspur tells
Douglas after he has killed both Lord Stafford and Walter Blunt
dressed, like the king himself, in "borrowed robes." This was
common medieval practice in warfare, and both Holinshed and
Daniel report its use at Shrewsbury.[66] However, as Winny remarks, Bolingbroke's use of "counterfeits" symbolizes his own
illegitimacy as king, and associates him with Falstaff, who also
counterfeits at a crucial moment.[67] Even in warfare, Bolingbroke is an enigmatic leader whose use of counterfeits who die
in his place undermines his authority. Indeed, the very idea that
the king's forces possess leadership is effaced; Stafford and Blunt
are impostors of an impostor. This "counterfeiting" contextualizes Falstaff's initial appearance in battle and his third, brief
soliloquy. Standing over Blunt, a scapegoat who died for a thief,
Falstaff proclaims flatly: "There's honor for you. Here's no van-
ity!" (5.3.32–33). Because "Honor hath no skill in surgery," and
it "will not live with the living," what value can it possibly have?
Blunt will not revive; Falstaff looms on stage. Morgann's argument that we should praise Falstaff as a soldier because he "led"
his "ragamuffins where they are peppered" is completely beside
the point.[68] The "honorableness" of an action matters not; what
matters for Falstaff is survival. When Hal enters, pursuing
honor, history and carnival collide. Hal rages at Falstaff for being
"idle," while "Many a nobleman lies stark and stiff / Under the
hoofs of vaunting enemies" (5.3.39, 40–41). Falstaff immediately
creates his own *heroic* history:

> *Falstaff.*  O Hal, I prithee, give me leave to breathe awhile. Turk
>       Gregory never did such deeds in arms as I have done
>       this day. I have paid Percy, I have made him sure.

*Prince.*   He is, indeed, and living to kill thee.
            I prithee, lend me thy sword.

*Falstaff.*  Nay, before God, Hal, if Percy be alive, thou gets not my
            sword; but take my pistol, if thou wilt.

*Prince.*   Give it me. What, is it in the case?

*Falstaff.*  Ay, Hal, 'tis hot, 'tis hot. There's that will sack a city.

*Prince.*   What, is it a time to jest and dally now?

                                                    (5.3.44–55)

Sure! Why not? Is not the battlefield—the court—the tavern, and are not all theater? Are not all such theatrical "places" fit for acting? As in the tavern scene of 2.4, spectators again see Hal and Falstaff, now on the downstage *platea,* fighting for control of the genre of this "play," as if the upstage *locus,* at once royal court and roguish tavern, were finally to be defined by the outcome of this battle between the prodigal prince and his ton of a companion who prefers sack to pistols. At this moment, on this stage, in this theater, the tavern is, indeed, *everywhere.* As after Gad's Hill Falstaff revised the history spectators had seen, so here, again for his and their "recreation's sake," he creates a history they have not seen. History is but improvised, theatrical words, and as each of these histories is outrageously fanciful, so in each Falstaff is outrageously "heroic." (Falstaff's wielding here the same sword he "hacked" after the debacle at Gad's Hill would symbolize visually his contempt for traditional honor, such as the code for which Hotspur actually dies.) His own impromptu history includes the death of Percy, who is doomed because he cannot "act" (i.e., counterfeit, in this theater), which ironically will be "confirmed" when Falstaff spies the dead Percy lying next to him in 5.4. Fearing thirst, Falstaff totes into battle the bottle of sack, and this, his wit, and an incorrigible contempt for the history that the play is enacting all around him demolishes Hal's assertion that there are times—historical moments in men's lives—that are not suited for jesting and dallying. Are not all times in this corrupted kingdom, even battle, suited for jesting and dallying—for acting?

Falstaff's brief, fourth soliloquy closes 5.3:

> Well, if Percy be alive, I'll pierce him. If he do
> come in my way, so; if he do not, if I come in his
> willingly, let him make a carbonado of me. I like not

such grinning honor as Sir Walter hath. Give me life,
which if I can save, so; if not, honor comes unlooked
for, and there's an end.

(lines 56–61)

Falstaff's third and fourth soliloquies, both spoken over the dead
Blunt, surround Hal's brief appearance as he angrily fights to
maintain his father's illegitimate reign. Shakespeare carefully
structures act 5 to prevent the play's historical material, and its
claim on the audience, to dominate the stage action. Just as the
play's history becomes most serious and relevant to Elizabethan
authorities' efforts to maintain their historical claim to power,
carnival undermines that history and appeals to plebeian culture's refusal to succumb to that power. As the gigantic, irrepressible symbol of the marginalized life of theater itself, Falstaff
ridicules the historical basis of that power that continually
threatened his theatrical existence: "[A]s who woulde say,
'There, let them saye what they will say, we wil play.'"[69]

In stark contrast to Falstaff's "history," that in which Hal must
act, which forces him to pay a debt he never promised, demands
much death: "And God forbid a shallow scratch should drive /
The Prince of Wales from such a field as this, / Where stained
nobility lies trodden on / And rebels' arms triumph in massacres" (5.4.11–14). Here, near the play's end, with Falstaff and
Hal embodying increasingly disparate "roles," Shakespeare reminds his audience of the carnage of history from 1.1: "Ten
thousand bold Scots ... balked in their own blood" (lines 68–
69). As Douglas and the King meet, Douglas's ironic claim, "I
fear thou art another counterfeit" reminds spectators of Bolingbroke's counterfeit kingship for which such massacres have occurred. Again, Shakespeare carefully contextualizes the action.
Hal enters, drives away Douglas, and then rescues his father
because he must; having thus "redeemed" his lost opinion with
him, Hal is now released from the Oedipal struggle[70] and can
now fight his real adversary, Hotspur. As Hal and Hotspur fight,
Falstaff again stumbles into their history, as he has throughout
act 5. In 5.1 he visually embodied a huge antagonism toward the
history behind Bolingbroke's quarrel with Worcester; here, his
actions denigrate history completely. As Hal fights Percy, Douglas, who has already killed two counterfeits of the King, Stafford
and Blunt, enters and fights Falstaff. Shakespeare's dramatic
purpose and symbolism here warrant scrutiny. As the most important historical scene of the play unfolds, Douglas encounters

another counterfeit on the battlefield. Like Bolingbroke, Falstaff is a "player king" who, in 2.4, became in his tavern regalia an appropriate image of the thieving king whose land was infected by thieves and thus no better than the tavern he despised. Falstaff, with his hacked sword, plays cheerleader to his "son" in battle: "Well said, Hal. To it, Hal!" With Bolingbroke off stage, Falstaff, the surrogate father and king from Eastcheap, now symbolizes physically the gigantic moral corruption of the kingdom that Hal is defending. Then, as Falstaff and Douglas fight, Falstaff's counterfeit death caricatures the play's most serious attempt at history. The "dumb show" of Falstaff's fight with Douglas[71] allows Kempe to mock Burbage's final attempt to "play" history seriously. Indeed, given Kempe's reputation for improvisational clowning, one can imagine this as one of those stage moments that finally severed Kempe from Shakespeare and his company, especially, one suspects, from Richard Burbage. On the Elizabethan stage, this moment may, indeed, have become a scene of high comedy; Falstaff's parody of history's most egregious demand, that men die for the state, becomes in the Liberties outside London's gates a roundly carnivalesque rebuke to the state's authority over men's lives.[72]

Calderwood argues that when Hal bestrides the prone bodies of Hotspur and Falstaff, his mediating "the claims of Hotspur mimesis and Falstaff theatrics" is shown metadramatically: "[S]ince Hal's ultimate function in history is to reunite an England torn throughout his father's reign by dissension, it is appropriate that his dramaturgical function at this point be to reunite a play that is itself splitting into antagonistic factions."[73] This tableau visually suggests Hal's ascendancy over both Hotspur and Falstaff, as if Hal's conquest of the former, and his acquisition of honor, finally grants him freedom from the latter. But again Shakespeare's structure is crucial here to audience response. Just as in 5.3 Falstaff's short third and fourth soliloquies surround Hal's entry on stage and his request for Falstaff's sword, so here Falstaff's evasion of death from Douglas and then his longer fifth soliloquy surround Hal's conquest of Hotspur and his eulogies over the two bodies. Shakespeare again gives Falstaff the concluding soliloquy within a strategic dramatic segment spoken directly to spectators; Falstaff, that is, gets the final "words" with which he directs spectators' responses to the history they have just seen.

Falstaff's "resurrection" exemplifies a major Elizabethan complaint about players: their protean abilities to transcend via acting political, social, gender, and even physical boundaries. Like Marlowe's Barabas, who in 5.1 is thought dead and then thrown "o'er the walls" of Malta only to rise again, Falstaff rises in a theater "outside" the walls of London to mock not only history but also death. Mullaney asserts that in an Elizabethan public theater "[W]e are in a place . . . where classes, occupations, states of being, even definitions of place come together to form an incongruous composition; where life and death reach an ambivalent congruence."[74] Because Falstaff's singular goal is the maintenance of life, one cannot fault him for counterfeiting to save that life:

> To die is to be a counterfeit, for he is but
> the counterfeit of a man who hath not the
> life of a man; but to counterfeit dying, when
> a man thereby liveth, is to be no counterfeit
> but the true and perfect image of life indeed.
>
> (5.4.115–19)

Falstaff's resurrected vitality, enunciated in a soliloquy, is unequivocally the dominant stage image at the end of *this* play; in Shakespeare's plebeian, public theater, this moment obliterates all order, all history, all time, all disparate "states of being," all conceivable limit. Situated on the downstage *platea,* Falstaff now declares the *locus* of this staged history as *primarily* a "place" of carnival resurrection even in the midst of medieval slaughter. As during the "ferocious" assault he faced at Gad's Hill, Falstaff has escaped the horrible carnage of Shrewsbury as if "by miracle." Having swindled history, Falstaff now casually debunks it by substituting for Hal's "historical" killing of Percy the final chapter of his own farcical version of Shrewsbury in which he breathlessly surpassed Turk Gregory in "deeds in arms." Spying the dead Hotspur, Falstaff suspects he too may be counterfeiting (i.e., he suspects that Hotspur may also have cheated history):

> Therefore I'll make him sure; yea, and I'll
> swear I killed him. Why may not he rise as
> well as I? Nothing confutes me but eyes, and
> nobody sees me. Therefore, sirrah [*stabbing
> him* ], with a new wound in your thigh, come you
> along with me.
>
> (5.4.124–28)

Modern audiences may agree with Robert Hapgood that Falstaff's stabbing of Hotspur is a "desecration,"[75] but in the Theatre

Falstaff's action perpetuates a fantastically successful challenge to authority and political hierarchy. Certainly his claim that "nobody" sees him means nobody who will betray him; upward of three thousand people in the Theatre see him, and he makes them complicit in his consummate theatrical "revising" of history.[76] Falstaff "takes up Hotspur on his back" (s.d.), lugging defeated honor and death ignominiously off his stage, and is for the last time challenged by Hal.

The Prince affirms "Thou art not what thou seem'st." Relying solely on his wit, Falstaff again, as after Gad's Hill, invents (i.e., improvises) action and time to disprove Hal's assertion "Why, Percy I killed myself and saw thee dead":

> Didst thou? Lord, lord, how this world is
> given to lying! I grant you I was down and out of
> breath, and so was he; but we rose both at an instant
> and fought a long hour by Shrewsbury clock. If I may
> be believed, so; if not, let them that should reward
> valor bear the sin upon their own heads. I'll take it
> upon my death I gave him this wound in the thigh.
> If the man were alive and would deny it, zounds, I
> would make him eat a piece of my sword.
>
> (5.4.143–51)

Prefacing his "history," Falstaff throws down Percy's body, "There is Percy," and claims "I look to be either earl or duke, I can assure you" (5.4.138,141). How? From lying about history, savaging chivalry, and cheating death—that is, from *acting* "here in this house"—Falstaff expects a significant political promotion that would explode hierarchy and its assumed authority. Falstaff looks to "steal" again from the commonwealth, using a concocted history as his means. Yet part at least of this history is true: Falstaff did stab Percy, and, as Falstaff boldly asserts, there is no one alive, on stage or in the Theatre, who can deny his claim. No one, that is, who *would* deny his claim, or eat his "hacked" sword! Falstaff has complete control of his spectators and knows it. Thus history itself becomes a carnival, a purely theatrical, topsy-turvy, *improvised* mix of fact, fiction, and invented time in which counterfeiting to preserve life becomes a means to political power, to being either earl or duke. Having been invited into history by Hal, by Richard Burbage, Falstaff (i.e. Will Kempe), uses it, and then dismisses it. For Will Kempe, for Falstaff, for theater, all places and times shall be carnival.

Hal tells Falstaff to "bring your luggage nobly on your back. /

For my part, if a lie may do thee grace, / I'll gild it with the happiest terms I have" (5.4.154–56). Calderwood argues that Hal's lying for Falstaff is the price Hal has to pay for "a restoration of the mode of dramatic reality to which Percy was so totally committed. Historical truth may be violated . . . but the mimesis of historical life is preserved. If theatrical illusion is a lie, it is a lie that must be countenanced, for there can be no theater without it."[77] Calderwood isolates the essential theatricality of Falstaff's character, and Hal's need to acknowledge it so that Hal may pursue his role in *I Henry IV* as historical mimesis. Hal and Lancaster must go to "the highest of the field, / To see what friends are living, who are dead" (5.4.158–59), resulting from the "rebels' arms'" earlier "triumph in massacres." As Falstaff's existence is essentially theatrical, one should ask, here at the close of his role, what his final status means in the Theatre, an Elizabethan playhouse existing in the Liberties, beyond the city walls and its jurisdictions. Falstaff's sixth and final soliloquy, again placed *after* Hal leaves the stage so that Falstaff again can direct spectators' responses, triumphs his abuse of and profit from history:

> I'll follow, as they say, for reward. He that rewards
> me, God reward him! If I do grow great, I'll grow
> less; for I'll purge, and leave sack, and live cleanly
> as a nobleman should do.
>
> (5.4.160–63)

Having defied and mangled history for his own benefit, Falstaff predicts a future history in which he is rewarded, and has become a nobleman. He speaks in a plebeian institution, a public playhouse, hounded throughout its existence by critics who, like Stephen Gosson, believed that "We are commanded by God to abide in the same calling wherein we were called, which is our ordinary vocation in a commonweale."[78] Falstaff will have none of this. After all, Bolingbroke, a thief, is still king. What matter hierarchy? And just as in the tavern one could ridicule kingship with a joint stool and a cushion, do so with the heir apparent, and fall calmly asleep with absolutely no fear of authority, so here, pontificating from the same place on stage where he counterfeited the king in 2.4, Falstaff speaks of growing great and becoming respectable. *I Henry IV* dramatizes the ease with which traditional authority and hierarchy in England may be made into absolute carnival. Falstaff violates this hierarchy and frustrates its authority, and his gargantuan energy emboldens his spectators to similar disregard for contemporary Elizabethan authority. Falstaff "re-creates" his spectators into thieves.

In *The End Crowns All,* Barbara Hodgdon writes:

> [J]ust as the history play inscribes the *idealized* dominance of the institution of kingship, it also interrogates that ideal by representing alternative values, meanings, and practices capable of contesting its hegemony, thus inviting, by its continuing reproduction, the potential redefinition of the relations between sovereign and subjects. . . . [T]he theater, positioned as a marginal institution that nevertheless forms one central term in the pervasive metaphor equating world with stage, was ideally suited to recuperate and mediate the conditions as well as the contradictions endemic to power relationships.[79]

Falstaff embodies a complete "redefinition of the relations between sovereign and subjects." Falstaff's inventions prove both history and time, the narrative basis and temporal heritage of contemporary authority, to be less stable and thus less reliable as political constructs than his own improvisational wit. As we know *I Henry IV* to have been very popular with Elizabethan audiences, we can imagine its continual playing at the Theatre (or perhaps the Curtain) to have energized significant reconsideration of traditional political hierarchy and its hegemony. For although the "history" of the play ends with royalty victorious, Hotspur dead, and the King, Lancaster, and Hal planning their next advances against Northumberland and Scroop (5.5), Falstaff's comically disruptive exit, lugging "honor" off the stage and his looking to be earl or duke by stealing and lying, undermine the authority on which Bolingbroke and his sons pretend to rule. At the close of this play, Hal gilds with a lie the stupendous theatrical energy that has trashed the history that he has struggled to enact.

Returning now to my earlier point about Kempe playing Falstaff and Burbage playing Hal, we can imagine the theatrical energy of this play as a virtual contest between Kempe and Burbage for on-stage supremacy. If Bryant and Wiles are right, as I believe they are, about Kempe's inheriting the "mantle" of Tarlton as an improvising jester, then, indeed, the contest between Carnival and History writ large in this play[80] is also a contest for supremacy within an acting company and its ability to "stage" a play according to a "script." As Falstaff's theatrical energy threatens both the historical basis of Elizabethan authority and its power to control the time of men's lives by ordering when they must die in the service of the state, so Kempe's improvisational energy, which I imagine his lavishing at every moment in an Elizabethan production of this play, threatens the ability of the Chamberlain's Men to perform a "script" with even moderate predictability. This feature of the play would have been most evident in 2.4. ca. 112–280, when Falstaff thunders into the tavern after his humiliation at Gad's Hill. As the Bergsonian "house of cards" builds (see n. 43), one imagines Burbage, in successive performances, becoming increasingly frustrated at his inability to "trap" Kempe, and Kempe becoming increasingly improvisational as he exploits the script to evade Burbage's efforts to "contain" him. Thus, Kempe uses the script to his advantage just as Falstaff uses history to his. The Chamberlain's Men, trying to stage a serious history play called *I Henry IV,* are repeatedly foiled by Kempe's continual re-creation of Falstaff's immortal carnival energy; on an Elizabethan stage the players thus replicate *during performance* the very instability of social structure that their play so vividly dramatizes.

If, as theater scholars believe, Hamlet's criticism of clowns' parts stems from Shakespeare's experience with the Chamberlain's Men, and Burbage played Hamlet, as we know he did, then Hamlet's complaints about clowns' urging laughter when "some necessary [historical?] question of the play be then to be considered" (*Hamlet,* 3.2.42–43) may, indeed, refer to Kempe's playing of Falstaff. As Humphreys demonstrates, Falstaff was immensely popular with Londoners (see n. 2), and it is conceivable that Kempe's playing of Falstaff made both character and actor more popular than either Shakespeare or Burbage could tolerate. Indeed, in creating Falstaff, Shakespeare may have created more disruptive theatrical energy than even his own highly professional company could contain.

# 6

## Disabling Joy: Dramatic Structure and Audience Response in *Twelfth Night*

A principal tenet of Shakespeare criticism is that his plays are composed of clearly distinguishable "major" and "minor" plots, with separate sets of characters, often taken from separate sources, which may be linked thematically, poetically, or analogically but which nonetheless remain distinct.[1] One notes, for example, that in *Twelfth Night* Shakespeare has created a group of downstairs roisterers whose antics often parallel, mimic, or mingle with those of the upstairs aristocracy. However, a different approach to Shakespearean structure, more theatrically orientated, is found in Jonathan Miller's recent statement:

> There are no subplots in Shakespeare; all of the "subplots" are, in fact, the other side of a very carefully cantilevered structure. Shakespeare's plays are written like the domes of Renaissance cathedrals in which if you disregard one side and think of it as minor, you upset the structure.[2]

Miller's statement reflects the director's mind and directs our attention where it should be anyway: to the theater and its audience. He suggests that spectators' experience of a play in the theater is more holistic than a scholar's in the study. Spectators experience the flow of a play within theater time, and are far less conscious of "divisions" within a play's structure between acts, scenes, and sets of characters than one is sitting in a study pouring over the endlessly annotated pages of a modern Shakespearean text.

In this chapter, I will explore *Twelfth Night* from the perspective that Miller proposes; i.e., as a continuous, holistic dramatic *process* rather than as a literary artifact divided into "major" and "minor" plots to be studied separately. As with the other chapters in this book, I shall initially consider *Twelfth Night* as an Elizabethan play, written and designed ca. 1600–1601[3] for production at the newly opened Globe Theatre. As I have argued in previous chapters, a primary feature at productions in Elizabethan public theaters, such as the Theatre and the Globe, is the phenomenon of multiple perspectives among the spectators, and I shall argue that the audience reactions that I believe the dramatic structure of *Twelfth Night* creates in performance brilliantly exploit this feature of the Globe Theatre, especially in the play's latter half. The structural features that I discern certainly ought to produce similar reactions among any group of spectators at any time in any theater. Although this claim is implicit in my arguments, I shall contend that these features of *Twelfth Night* would have been most evident in performances at the Globe Theatre for which Shakespeare initially designed the play.

Barring major cuts,[4] all audiences at any production of a play would see the same script performed. I define script as the sequence, or structure, of dramatic events that dictates action and dialogue on stage: for example, character A enters at 1.1 and speaks eighteen lines, to be followed on stage at line 19 by character B, who speaks with A for twenty lines, moves or gestures appropriately, then exits with A at line 39, and so forth, throughout the play. The script of *Twelfth Night* is the common denominator of all performances of the play, and it creates the theatrical experiences among spectators. Because only this sequence itself[5] is commonly experienced by all spectators, any analysis of audience responses to *Twelfth Night* should focus on this sequence, the structure of the play as it unfolds on stage during performance. In exploring this structure I shall stress two principal features of *Twelfth Night*. First, Shakespeare carefully modulates its pace. The structure of acts 1 and 2 is similar. Each features several relatively short, uncomplicated scenes succeeded by more intense and dramatically complex scenes in which serious emotions or concerns are examined. 1.5 concludes with Olivia's first meeting with Viola, and 2.4 is Viola's long scene with Orsino.[6] Act 3, however, differs significantly; after the passionate dialogue between Viola and Olivia, shorter, rapidly changing scenes featuring numerous spontaneous plays-within-plays, or "inner-plays" as I shall term them, suddenly dominate, creating a maddening[7] pace that persists throughout act 5. Second, scrutiny of these inner plays reveals that they actually begin to disintegrate before our eyes, thus imaging the gradual disintegration of the larger artifact. From these analyses I shall argue that Shakespeare has inscribed into the play a con-

tinually increasing sense of structural collapse that finally disables spectators' acceptance of the romantic, festive mood that
the play struggles to enact in its final moments. As my main
structural arguments concern the second half of the play, I shall
discuss acts 1 and 2 rather briefly and then examine acts 3 to 5
more fully.

Both Orsino and Olivia have violated what Thomas Van Laan
calls their proper "social roles"[8] for wholly imaginary ones: Orsino the naive, befuddled Petrarchan wooer unwittingly drown-
ing in his own verbal folly;[9] Olivia the hermetically sealed
cloistress oblivious to her surroundings. Unlike Orsino and
Olivia, but like her brother, Viola is "Most provident in peril"
(1.2.12). Her deliverance from the sea, with her gold in tact, no
less, and her brother's riding "a strong mast that lived upon the
sea . . . like Arion on the dolphin's back" (1.2.14, 15), suggest
their status as almost mythic saviors of romance and legend.
Though she initially wishes to serve Olivia, who, the captain
tells her, has also lost a brother and a father, she chooses to be
"adventurously epicene"[10] in Orsino's service. Viola is a strong-
willed woman whose self-determination immediately contrasts
her with Orsino and Olivia. Although Viola's disguise is initially
an external impediment to her own romantic desires, it becomes
the means by which she provokes in both Orsino and Olivia
critical self-examination of their internal impediments to
desires.

In 1.3 Shakespeare introduces the Saturnalian spirit that initially undermines Olivia's household and eventually "invades the
whole play."[11] Toby is sure that "care's an enemy to life," whereas
Maria is certain that Toby must confine himself "within the modest limits of order" (1.3.2–3, 8–9). Shakespeare here establishes
the fundamental tension between revelry and restraint in the
play,[12] and introduces the first of the many instantaneous inner
plays that occur throughout *Twelfth Night,* especially in acts 3 to
5. Toby the "director" instructs Andrew the "actor" in "accosting"
Maria, who refuses to cooperate in Toby's and Andrew's game
and instead easily proves her earlier claim that Andrew is a
"foolish knight." Andrew is hilariously inept and completely bewildered by Toby's and Maria's sexual jests. As a potential wooer
of Olivia he is pathetic, and, as if confirming his claim that he
is "a fellow o' the strangest mind i' the world" (1.3.110–11), decides on Toby's bald (and perhaps drunken) assertion that Olivia
will not "match above her degree, neither in estate, years, nor
wit" (1.3.107–8) to stay a month longer. Jerked by Toby's invisi-

ble strings, Aguecheek dances giddily off the stage, spurred by a self-delusion that he can be the lover of the woman he thinks he has chosen.

In 1.4 and 5, Viola's situation becomes far more complicated. As Cesario she shall "act" Orsino's woes, and, unlike Orsino himself, "Be clamorous and leap all civil bounds / Rather than make unprofited return" (1.4.21–22). Ironically Orsino's conviction that Cesario's youthful, androgynous appearance will aid "his" mission to Olivia compounds it immensely and instigates the play's elaborate love triangle. The intensity and complexity of the passions aroused within this triangle increase as the play progresses, and I shall argue that the contrast between these vehement feelings and the means of their resolution in the final scene is central to spectators' experiences of the play. As Viola playing Cesario begins her mission to Olivia, her own division within herself heralds the play's romantic entanglements: "I'll do my best / to woo your lady. [Aside.] Yet a barful strife! / Whoe'er I woo, myself would be his wife" (1.4.40–42).

1.5 is 306 lines long, by far the longest and most involved scene of act 1. It begins in rancor between Maria and the apparently long absent Feste, modulates to Feste's quickly proving Olivia a "fool" for mourning her dead brother whose soul is in heaven, and thence to Malvolio's quarrel with Feste, whom Malvolio labels a "barren rascal." The tension between Malvolio and Feste is palpable, as is that between Olivia and Malvolio, whom Olivia, perhaps angered by Feste's proving her a fool, suddenly ridicules as being "sick of self-love." When Toby enters to announce Cesario's presence at Olivia's door, he is already "half drunk" and is presumably such (or probably fully drunk) for the rest of the play. Even as Shakespeare prepares his spectators for the first pensive dialogue of the play, he stresses Toby's and Feste's Saturnalian revelry and their antagonism toward Malvolio, which escalate significantly in act 2. Shakespeare thus contrasts here two disparate energies in the plot: the centrifugal, disruptive energy of Toby's increasing drunkenness that is abetted by Feste's sudden return to Olivia's household; and Viola's centripedal effort to woo Olivia for Orsino. Spectators will see the former energy explode and overwhelm the latter, especially during the final moments of act five.

When she confronts Olivia in the upstage *locus* of her house, Viola, wearing her apparently wholly innocent disguise of "Cesario," is not that she plays. As she labors to speak the "script" she has learned from Orsino,[13] Viola's determination to penetrate Olivia's veiled appearance immediately, and ironically, attracts her to Olivia. Viola insists on being alone with "the lady of the house" before she speaks her memorized praises. Olivia claims that "'tis not the time of moon with me to / make one in so skipping a dialogue" (1.5.196–97); however, when Viola insists that "What I am and what / I would are as secret as maidenhead—to your ears / divinity; to any other's, profanation" (1.5.210–12), Olivia relents, certainly flattered by Viola's insistence that she indeed identify herself as the lady of the house. Robert Westlund asserts that Viola has "touched on just the right topic—on who and what Olivia is—and thus appears to understand her on the deepest level."[14] Olivia is suddenly being praised for features she momentarily will admit she knows she has and thus would like to be recognized. Once they are alone, "Cesario" tries to return to his "script" from Orsino, but is checked by Olivia's terse remark that it is all "heresy." Intrigued by her competition, Viola, the woman behind the mask of Cesario, then radically changes her approach: "Good madam, let me see your face." Olivia reveals herself to "Cesario," who she supposes a man to whom she is rapidly becoming attracted, whereas Viola, a woman and her competition for Orsino, admires the face of another admittedly attractive woman:

> 'Tis beauty truly blent, whose red and white
> Nature's own sweet and cunning hand laid on.
> Lady, you are the cruel'st she alive
> If you will lead these graces to the grave
> And leave the world no copy.
>
> (1.5.234–38)

Prompted by Viola's criticism of her refusing to leave the world a copy, Olivia immediately begins itemizing her beauty. Such self-praise, however tersely delivered on stage, questions Olivia's plan to shield her beauty for seven years. This brief self-awareness also prompts Viola's most stinging criticism of Olivia:

> I see you what you are: you are too proud.
> But, if you were the devil, you are fair.
> My lord and master loves you. O, such love
> Could be but recompensed, though you were crowned
> The nonpareil of beauty!
>
> (1.5.245–49)

Viola's emotions tumble as she speaks these lines: she admits Olivia's beauty, urges again Orsino's love for Olivia, and increasingly despairs of her own love for Orsino. This emotional anguish is surely increased when Viola hears Olivia praise Orsino as "virtuous . . . noble . . . of great estate . . . free, learned, and valiant." (To this praise should be added Valentine's remark in 1.4. that Orsino is not "inconstant . . . in his favors," a claim that will be severely tested in act 5.) Olivia's praising Orsino encourages Viola's own love for him; yet, as the scene climaxes, "Cesario" unwittingly becomes Olivia's desired lover. In her "willow cabin" speech, Viola is intense and passionate; she is also convincing. Olivia has not heard from Orsino himself or his dictated "texts" anything like Viola's

> Make me a willow cabin at your gate
> And call upon my soul within the house;
> Write loyal cantons of contemnèd love
> And sing them loud even in the dead of night;
> Hallow your name to the reverberate hills,
> And make the babbling gossip of the air
> Cry out "Olivia!" O, you should not rest
> Between the elements of air and earth
> But you should pity me!

> (1.5.263–71)

When "Cesario" invites Olivia to pity "him," Olivia's reaction intensifies Viola's predicament. Olivia begins to pity a young "man" to whom she is rapidly becoming attracted and whom she sees being forced to speak for another. Westlund observes that "By the end of the scene Olivia begins to be what she admires in others (as we know from her chiding Malvolio for 'self-love'): she is 'generous, guiltless, and of free disposition.'"[15] Viola exits cursing Olivia, a reaction to Olivia's seemingly irrational rejection of a man whom she praises highly and to Viola's own anger at another woman who could have for the asking the love of a man whom Viola herself desires yet believes unattainable: "Love make his heart of flint that you shall love, / And let your fervor, like my master's, be / Placed in contempt! Farewell, fair cruelty" (1.5.281–83).

Viola's angry, oxymoronic parting crystallizes the emotional complexities inherent in this dialogue, especially within Viola's dual roles as willing lover of and unwilling messenger for Orsino, and initially identifies the upstage *locus* of *Twelfth Night* as a place of comic disguise and uncertain consequences. The latter portion of scene 5 dominates act one, and establishes a distinct rhythm: four generally short, lighter scenes presumably played in the downstage *platea,* followed by a much longer scene that begins with Feste's witty dismissal of Olivia's mourning, modulates to his rivalry with Malvolio and Toby's increasing drunkenness, and then concludes with the far more compelling and intricate dialogue between Olivia and Viola. Shakespeare repeats this pattern in act two: Antonio and Sebastian appear in 2.1;[16] Malvolio gives Olivia's ring to Viola in 2.2; and the raucous "caterwauling" of 2.3 establishes the dangerously unpredictable vitality of the play's Saturnalian energy. These scenes are then followed by the long, compelling dialogue between Viola and Orsino in 2.4. This rhythm, and Shakespeare's alteration of it later in the play, are seminal to the *theatrical* experience of *Twelfth Night.*

Also seminal are two lines of Viola's long soliloquy that she speaks after receiving the ring from Malvolio. After realizing what the ring probably means—"I am the man" and thus Olivia "were better love a dream" (2.2.25, 26)—Viola remarks, "Disguise, I see, thou art a wickedness / Wherein the pregnant enemy does much" (lines 27–28). Viola now realizes that her initially innocent disguise of Cesario has created a potentially embarrassing and possibly "wicked" sexual consequence: Olivia has fallen in love with a woman, not the engaging, energetic young man she thinks Cesario to be. Although the "wickedness" of Viola's disguise at this moment in the play is qualified by its place within a tradition of romantic comedy disguise, Toby's unleashed Saturnalian energy will soon compound Viola's disguise and lead to a scene whose "wickedness" is theatrically far more frightening.

The tension between the disparate energies of 2.3 and 2.4 is critical to appreciating this dramatic rhythm. Toby's midnight drinking party apparently repeats the previous night's revelry,[17] during which Feste, according to Sir Andrew, "wast in very gracious fooling" (2.3.22). (Feste has apparently regained his comic form in just three days.) Occurring presumably in the upstage *locus* where earlier Olivia and Viola had spoken, Toby's midnight revelry now identifies this theatrical space with his Saturnalian energy, which will culminate in the baiting of Malvolio in 4.3. The scene begins and ends with denials of the limitations of time and holiday itself; Toby initially insists that "Not to be abed after midnight is to be up betimes," and after plotting against Malvolio, he beckons Andrew to further quaffing: "Come, come.

I'll go burn some sack. 'tis too late to go to bed now. Come, knight; come, knight" (2.3.2–3, 189–90). Like the great comic energy of Falstaff's defense of his Gad's Hill heroics, the energy of Toby's midnight party explodes on stage; just as the party itself extends past midnight, past the assumed limits of festivity, past the twelfth night of the Christmas revels that Shakespeare's title recalls, so this revelry and its accompanying revenge extend past the "end" of this scene to infect the rest of the play. For spectators, the remainder of the play is a theatrical *agon* between this disorderly Saturnalian energy and the sober trappings of romantic comedy.

The shift from Olivia's basement tavern to Orsino's subdued court is the most extreme of the play.[18] Again as in 1.5, the upstage *locus* of this play is a place of intense romantic dialogue. As in 1.1, Orsino again asks for music, here an image of order after the spontaneous "catches" of 2.3. Like Sir Andrew in 2.3, Orsino also speaks of "last night," here asking for "That old and antique song we heard last night. / Methougt it did relieve my passion much" (2.4.3–4). We do not know what Viola has told him of her first dialogue with Olivia, and so spectators cannot ascertain his mood from what they have seen in 1.5. Orsino assumes that he is the model of all "true lovers": "For such as I am, all true lovers are, / Unstaid and skittish in all motions else / Save in the constant image of the creature / That is beloved" (2.4.17–20). Because Orsino's love for Olivia is wholly illusory, his claim is absurd. When Orsino suspects by Viola's "masterly" remark about the music—"It gives a very echo to the seat / Where love is throned" (2.4.21–22)—that "he" is in love, Viola as Viola describes her desired lover as resembling Orsino in age and complexion, which Orsino then interprets as "Cesario's" conception of an ideal woman—hence, Orsino's further advice:[19]

> Too old, by heaven. Let still the woman take
> An elder than herself. So wears she to him;
> So sways she level in her husband's heart.

(2.4.29–31)

Viola then hears from the man she loves his own confession about men's unstable passions:

> For, boy, however we do praise ourselves,
> Our fancies are more giddy and unfirm,
> More longing, wavering, sooner lost and worn,
> Than women's are.

(2.4.32–35)

Orsino does not recognize his self-indictment; Viola does: "I think it well, my lord." Whereas Viola's line is comic, Orsino's reply is cruel:

> Then let thy love be younger than thyself,
> Or thy affection cannot hold the bent;
> For women are as roses, whose fair flower
> Being once displayed, doth fall that very hour.
>
> (2.4.36–39)

Viola's response, "And so they are. Alas that they are so, / To die even when they to perfection grow!" (2.4.40–41), echoes the sexual innuendo in Orsino's metaphor of displayed and fallen roses; Viola as Cesario attempts a camaraderie with Orsino even as she acknowledges the seriousness and irrevocability of a woman's sexual commitment.

Feste's song of a pathologically melancholy lover "slain by a fair cruel maid" who wants an obscure, unmarked grave pleases Orsino. Also, Orsino simply does not grasp Feste's accurate description of his mind as a "very opal" nor his severe sarcasm in the lines concluding this brief interval: "I would have men of such constancy put to sea, that their business might be everything and their intent everywhere, for that's it that always makes a good voyage of nothing" (2.4.75–78). Wallowing in his lovesickness, Orsino immediately redirects the dialogue, sending Cesario back to Olivia: "Get thee to yond same sovereign cruelty" (l.80). Viola's effort to interject some reality, "But if she cannot love you, sir?" is irrationally dismissed: "I cannot be so answered." Ruth Nevo identifies Orsino's "disequilibrium" as partly a conviction that men are the superior martyrs to love,[20] and his refusal to abandon either his illusory passion or his morose martyrdom multiplies his contradictions. Trying to draw Orsino out of his romantic lethargy, Viola creates a supposedly fictional situation, although painfully related to her own, in which a lady has for his love "as great a pang of heart / As you have for Olivia. You cannot love her; / You tell her so. Must she not then be answered?" (2.4.90–92). Orsino's response is marvelously confused:

> There is no woman's sides
> Can bide the beating of so strong a passion
> As love doth give my heart; no woman's heart
> So big, to hold so much. They lack retention.
> Alas, their love may be called appetite,

No motion of the liver, but the palate,
That suffer surfeit, cloyment, and revolt;
But mine is all as hungry as the sea,
And can digest as much. Make no compare
Between that love a woman can bear me
And that I owe Olivia.

(2.4.94–103)

Feste said Orsino's brain was a very opal. Actually, it is a lot worse: Orsino wears motley in his brain. Having called men's fancies more "giddy and unfirm" than women's, and having credited women with more constancy than men, he now dismisses woman's love as mere appetite. If a woman's love is mere appetite, and soon "revolts," one wonders why he so ardently craves Olivia's.

Exactly as she had done in 1.5, Viola concludes 2.4 with a supposition: were Viola as "Cesario" to love Olivia in her "master's flame," she would construct a willow cabin at her gate and call upon her constantly; were Viola a "woman," she would prove to Orsino that woman's love is as "true of heart" as men's. Viola supposes herself her father's only daughter who "sat like Patience on a monument, / Smiling at grief" (2.4.114–15). Yet, as a real daughter playing a man who resembles someone she believes is drowned, she "knows not" (yet) whether her sister died (i.e., will die) of her love. Viola's projection is a self-defense, an image of herself at this moment experiencing an incorrigible paradox, loving a man as self-deluded and immature as she is confused and frustrated. Her rhetorical question, "Was not this love indeed?" is left unanswered, drawing spectators deeply into the ambiguity and pathos of her situation.[21]

Orsino does not return until 5.1, when he appears at Olivia's house with Viola. When Orsino reappears, spectators rightly assume that his self-delusion has not abated, for nothing happens between the end of 2.4 and 5.1 to change this assumption. Furthermore, this assumption affects spectators' reaction there to his sudden, passionate and threatening jealousy. Between the end of this scene and act 5, Shakespeare interjects Maria's and Toby's plotting, which creates the tumultuous and dangerous context in which Orsino and Viola meet again and pledge their love. Thus, Shakespeare's structure dictates that spectators experience Orsino's and Viola's "romantic reunion" in the midst of immense Saturnalian energies wholly antithetical to such romance.

From the subdued tones of 2.4, Shakespeare turns abruptly to Malvolio's hysterical letter reading, the first of the numerous inner plays originating in Toby's party that dominate the rest of *Twelfth Night*. Note that Malvolio has an onstage audience, as will many of the "actors" in later playlets, and even as Toby, Andrew, and Fabian watch Malvolio's antics, their own roles within this playlet change instantaneously. Even before he finds Maria's forged letter, Malvolio's "practicing behavior to his own shadow" so infuriates the conspirators that they nearly destroy the "sinews" of their plot; Fabian's "O peace, peace, peace! Now, now" rings throughout their baiting of Malvolio. Toby's and Andrew's anger rises as quickly as Malvolio's bloating of his authority. The eavesdroppers become unwitting participants in their own game.[22] Malvolio refashions Toby completely:

| | |
|---|---|
| *Malvolio.* | Saying, "Cousin Toby, my fortunes having cast me on your niece give me this prerogative of speech—" |
| *Sir Toby.* | What, what? |
| *Malvolio.* | "You must amend your drunkenness." |
| *Sir Toby.* | Out, scab! |

(2.5.68–73)

Toby's is a disorderly, and thus predictable, reaction to Malvolio's recreation of him in this vision of an ordered household.[23] Toby is still a drunken rogue, but Malvolio has momentarily altered his identity within the bounds of Maria's playlet in which Toby's "role" as uproarious eavesdropper at the baiting of a pathetic "affection'd ass" was supposedly set.

2.5 is crucial to Shakespeare's structuring of *Twelfth Night*. Like 1.5 and 2.4, it is fairly long (203 lines), focusing rather intently, although comically, on few characters—mainly Malvolio and Toby. However, as the final scene of the first portion of the play (i.e, acts 1 and 2), 2.5 differs in being the first of the series of spontaneous playlets that verges on self-destruction; the "sinews" of the plot are stretched perilously thin, as Andrew and especially Toby become increasingly angry. Like nearly everyone else later in the play, they become unwitting participants in a game they thought they controlled or at least understood. This dramatic phenomenon occurs repeatedly throughout the rest of the script, as numerous "plays" crisscross and hurl bewildered characters into situations they could not possibly have anticipated, thus creating the "mid-summer madness" from which no sane escape seems possible. In the second half of this comedy,

*What You Will,* the conflicting and relentless energies of the many inner plays cumulatively conspire to devour the larger artifact and increasingly involve theater spectators as reluctant participants in that devouring. The Saturnalian energy released by Toby's revels, which he extends well past midnight by burning sack, consumes the play itself and with it spectators' sense of the play's presumed aesthetic form.

When Viola returns to Olivia's house in 3.1, she is treated rudely by Feste, who tells Viola flatly, "I do not care for you" (3.1.29), and then is further badgered by Toby and Andrew.[24] The latter are summarily dismissed: "Let the garden door be shut, and leave me to my hearing" (3.1.92–93), thus perhaps fueling Toby's and Andrew's later wish for revenge against Viola. Viola says she has come to Olivia to "whet your gentle thoughts / on [Orsino's] behalf" (3.1.105–6). Like Orsino in 1.1, Olivia uses violent images to express her predicament:

> Under your hard construction must I sit,
> To force that on you in a shameful cunning
> Which you knew none of yours. What might you think?
> Have you not set mine honor at the stake
> And baited it with all th' unmuzzled thoughts
> That tyrannous heart can think? To one of your receiving
> Enough is shown; a cypress, not a bosom,
> Hides my heart. So, let me hear you speak.
>
> (3.1.115–22)

Olivia's imagery accuses Viola as "Cesario" of a violence that she, as a woman, could never have intended. The initial emotional simplicity and sexual innocence of 1.2—she was to be presented as a eunuch—have deepened and darkened. Viola's "I pity you" is not a "degree to love," as Olivia maintains; "for 'tis a vulgar proof / That very oft we pity enemies" (3.1.123,124–25). How are spectators to take Viola's "pity" for Olivia? Certainly she speaks to Olivia as Viola here, and "enemy" is ambiguous, echoing obliquely Viola's view of disguise as a wickedness, "Wherein the pregnant enemy does much" (2.2.28). Olivia is still Viola's competition for Orsino, and she is also unknowingly inimical to Viola's sexual integrity as a woman. At this moment the *locus* of *Twelfth Night,* here and for the remainder of the play Olivia's household, is identified as a place where disguise itself as a theatrical energy may suddenly propel characters into antagonistic and unpredictable roles.

The scene concludes with questions of identity and expressions of passion:

> *Olivia.* I prithee, tell me what thou think'st of me.
> *Viola.* That you do think you are not what you are.
> *Olivia.* If I think so, I think the same of you.
> *Viola.* Then think you right. I am not what I am.
> *Olivia.* I would you were as I would have you be!
>
> (3.1.138–42)

Both women are frustrated, even angry. Viola, utterly bewildered by Orsino's obtuseness in 2.4, is still playing messenger for him in what she knows is a hopeless "courtship." Olivia is not in love with a man, as she thinks she is, and thus her desires must remain, for now, unfulfilled. Yet Olivia's Petrarchan aside—"O, what a deal of scorn looks beautiful / In the contempt and anger of his lip! / A murderous guilt shows not itself more soon / Than love that would seem hid" (3.1.145–48)—indicates the overwhelming passion that she can no longer suppress:

> Cesario, by the roses of the spring,
> By maidhood, honor, truth, and everything,
> I love thee so that, maugre all thy pride,
> Nor wit not reason can my passion hide.
> Do not extort thy reasons from this clause,
> For that I woo, thou therefore hast no cause.
> But rather reason thus with reason fetter:
> Love sought is good, but given unsought is better.
>
> (3.1.149–56)

L. G. Salingar calls this speech the "turning point of *Twelfth Night*"; he argues that the first half of the play "dwells on self-deception in love," while "the second half stresses the benevolent irony of fate."[25] Salingar adds that "love now appears to Olivia as a startling paradox: guilty, even murderous, an irruption of misrule; and at the same time irrepressible, fettering reason, and creating its own light out of darkness".[26] Olivia's words certainly indicate intense love for "Cesario." Yet this very intensity, even for a disguised woman, complicates severely Shakespeare's use of identical twins to "solve" the romantic confusions which his plot creates. Olivia's declaration of love here reminds one of Rosalind's "O coz, coz, coz, my pretty little coz, that thou didst know how many fathom deep I am in love!" (*As

*You Like It,* 4.2.197–98; Bevington 4th ed.). Rosalind does indeed marry Orlando, the object of her passion; Olivia marries a substitute. Can love as ardent as Olivia's words portend be so readily transferred to another, even an exact twin, given disguise's evident power to deceive? I shall argue that Shakespeare's reliance on this romance formula amid the chaotic circumstances that his plot produces in act 5 significantly complicates spectators' theatrical experience of the final moments of *Twelfth Night.*

After this impassioned moment, Shakespeare radically alters the mood and pace of his play. The remainder of act three is a series of "inner plays" complete with their own actors, directors, and onstage audiences during which Shakespeare carefully juxtaposes both "major" and "minor" plots and establishes the primary rhythm for the rest of the play. These "inner plays" develop rapidly, funneling Toby's unruly midnight energy straight toward the romantic comedy formulas of act 5 and thereby establishing clearly on the *platea* the theatrical legitimacy of Saturnalian improvisation and play, of what Weimann terms an authority "residing within the textual and theatrical activity itself . . . *representing* . . . theatrical production."[27] Within the Globe, spectators ranged around and above the stage watch from their disparate perspectives theatrical activities and productions contrived by Toby, Maria, and Fabian that eviscerate with increasingly frenetic energy the dramatic artifice itself. 3.1, which features Viola and Olivia, is 164 lines long. 3.2, which launches Fabian's and Toby's intrigue against Cesario and includes Maria's report about Malvolio in yellow stockings and cross-gartered, is 82 lines, just half of 3.1. Toby and Fabian begin by convincing dimwitted Andrew that Olivia's gentleness toward "Cesario" in her orchard, during which she saw Andrew observing them, was really "a great argument of love in her towards you" (3.2.10–11). Their plot thus involves Olivia once again in a part she does not know she is supposed to play and also creates another one for Cesario: the fierce fighter whom Andrew must challenge in order to win Olivia's favor and save his honor. (The sheer absurdity of all this will be plain to spectators who recall Andrew's pathetic encounter with Maria in 1.3. This absurdity will also highlight the childishness and probable maliciousness[28] in Toby's actions.) Toby knows that both Andrew and "Cesario" are feeble warriors; yet the show—his theatrical production—must go on. As Andrew dashes off stage to pen his "horrid" challenge, Maria explains that another letter, her forgery in Olivia's hand, has worked: Malvolio "most villainously" obeys "every point of the letter that I dropped to betray him."[29] Within eighty-two lines, one playlet has commenced, and another has reached its second stage. The pace of *Twelfth Night* is rapidly increasing.

3.3 with Antonio and Sebastian, absent since 2.1, totals forty-nine lines, again about half of 3.2. Shakespeare's halving of scene lengths through 3.3 rapidly hurls the play toward the chaos of 3.4 and act 4. Sebastian and Antonio may appear independent of the maelstrom swirling around them, but in their next appearance, they will simply drown in it. The energies of the various "plots" are accumulating rapidly and will soon overwhelm the theatrically artificial distinctions between "major" and "minor" actions.

When 3.4 opens, Olivia seeks Malvolio because she wants him to arrange a "feast" for "Cesario," who is about to return. Maria, who says Malvolio approaches, thinks Olivia still mourns her brother and does not know she loves "Cesario." Thus, when Malvolio appears ridiculously appareled, the "major" and "minor" plots collide, leveling Olivia and Malvolio to players in games (i.e., "theatrical productions") similarly unreal. Malvolio thinks Olivia loves him, while she anxiously awaits the return of Cesario and expects Malvolio to remain a sober, reliable steward. She has no idea why Malvolio makes an ass of himself, because she is unaware that she is supposed to be his lover in Maria's "play." Yet Malvolio plays his part in this playlet so well that, after repeating the instructions he believes Olivia has written for him, he continues "playing" even after his intended audience—Olivia—exits. Malvolio bends Olivia's words to fit his own delusions,[30] including her desperate order that Toby and others "have a special care" of him: "Oho, do you come near me now? No worse man than Sir Toby to look to me!" (3.4.66–67). His rash assumption of divine protection—"Well, Jove, not I, is the doer of this, and he is to be thanked" (3.4.84–85)—is rudely greeted by his adversaries as this playlet rushes to its next scene and becomes rather frightening and cruel. Not only its principal player but also Maria's entire playlet is out of control. Malvolio is "surly with servants" and thus ironically inspires more cruelty among his tormentors: for their pleasure, they will bind him "in a dark room" and thus punish him for being in "disguise," for donning the cross-gartered yellow apparel he believed preferred by his supposed lover in a romantic game he thought they were both playing.

3.4 opened with spectators expecting one action to dominate—Olivia expects Cesario—but Malvolio's sudden appearance usurps the previous action. This pattern dominates the remainder of act three. Andrew enters at line 145 with his witless challenge to Cesario. Toby again assumes control; he will, as Maria has done earlier, forge a letter that will replace Andrew's "excellently ignorant" scribbling, portray Andrew as a fierce fighter, and petrify Viola. Again evident is Shakespeare's careful modulation of *Twelfth Night*'s rhythm: the "Malvolio plot" runs 125 lines, to line 143; Andrew's "challenge" totals fifty-four, or about half, to line 198; the meeting of Olivia and Viola, expected since 3.4.1, is brief, only twenty-one lines, again about half of the preceding segment. Thus, the structure of 3.4 itself, up to Antonio's entrance at line 311, repeats the overall structure of scenes one through three: as each scene becomes progressively shorter by about one-half, so do the segments within scene 4. As the increasingly shorter scenes in act 3 hurl the entire play toward 3.4, so the segments within scene 4 shorten regularly and rush the scene toward its most bizarre episode, the encounter between Cesario and Andrew. Thus, the pattern and pace of act 3, noticeably different from those of acts 1 and 2, become significant features of spectators' experience of the total artifact. The rapid multiplication of "plots," or "plays," and their steamrolling of serious human emotions continues unabated through act 5, continually reinforcing on the stage *platea* the theatrical legitimacy of improvised and increasingly dangerous "play," and thereby creating the dramatic context within which spectators experience the final moments.

Shakespeare's juxtaposition of segments within 3.4 is as theatrically effective as his modulation of pace. The brief meeting between Olivia and Viola is a calm interlude squeezed between Toby's meditation of "some horrid message for a challenge" (3.4.201–2) and his actually hurling it at Cesario at line 222–27. In this interlude, Olivia again confesses her love for "Cesario," who again refuses her love and again pleads for Orsino. Yet Viola keeps her disguise. Shakespeare's sustaining of this romance motif, during which Olivia gives Cesario her picture, stimulates in spectators the multiple exasperations being experienced by both Olivia and Viola. Neither is what she plays; Viola continues to urge a hopeless emissary from Orsino, while Olivia pursues a chimera. The longer they "play" their parts, the more theater spectators' experience parallels what they observe on stage. Shakespeare's prolonging of Viola's disguise and its severe sexual

complications leaves it immensely vulnerable to Toby's increasingly darkening ideas of "sport" and (post) midnight revelry.

Toby's sudden challenge to Cesario increases spectators' sense
that, by this point, no feelings, regardless of how urgent or powerful, are intrinsically valuable in the frenzy of this play. Shakespeare refuses to give Viola, and thus spectators, time to
contemplate the pathos of Olivia's gift before Toby ludicrously
complicates her situation. Viola recoils at the prospect of sword
play, yet her alternative—"I will return into the house, and desire some conduct of the lady"—might imply affection for Olivia,
a suggestion that Viola must avoid. Viola is "no fighter"; neither
is Andrew. Both are trapped. Yet Toby's plot demands that both
must be what they are not, and so Viola's disguise suddenly
becomes a "wickedness" with potentially lethal consequences.
Toby's and Fabian's frantic dashes between the reluctant warriors signal not only their furious determination to maintain
their sport but also the dizzy pace now assumed by *Twelfth Night*
itself. Distinctions between "plots" blur, for spectators see complex emotions trivialized by drunken fools and the central character of the "main plot" as victimized by childish games as the
most pathetic character in the "subplot." In the theater, spectators see identity and purpose become equally malleable in characters as intellectually and emotionally diverse as Viola and
Andrew.

Toby is drunk; so, apparently, is fortune. Just as Viola and
Andrew are about to fight, Antonio suddenly appears, mistakes
"Cesario" for Sebastian, rescues "him" from Toby's humiliating
sport, and finds himself promptly arrested. Toby threatens Antonio, thus initiating Toby's fight with Sebastian in 4.1 that continues into act 5, and Antonio's bewilderment is matched only
by Viola's amazement at his calling her Sebastian. Viola is jarred
by Antonio's accusation of ingratitude for not returning his
purse, and this accusation follows by only 146 lines her "acquit-
ting" Olivia of her love for "Cesario," and then being challenged
by Andrew and Toby. Within this segment of 3.4, Shakespeare
is again overloading characters' experiences and thus com-
pounding spectators' responses. The pace of the emotional
changes in Viola and Antonio is as rapid as the entrances and
exits of the various characters whom fortune thrusts onto the
stage.[31]

Just as in 3.4 Shakespeare rapidly alternates interlocking
"plots" involving both "major" and "minor" characters, so in 4.1
he repeats this pattern with Sebastian's entrance. As Van Laan

notes, everyone who greets him thinks him "Cesario,"[32] and from this forcing an identity on Sebastian emerges another series of rapidly developing inner plays in which he is never who he is forced to "play." Feste thinks him "Cesario," to whom he was sent by Olivia; Andrew strikes him, thus ludicrously overplaying his "role" as a "devil in [a] private brawl"; Toby, the erstwhile director of this "scene," again becomes an actor in his own plot by also threatening Sebastian, who he believes is "Cesario," Andrew's "rival" for Olivia; and Olivia rushes to rescue "Cesario" from her drunken uncle. As in 3.4, Shakespeare refuses to allow his spectators to dwell on what they see. Emotions, identities, and the "parts" being played, as well as the "plays" themselves, are fluid and illusive, a kaleidoscope of illusion within illusion in which spectators' grasp of any one character's sense of reality, much less of what constitutes a "plot" in *Twelfth Night,* is virtually impossible. The "authority" of theatrical activity itself on the *platea,* of the "improbable fiction[s]" colliding on stage, dissolves. Sebastian simply bounces from Feste to Toby's motley crew to Olivia, and spectators' knowledge of why he is so emotionally battered—he is Viola's twin—is overwhelmed by their effort to assimilate what they witness. As Feste remarks, "Nothing that is so is so" (4.1.8).

As 4.1 concludes, images of anger, haste and madness dominate. Olivia rages at Toby's drunkenness: "Will it be ever thus? Ungracious wretch, / Fit for the mountains and the barbarous caves, / Where manners ne'er were preached! Out of my sight!" (4.1.46–49). She is also anxious to console "Cesario":

> Go with me to my house,
> And hear thou there how many fruitless pranks
> This ruffian hath botched up, that thou thereby
> Mayst smile at this. Thou shalt not choose but go.
> Do not deny. Beshrew his soul for me!
> He started one poor heart of mine, in thee.

> (4.1.53–58)

Sebastian is confused: "What relish is in this? How runs the stream? / Or I am mad, or else this is a dream" (4.1.59–60). Ironically, Olivia succeeds where others have not: she convinces someone to cooperate with her completely. Yet, as so often in the play, she does not know to whom she speaks, even though this time she is speaking to a man, not to a woman disguised as a man. Sebastian, who has told Antonio that his voyage was "mere extravagancy," speaks for his own immediate experience, but he summarizes as well an audience's experience of this play since the beginning of 3.3. In Illyria, strangers no sooner enter than they are attacked and wooed by other strangers almost simultaneously. This play and its characters are out of control—mad.[33]

Malvolio's imprisonment and interrogation by Feste as Sir Topas concludes the series of "plays" begun by Maria's forged letter in 2.5. Toby has been dismissed angrily by Olivia as a "Rudesby" just twenty-five lines before, so he drunkenly wanders off to seek another diversion, another gull to maintain his "sport." Maria, whose last line on stage was "Nay, pursue him now, lest the device take air / and taint" (3.4.133–34), arrives in 4.2 with Feste's disguise. She is determined to humiliate Malvolio, if not drive him mad; Fabian had earlier feared that their "device would make [Malvolio] mad indeed," to which Maria ironically responded "The house will be the quieter" (3.4.135–36). Feste apparently now has nothing else to do, and remembers Malvolio's ridicule of him in 1.5 before Olivia.

Thus, the motives propelling Toby, Maria, and Feste in their "play" are hardly benign. On the Globe stage, if Malvolio's "prison" was a discovery space[34] behind curtains at the back of the stage, then Malvolio would actually be in "darkness" far upstage when he cries out about the "hideous darkness" in which he is being kept against his will. The upstage location of this scene suggests the principal *locus* of the play, Olivia's house, already a "place" of disguise and narcissistic self-delusion, which now suddenly and frighteningly embodies a real wickedness of disguise in which an avowed enemy does much indeed. Further, when he twice asserts that "this house is dark" Malvolio symbolically includes the playhouse, the Globe, as a place of darkness, i.e, evil, because all spectators participate in, and many probably enjoy and thus approve, his baiting. Indeed, the difficulty of predicting spectators' reaction to this scene at this moment *in performance*—the play's most witty character ridiculing its most oppressive—is its principal theatrical value for *Twelfth Night*. In the open, naturally lighted Globe, spectators would not be at all "in the dark" about their participation in this scene: sitting around and above the thrust stage, some spectators in all areas of the theater may be appalled by Feste's actions; others, who may enjoy it, are seen enjoying, and watch others enjoying, watching a man being cruelly humiliated. Indeed, as the scene progresses, any laughter it generates may be contagious among spectators throughout the playhouse, thus increasing among others a sense of rising cruelty as more spectators "join in" and thus approve Feste's mockery of one who, after all, is not "any more than a steward" and foolishly believed he could be a noblewoman's lover. Malvolio's treatment in this scene is thus psychologically central to spectators' communal experience of the play. Logan argues that in a play devoid of parents[35] Malvolio "fills the dramatic function of the senex and the blocking figure."[36] With the sort of consciousness Malvolio embodies literally locked in the dark, Saturnalia is now freed from all restraints; to the extent that spectators enjoy Malvolio's imprisonment in their "dark house" (i.e., the Globe), they approve an unrestrained Saturnalian cruelty that mocks not only comedy but also their own laughter.[37]

During the scene itself, Feste the actor, the clown, the jester from Olivia's basement who has, as players do, acted for money throughout the play, now acts to hurt viciously another man who thought also, like an actor, to wear a disguise and "play a role" for another's approval. Feste is not only part of Toby's larger plot to humiliate Malvolio but also as Sir Topas the Curate an actor within his "role" of co-conspirator:

| *Malvolio.* | Sir Topas, Sir Topas! |
| *Sir Toby.* | My most exquisite Sir Topas! |
| *Feste.* | Nay, I am for all waters. |
| *Maria.* | Thou mightst have done this without thy beard and gown. He sees thee not. |

(4.2.61–65)

After Toby and Maria leave, Feste at one point plays both himself and Sir Topas within one set of lines: "Maintain no words with him, good fellow. Who, I, sir? Not I, sir. God b' wi' you, good Sir Topas. Marry, amen. I will, sir, I will" (4.2.99–102). Further, this playlet, like so many others in *Twelfth Night,* self-destructs. Sir Toby wishes he were "well rid of this knavery," but Feste, as the chief actor in this farcical inquisition, simply cannot restrain himself; as in the preceding lines, he continues abusing Malvolio even after Toby has urged him to stop. He sings and jokes to a helpless man who traps himself by speaking to a jester whose principal interest in his improvised play is revenge. The upstage *locus* of *Twelfth Night* is now a place where disguise, Malvolio's cross-gartered yellow stockings unknowingly and Feste's Sir Topas gown knowingly, is truly a wickedness:

>| *Malvolio.* | Fool, there was never man so notoriously abused. I am as well in my wits, fool, as thou art. |
>| *Feste.* | But as well? Then you are mad indeed, if you be no better in your wits than a fool. |

>                                                        (4.2.87–90)

Malvolio's prison may be partly self-made, the result of excessive egotism,[38] or the failure of his imagination.[39] Nonetheless, he is taunted cruelly in a type of public place where bull and bear baiting had often been "staged," and his imprisonment and "baiting" by Feste may have reminded many Elizabethan spectators of such "sport" or of the public parading of idiots.[40] Feste wears not motley in his brain;[41] he knows an easy target when he sees it.

As plays within plays multiply, consume characters, and then collapse, the "inner plays" as images of the sequence of dramatic events we call *Twelfth Night* presage its disintegration. As the final episode in this snowballing madness initiated by Maria's letters, Malvolio's interrogation symbolizes the kinds of forced, unnerving role playing spectators have witnessed since 3.2. However much revelry was intended by Maria and Sir Toby, revenge was always a prime motive, and in 4.2 spectators see how plots begun in fun can end in fear. Further, the dramatic prominence of this scene compared with the previous and succeeding scenes would be quite evident in a Globe performance, and would superbly exemplify J. L. Styan's point about Shakespeare's creating visual as well as aural stage contrasts "on the assumption that an audience will deduce meaning from them."[42] Feste's trial of Malvolio is twice as long as 4.1. It is also three times longer than Sebastian's soliloquy and his hasty exit for his secret marriage with Olivia in 4.3. Sebastian's rhapsodic musings about the air, the glorious sun, and the pearl Olivia gave him certainly alter rapidly the play's mood, but Globe spectators watching and hearing him speak probably downstage center could simultaneously still see the upstage "prison" behind the central arras from which Malvolio had only seconds earlier pleaded for help from Feste and behind which Malvolio might well be imagined to remain standing; recall that the Folio script has no "exit" for Malvolio at the end of 4.2, only the singular stage direction "Exit" for Feste as he sings "Adieu, goodman devil." One assumes that because Malvolio probably spoke at the Globe from "off-stage" he needed no scripted "exit," but the discomfort that Feste's sardonic joy probably created among many spectators could easily provoke their "visual imagination"[43] to contrast explicitly Sebastian's conviction that here in Illyria he is experiencing "some error, but no madness" (4.3.10) with Sir Topas's assertion that Malvolio in his madness spoke "vain bibble-babble" (4.2.97) and is thus still imprisoned as "mad" by his tormentors behind the central arras, "on-stage," although invisible. Thus, both visually and aurally, because of its greater length and its visual tempering of Sebastian's meeting and joyous departure with Olivia, Malvolio's humiliating ordeal tarnishes the gradual resolution of the "major" plot afforded by Olivia's and Sebastian's impending marriage and creates anxiety among spectators expecting a traditional comic conclusion to *Twelfth Night*'s careening theatrical energies. In act 5 the accelerating collision between "major" and "minor" plots eradicates completely this artificial distinction within the play and brilliantly crystallizes this anxiety.[44]

When Orsino enters with Viola, spectators see them together for the first time since 2.4. It is an unchanged Orsino whose actions in act 5 epitomize Feste's description of his mind as a "very opal." After his witty chat with Feste, Orsino's mood immediately changes as he spies Antonio, and his anger at seeing Antonio may partly explain his sudden and much greater anger when Olivia enters. Confusion reigns. Antonio still believes "Cesario" to be Sebastian, as will Olivia when she enters. Orsino has come seeking Olivia, still hoping to "woo" her. Yet his latest courtship is interrupted first by the Officer's talk of Antonio's part in pirating the *Phoenix* when Orsino's nephew Titus lost his leg, and then by Antonio's mistaken attack on "Cesario" as Sebastian for denying his friendship and his purse in 3.4. Viola is again trapped. Antonio is furious at Viola, and after just a few harsh words between Olivia and Orsino, Orsino's anger suddenly and violently confounds her situation and heralds the most inexplicable moment in the play. Still thinking "Cesario" a man and suspecting his complicity in Olivia's continual rejection of him, Orsino turns on Viola viciously.[45] The "place" where Globe spectators last saw them speaking gently about love suddenly becomes deadly:

> Why should I not, had I the heart to do it,
> Like to th' Egyptian thief at point of death
> Kill what I love?—a savage jealousy
> That sometimes savors nobly. But hear me this:
> Since you to nonregardance cast my faith,
> And that I partly know the instrument

That screws me from my true place in your favor,
Live you the marble-breasted tyrant still.
But this your minion, whom I know you love,
And whom, by heaven I swear, I tender dearly,
Him will I tear out of that cruel eye
Where he sits crownèd in his master's spite.—
Come, boy, with me. My thoughts are ripe in mischief.
I'll sacrifice the lamb that I do love,
To spite a raven's heart within a dove.

(5.1.115–29)

How are spectators to respond to this speech? Does Orsino
threaten murder? Homosexual rape? The violence of his images
is unequivocal; his jealousy is "savage," and his image for taking
Cesario from Olivia is to tear "him" from her "cruel eye." Is
Orsino's anger such that he will violently sacrifice Viola to his
will merely to satiate a rapacious, egotistical jealousy? Shakespeare creates a structurally similar version of the comic moment in 3.4 when "Cesario" was trapped between Toby and
Andrew in the mock sword-fight. But here the passions and
anger are frighteningly real, and Viola's situation is perilous. In
view of her situation, Viola's response to Orsino is astonishing:
"And I, most jocund, apt, and willingly, / To do you rest, a thousand deaths would die" (5.1.130–31). The latent sexual pun in
"die" only heightens the seeming impossibility of this moment.
Given what Viola has heard from Orsino in 2.4, especially his
self-indulgent claims about the depth of his passions for Olivia
and his assertion of the shallowness of women's love, why does
she agree to accompany him? No simple answer, however generic
or reductive, will suffice.[46] And that, *in the theater,* is precisely
the point! How much sense does this relationship now make?
Are the comic conventions of disguise and mistaken identity
sufficient to counter this unconventional and possibly violent
moment? Does Orsino's explosive jealousy warrant Viola's immediate forgiveness, even her sexual acquiescence to his will? Elizabeth Donno claims that "This (short-lived) vehemence on
Orsino's part, suggesting some degree of violence, is to be compared with his posture as the moody lover in the opening scene
of the play."[47] This is a "literary" reaction to the text, a "looking
backward" that asks us to compare one moment in a script happening immediately on stage with another that occurred perhaps two hours earlier. But during performance, when
spectators must react to continuous stage action, they witness
in Orsino a "vehemence" for which they are unprepared by any-

thing Orsino said during his last appearance in 2.4. If during this stage moment spectators do "think back" to Orsino in 2.4, what they find in comparison is a character whose mental stability now appears questionable. In performance the fierce realism of Orsino's sudden, vicious outburst severs this moment from its "conventional" surroundings.

Shakespeare immediately complicates the love triangles. Olivia is horrified at "Sebastian's" apparent homosexual desire for Orsino: "Ay me, detested! How am I beguiled!" To her calling Viola "husband," Viola, bewildered, can only respond "No, my lord, not I." When the priest confirms the marriage of Olivia and Sebastian, Viola is again attacked by the man she protests she loves:

> O thou dissembling cub! What wilt thou be
> When time hath sowed a grizzle on thy case?
> Or will not else thy craft so quickly grow
> That thine own trip shall be thine overthrow?
> Farewell, and take her, but direct thy feet
> Where thou and I (henceforth) may never meet.
>
> (5.1.162–67)

As the Malvolio game begun by Maria's letter in act two became ugly, so the innocent donning of disguise by Viola herself in 1.2 now verges on chaos, on another kind of "wickedness." Even as Viola again protests to Orsino, "My Lord, I do protest—" Olivia accuses her, as Sebastian, her presumed husband, of a lack of will: "O, do not swear! / Hold little faith, though thou hast too much fear" (5.1.168–69).

Just as the lovers from the "main" plot attempt to resolve their frustrations and increasingly dangerous anger, the bloodied,[48] steamrolling rogues of the "subplot" immediately flatten all artificial plot divisions, again crashing into Viola's life and accusing her of being a "coward" or "devil incardinate" who breaks peoples' heads for nothing. Again, just as in acts 3 and 4, Shakespeare refuses to allow spectators to dwell on an emotional crux. As the frightened, pathetic Andrew calls for a surgeon for himself and, importantly, also for Toby—"For the love of God, a surgeon! Send one presently to Sir Toby"—whom should observers pity more, Viola or Andrew? Whose fear is greater, Viola's or Andrew's? Viola is again accused of something she did not do: "You broke my head for nothing, and that that I did I was set on to do't by Sir Toby" (5.1.182–84). Just as Viola attempts to defend herself, Feste and Toby, the latter bleeding and, as he has been since 2.3, drunk, stagger onto the increasingly crowded stage; again, in Styan's term, they "violently reorientate" the theater audience.[49] In the final moments of its increasingly violent "festivity," Shakespeare plunges the stage, the *locus* of *Twelfth Night,* into chaos: Toby asks Feste "Sot, didst see Dick surgeon, sot?" only to learn that he too is drunk, consumed by Saturnalian excess: "his eyes were set at eight i' the morning" (5.1.196,197–98). Toby, oblivious to his condition, protests he hates a "drunken rouge," and then angrily dismisses Andrew's offer of help:

*Sir Andrew.* I'll help you, Sir Toby, because we'll be dressed together.

*Sir Toby.* Will you help? An ass-head and a coxcomb and a knave, a thin-faced knave, a gull!.

(5.1.203–6).

The "festive" entertainers of the play, who entered 1.3 with jovial drinking and exited with Andrew's jocund "dancing," and celebrated "cakes and ale" in their caterwauling scene and burned sack for nightcaps, now stumble off stage amid vicious, drunken quarreling, and with no promise of help; Dick Surgeon's eyes are far too "set" for him to mend wounds. With what Logan calls the "controis of the super-ego" symbolically imprisoned with Malvolio in this "dark house" of the Globe, the revelers' unchecked determination to maintain "what they will" past all sensible bounds has cost them bloodshed and pain; and while Andrew still cares enough for Toby to urge that a surgeon be sent to him, Toby now belittles Andrew for being the gull who fueled and financed so much of their "matter for a May morning." This sudden dissolution among the Saturnalians who cannot be true to one another intensifies spectators' sense of the dissonance they witnessed among the lovers. The biggest fools of this play disappear into its catacombs, but their final violent, disruptive appearance jars spectators who only moments before had tried to comprehend and pity Viola as she was battered between Orsino and Olivia. The witty gaiety of Orsino's dialogue with Feste modulates into moments of confusion, then pity, and then fear, followed rapidly by verbal and physical images of the violence that Viola has apparently only narrowly escaped.

On the Globe stage, the theatrical experience of the first half of 5.1 as I have analyzed it would have been intensified.[50] Although we cannot be certain how this scene would have been staged, one can reasonably conjecture how it might have represented visually the dissonance present in the script. Probably Orsino and Viola and then Olivia would have entered from separate doors, symbolically representing their continued enmity, and during their angry exchanges from ca. line 98 to Andrew's entrance at line 169, one imagines Viola standing downstage center between her warring adversaries. Orsino, perhaps stage left, and Olivia then stage right, would visually symbolize the rapidly growing emotional distance between them and between each of them and Viola as they verbally attack her. Antonio, meanwhile, is off to one corner of the stage as ordered by Orsino ("Take him aside"), restrained by the officers and ignored until Sebastian's entrance at line 208. Antonio, not knowing he is speaking to Viola, not Sebastian, speaks of broken promises and friendships, and his disillusion and isolation symbolize the increasing disharmony on stage.[51] When first Andrew and then Toby and Feste enter, again presumably from separate doors, the stage picture is immediately complicated, as another warring trio now commands spectators' attention. As Andrew urges help, and Toby fulminates and then attacks his "gull," their exits through separate doors would reinforce the isolation and disharmony now metastasizing on stage.

Shakespeare's placing of Sebastian's reentrance (line 208), and the order and duration of the final segments of act 5, emphasize my main point in this essay: the relation between dramatic structure and, at this moment in the play, not only audience response but also audience belief. Viola's lyrical reunion with Sebastian is necessary; their survival and similarity are "improbable fictions" of another sort become reality. Viola's "disguise" ends here; she can return to her "maiden weeds" and be Orsino's wife.[52] Olivia presumably "sees" in Sebastian those qualities she has loved in "Cesario"; the wonder of "One face, one voice, one habit, and two persons" (5.1.215) miraculously blesses her having taken Sebastian for Cesario. The exchanges between Olivia and Sebastian exhibit emotional growth and, presumably, some permanent change: Viola as "Cesario" has ignited within Olivia passions that she can now enthusiastically indulge. Orsino, spectators must presume, recognizes in himself a love for Cesario/Viola regardless of gender.

However emotionally gratifying this tableau may seem, it is nonetheless, as Anne Barton contends, noticeably artificial and schematized, the final pairings-off "perfunctory."[53] If one recalls Olivia's obviously passionate confession of love to "Cesario"

(3.1.149–56), one senses, especially in performance, the difficulty of believing Olivia's instantaneous acceptance of Sebastian. Furthermore, what one expects would be the most emotionally gratifying occurrence in this segment—Viola's exchange of vows with Orsino—is the least explored and thus theatrically the least convincing. Their entire dialogue is only eleven lines long, and its core appears simplistic after Viola's reunion with Sebastian:

> *Orsino.* [To Viola.] Boy, thou hast said to me a thousand times
> Thou never shouldst love woman like to me.
>
> *Viola.* And all those sayings will I over swear,
> And all those swearings keep as true in soul
> As doth that orbèd continent the fire
> That severs day from night.
>
> (5.1.267–72)

The commitment evident in Viola's lines intensifies spectators' realization that she is speaking to a man who only moments before had threatened her with violence, possibly sexual in nature, and had insisted that woman's love was but "appetite, / No motion of the liver, but the palate, / That suffer surfeit, cloyment, and revolt" (2.4.97–99). Are spectators to believe that Orsino's fierce jealousy can so rapidly dissipate? Shakespeare does not give to Orsino the long purgation he grants Leontes. Rather, as he has done throughout the play, here in arguably its most delicate moment, Shakespeare compels spectators to alter their expectations of Orsino's and Viola's relationship as suddenly as they alter their views of each other. Just 100 lines earlier Orsino had ordered "Cesario" to go where they "may never meet" (line 167). But having learned that "Cesario" is a woman, he suddenly offers her love, but only *after* he finally accepts that Olivia can never be his. Although the impending marriage between Olivia and Sebastian appears explainable, given the convention of Sebastian's resemblance to "Cesario," that between Viola and Orsino does not. Shakespeare strains his comic conventions perilously here. Are spectators to believe that this is the man Viola is to marry, given what they have seen and heard from him? Does this moment adequately compensate Viola for her instruction to Orsino in 2.4 on the love women may have for men and men should have for women?[54] Does Viola's being Orsino's "second choice" in this scene, and the woman chosen "at the latest minute of the hour" (*LLL* 5.2.783) convince spectators that Orsino's love is more than merely extemporaneous desire for any unmarried woman to placate his jealousy of Olivia's marriage to Sebastian? Viola's last lines in the play (5.1.274–77) are about her maiden's garments and Malvolio's "suit"; from here on, she is, like Antonio, who last speaks at 1.224, silent for the remainder of the play.

The final jolt to spectators is Malvolio's reappearance; he enters just as spectators expect Viola to respond to Orsino's remark "You shall from this time be / Your master's mistress" (5.1.325–26). The ultimate result of disguise being a "wickedness" crashes into the *locus* of romantic comedy and reminds spectators that this "place" of love was recently a "place" of cruel torment, as Elizabethan public theaters often were. The audience cannot dwell on Viola's emotions; jarred again by a severely disruptive energy from the play's underworld, spectators hurdle "plots" and see emotions and characters rapidly juxtaposed. Note that Sebastian's appearance and the resolution of the lovers' dilemmas are framed by events of the "sub plot": Andrew's and Toby's bloody heads and drunken accusations precede these events, and Malvolio's anger and threats follow them. This latter segment, from Feste's entrance with Malvolio's letter to Malvolio's threat to be "revenged on the whole pack of you" (5.1.378) is ninety-seven lines long, the longest segment of act 5. It darkens all of act 5 and, placed where it is, concludes this "comedy" equivocally. Which is the stronger emotion: spectators' confidence in Viola's marriage to Orsino, or fear of Malvolio's threat? As Ralph Berry shrewdly observes, Malvolio's word "pack" suggests bearbaiting, and his "whole pack of you" implicitly includes the theater audience as he storms off stage, signaling, like Antonio's isolation (everyone at the end of the play simply ignores him) and the exits of Toby and especially Andrew, the violent dissonance that undermines this play's and its lovers' struggle for festive, romantic harmony.[55] At this precise moment in performance, which predominates: the Duke's promise of a golden time, or the realities of human vice? Joy or apprehension? Romantic comedy or Saturnalian excess?

Burdened by its conflicting moods, act 5 disintegrates before spectators' eyes. Berry asserts that at the end "The minor action bids to overwhelm the major."[56] I would argue rather that this distinction disappears by the end of the play. Beginning especially in 3.2, the play *as experienced in performance* dissolves distinctions among the actions of the "major" and "minor" plots and equally tramples at several junctions both serious and trivial emotions. Act 5 recapitulates these structural features of the play; spectators are barely allowed to comprehend the range of emotions sweeping the stage, Viola's reunion with Sebastian or Orsino's jealous anger, before a totally dissonant action, Toby's drunken rage or Malvolio's departing curse, simply demolishes that emotion. The play's convulsive Saturnalian energy becomes the paradigm of the larger structure itself, whose rapid disintegration in act 5 disables the unified joy the lovers seek and spectators expect at its end.[57]

Feste's song concludes:

> A great while ago the world begun,
>     With hey, ho, the wind and the rain,
> But that's all one, our play is done,
>     And we'll strive to please you every day.

Begun a long time ago, the world here acted in the Globe is as often sad as merry. Feste speaks of a single play, within which there is much "playing"—often abetted by disguise—some of which, including his own as Sir Topas, leads to humiliation and physical injury; some to presumably happy marriages only because of romance conventions operating in fiercely unromantic surroundings; and some to questionable marriages that, the romantic conventions notwithstanding, are difficult to accept. In act 5, as throughout, plots merge, blend, and then blur previously distinct outlines of characters, identities, and emotions.[58] The "carefully cantilevered structure" of *Twelfth Night,* its numerous bizarrely interlocking episodes, brilliantly creates theatrical energies that in performance produce a deliberately intended anxiety among spectators entirely appropriate to the limits of festivity implied by the play's title; indeed, *What You Will* mirrors the multiple perspectives from which the Globe's spectators viewed the play. Malvolio's final intrusion into comic romance, the result of his own absurd delusions about love, implies that no "place," including the *locus* of this play, is immune from revenge, and collapses not only distinctions between major and minor plots but also the platform stage's performance distinctions between *locus* and *platea.*

In his final lines, standing perhaps in Malvolio's final place on the stage, Feste evokes for his spectators that outer world beyond the theater doors that his "play," including his ruthless taunting of Malvolio, his part in the "whirligig of time" that "brings in his revenges," has so faithfully mirrored. (Feste apparently believes that his participation in the cruelest game of the play is supposed to please.) Outside these doors the exigencies of time and fortune evoked by his song—the transience of youthful innocence, the unruliness and fear of man's estate, the uncertainty of marriage, and the despair and drunkenness of old age—await them. As he dismisses from the theater and sends into the wind and rain of an English winter the spectators who have paid him to act, to entertain them in this comedy, Feste himself disables joy.[59]

# 7

## Seeing and Believing: Audience Perception and the Character of Cressida in Performance

In this and the final chapter, I wish to examine specific issues of audience response at the Globe Theatre to eavesdropping scenes in *Troilus & Cressida* and *Hamlet,* probably written within a year or two of each other. In both 5.2 of *Troilus,* the notorious meeting between Cressida and Diomedes, and the "Mousetrap" in 3.2 of *Hamlet,* performance on the Globe's thrust stage—the actual, continuous interaction between actors and spectators during the entire scene—would have created a range of spectator reactions that cannot be duplicated in modern proscenium theaters. Although each of these scenes has been thoroughly scrutinized by literary critics, few critics have so thoroughly examined either scene in its original theatrical setting and thus have not considered their dramatic "meaning" as part of an actual theatrical performance at the Globe, the theater for which each scene was designed. As I remark in my introduction, Homer Swander has forcefully argued that to exclude specific theatrical circumstances when examining Shakespeare's plays, especially "the theatre space and the actor-audience relationship that he knew was a given for him" is to exclude "something important."[1] Central to my arguments in these last two chapters will be the plural and enormously complex actor-audience relationships these scenes created at the Globe, and Philip C. McGuire's reminder that "A play is not an artifact but a process, unique with each performance, of making physically present (of *realizing*) possibilities of perception and feeling that lie attenuated and frozen in the script."[2] I shall argue that these multiple "possibilities of perception" within 5.2 of *Troilus & Cressida* and 3.2 of *Hamlet* epitomize Shakespeare's creative use of the performance space that the Globe presented to him,

174

and that examining these two scenes at the Globe is essential to understanding fully their possibilities for *dramatic* meaning and their place within their respective plays.

J. L. Styan explains that the convention of eavesdropping, which illustrates clearly the freedom of Elizabethan stage groupings, requires a "special pattern of movement."[3] The complexity and staging of an eavesdropping scene, including the spatial relationship between observer and observed, are determined primarily by whether or not the observer speaks. In *Hamlet* 3.1, for example, Polonius and Claudius remain silent, so this scene requires only that they and Hamlet be visibly separated on the large platform because the convention dictates that Hamlet does not see his adversaries. However, as Styan remarks, if the observers do speak, the blocking and direction are far more demanding.[4]

Speaking eavesdroppers are dramatically more complex because their comments necessarily concern what they see, automatically complicating theater spectators' response to stage action. For the duration of most plays, spectators observe one stratum of action they can judge as they wish; however, in the presence of speaking eavesdroppers, the spectators must balance their own reactions against internal comments emanating from the staged action. Such internal comments may reinforce spectators' impressions of characters, or may reveal characters' own idiosyncratic reactions to stage action that may not necessarily agree with theater spectators' responses. Iago's "staged" interview in 4.1 between himself and Cassio, which Othello observes, illustrates this last point; everyone else in the theater knows Cassio is discussing Bianca, whereas Othello incredibly believes that Cassio is discussing his supposed liaisons with Desdemona.

Because a speaking observer is overheard by the theater audience but not by the observed stage character(s), the characters' relative proximity to each other and their positions on stage must be carefully designed for maximum dramatic effectiveness. On the Globe's thrust stage, an observer's position would determine immediately his relationship with the observed and with different segments of the theater audience, and the spaciousness and fluidity of the Globe's thrust stage would have permitted several different blockings of most eavesdropping scenes in Shakespeare's Globe plays. While this last assertion is simple enough, what are not so simple are the different interpretations that would have developed from these different blockings, and we can learn much about Shakespeare's dramatic art and how he adapted it to Elizabethan stage conditions by examining different possible stagings of some of his eavesdropping scenes and the equally different reactions to such scenes that these stagings would have created in the Globe playhouse. Because of the crisscross pattern of sight lines at the Globe,[5] a spectator seated anywhere in the theater during an eavesdropping scene, whether in the central portion of the theater (central audience) or along either side (side audience) of the thrust stage,[6] could watch not only the scene itself but also other spectators watching the same scene. Thus, the entire theatrical event—acting, observing, and observing of observing—became a visual analogue of the eavesdropping scene itself. This feature of eavesdropping scenes, especially in scenes as dramatically complex as 5.2 of *Troilus & Cressida* and 3.2 of *Hamlet,* illustrates superbly Stephen Orgel's assertion that essential to Renaissance theater is a "basic fluidity or disjunctiveness" that "depends for its truth upon its audience." "[Henry] Peacham's sketch of *Titus Andronicus* . . . persuades the viewer of the significance, position, status of its figures. It does not mime a consistent world but expresses an action. Its elements fit together only insofar as a viewer interprets and understands them."[7] At the Globe, spectators' involvement in and interpretations of staged action would have been especially pronounced and complex during 5.2 of *Troilus & Cressida.*[8]

In the theater, this scene inevitably chafes. Regardless of how one judges, or has prejudged, Troilus and Cressida in or before this scene, by its end one is deeply disturbed by Cressida's words to Diomedes and by Troilus's profound despair. The terrible conflicts inherent in the scene—Cressida's half-spoken, anguished fears; Troilus's sense of betrayal and shock at Cressida's actions; Ulysses's ambiguous motives in accompanying Troilus; and Thersites' roguish, cynical remarks—assault spectators almost too rapidly, and the flood of remarks from the five characters creates a dizzying sense of multiple realities analogous to the stage characters' own experiences.

Shakespeare's characterization of the lovers prior to 5.2 and the play in which they appear are equally essential to spectators' experience of this scene. Troilus and Cressida attempt to pursue love amid a protracted, absurd war fought for a whore by men who deliberately hide this fact from themselves in "ceremonies and formal rhetoric," especially in the two council scenes, while throughout the play "images of disease and devouring appetite," as well as the relentless, corrosive appetite of time, continually undercut their formality and expose their hypocrisy.[9] Further, as Gayle Greene astutely argues, the absence of order in the play imperils one's sense of an autonomous "self": "The disturbance of the hierarchical order leaves the individual not autonomous and free, but bound to definition by relation of a different, more destructive sort. Deprived of the legitimate sanctions of hierarchy, the individual must create his or her own value, an appearance to please the beholding eye, in what is essentially a selling of the self."[10]

Troilus initially disdains war "without the walls of Troy," overwhelmed by the "cruel battle here within" (1.1.2,3); while sounding a traditional Petrarchan hyperbole that suggests his "victimization" by love, he also immediately associates love with war, and in his initial soliloquy describes his love for Cressida in commercial terms: "Her bed is India, there she lies, a pearl. . . . Ourself the merchant, and this sailing Pandar / Our doubtful hope, our convoy, and our bark" (1.1.103, 106–7). In the Trojan council scene, Troilus will ask, "What's aught but as 'tis valued?"[11] and his own imagery suggests that Cressida is apparently valued as a merchant's prize;[12] because she is "stubborn-chaste against all suit," Troilus must venture with the sordid aid of Pandarus. As the object of Troilus's romantic venture, Cressida initially displays a sardonic, defensive wit[13] that gradually reveals a far more complex character who is profoundly aware of her precarious condition: a single woman, the daughter of a traitor, alone in a besieged kingdom ruled by men who have slaughtered casually for seven years to defend a faithless woman and, they believe, their "honor," as Hector and Troilus will argue in the Trojan council scene. During 1.2, as she and Pandarus view the returning troops, probably from above the upstage *locus* of Troy, she ironically undercuts not only Pandarus's praise of Troilus—"There is amongst the Greeks Achilles, a better man than Troilus" (1.2.249–50)—but also of all men, suggesting perhaps early in the play her fear that in war, especially *this* war, men are simply interchangeable because of their imminent death.[14] Attempting to praise Troilus, Pandarus catalogs his "birth, beauty, good shape, discourse . . . youth, liberality, and such-like, the spice and salt that season a man," all of which Cressida reduces to "a minced man; and then to be baked with no date in the pie, for then the man's date is out" (1.2.258–59). A dead man has no date, no time; all the men Cressida views, including Troilus, may soon be "minced" (i.e., "chopped up fine" [Bevington, 4th ed., note line 258]) by this hideous war. Cressida's sense of this possibility at least partially explains her initial defensiveness, but equally important to her character is her initial sense of her sexual vulnerability:

*Pandarus.* You are such a woman! A man knows not at what ward you lie.

*Cressida.* Upon my back to defend my belly, upon my wit to defend my wiles, upon my secrecy to defend mine honesty, my mask to defend my beauty, and you to defend all these, and at all these wards I lie, at a thousand watches.

(1.2.260–66)

Cressida's imagery reveals a witty, playful sexuality *completely* absent in Troilus, as well as a profound need, evident in her repeated, parallel use of "defend," to guard that sexuality. These elements in her character are heightened in her soliloquy, which emphasizes early in the play the significant differences between herself and Troilus. Although she loves Troilus, she will "hold off": "Things won are done, joy's soul lies in the doing. . . . Men prize the thing ungained more than it is. . . . Then though my heart's content firm love doth bear, / Nothing of that shall from mine eyes appear" (1.2.289, 291, 296–97). The sexual puns in Cressida's soliloquy perhaps emphasize her sense that men, even when loved, as she says she loves Troilus, only seek to purchase, as merchants do, a sexual commodity whose value only the purchaser can determine.[15] Spectators' awareness of the significant differences between Troilus and Cressida, especially Cressida's sense of her vulnerability so early in the play, is crucial to their later experience of them in 5.2.

Shakespeare accentuates these differences in 3.2, as on the downstage *platea* the lovers attempt to secure their sexual relationship amid the continuing war which the Greek and Trojan councils have reaffirmed in the twin council scenes. Troilus's sexual anticipation makes him "giddy," and "expectation whirls [him] round." His senses are enchanted by the "imaginary relish" which he finds "sweet"; however, actual sexual joy apparently frightens him:

> What will it be
> When that the watery palate tastes indeed
> Love's thrice repurèd nectar? Death, I fear me,
> Swooning destruction, or some joy too fine,
> Too subtle-potent, tuned too sharp in sweetness

For the capacity of my ruder powers.
I fear it much; and I do fear besides
That I shall lose distinction in my joys,
As doth a battle, when they charge on heaps
The enemy flying.

(3.2.19–28)

As Cressida repeats "defend," so Troilus repeats "fear." Although
Troilus may be "unable to distinguish one delight from another"
(Bevington, 4th ed., note line 26), his imagery also suggests fear
of losing a distinct "self," however imperfectly that "self" may be
realized so far in the play. Further, he again associates love with
war, here grotesquely linking his expected sexual joys with the
"joys" of slaughtering fleeing soldiers. After Pandarus leaves to
start the (sexually symbolic) fire in the bed chamber, Cressida
speaks of her fears, which are exacerbated by Troilus's litany of
the mythical tasks imposed by ladies on their knights: "to weep
seas, live in fire, eat rocks, tame tigers, thinking it harder for
our mistress to devise imposition enough than for us to undergo
any difficulty imposed" (3.2.77–79). Troilus believes that the
"monstrosity" in love is "that the will is infinite and the execu-
tion confined," whereas Cressida defines this monstrosity far
differently:

They say all lovers swear more performance than they
are able, and yet reserve an ability that they never
perform, vowing more than the perfection of ten
and discharging less than the tenth part of one.
They that have the voice of lions and the act of
hares, are they not monsters?

(3.2.83–88)

Beneath Cressida's witticisms about male sexual (im)potency is a
far deeper fear that men's love is but a "voice," an avowal lacking
commitment and not only sexual but also, and more ominously,
emotional strength. Troilus's simplistic question, "Why was my
Cressid then so hard to win?" intensifies her anguish even as
she moves towards an irrevocable commitment:

Hard to seem won; but I was won, my lord,
With the first glance that ever—pardon me;
If I confess much, you will play the tyrant.
I love you now, but till now not so much
But I might master it. In faith, I lie;

My thoughts were like unbridled children, grown
Too headstrong for their mother. See, we fools!
Why have I blabbed? Who shall be true to us,
When we are so unsecret to ourselves?
But, though I loved you well, I wooed you not;
And yet, good faith, I wished myself a man,
Or that we women had men's privilege
Of speaking first. Sweet, bid me hold my tongue,
For in this rapture I shall surely speak
Cunning in dumbness, from my weakness draws
My very soul of counsel! Stop my mouth.

(3.2.116–32)

Even as Cressida speaks, she wishes, not for a kiss, as Troilus assumes, but that she would not speak, lest she do what she already senses she will regret: commit herself sexually. Her "divided self" is frighteningly clear:

> Troilus.    You cannot shun yourself.
> Cressida.   Let me go and try.
> I have a kind of self resides with you,
> But an unkind self that itself will leave
> To be another's fool. Where is my wit?
> I would be gone. I speak I know not what.

(3.2.145–50)

Janet Adelman argues that the "self" of Cressida here is a woman utterly dominated by a fear of just what she commits in this scene: a self-betrayal.[16] She commits to Troilus a "self" that shall be "unkind" because even as it is given it shall be unkind to both the donor and the recipient. Cressida fears what she has done because she violates her earlier expressed fear that she shall be prized, and valued, only as "the thing ungained." If this is true, then the man she admits she loves shall prove to be no more than what, in fact, he is: another merchant seeking a sexual prize valued in only its mysterious elusiveness. Further, Cressida here denies her awareness of the wretched world in which she lives, and her loss of "wit" and sudden wish to leave suggest that momentarily at least she realizes this may be her greater error.[17]

In their dialogue concluding 3.2, both Troilus and Cressida speak more than they know. Troilus naively asserts "I am as true as truth's simplicity, / And simpler than the infancy of truth" (lines 168–69); he then assumes based on this chiasmatic assertion that he can claim to be the model of faithfulness. With Cassandra's ironic insight into the future, Cressida prophesies not only her own "unfaithfulness" but also the destruction of Troy by the very forces that began the war and have brutalized love:

> If I be false or swerve a hair from truth,
> When time is old and hath forgot itself,
> When waterdrops have worn the stones of Troy,
> And blind oblivion swallowed cities up,
> And mighty states characterless are grated
> To dusty nothing, yet let memory,
> From false to false, among false maids in love,
> Upbraid my falsehood!
>
> (3.2.183–190)

Given her subliminal awareness of what is occurring all around her, the gradual swallowing of cities, not just by time but by the blind oblivion of a war that "minces" men, her prophecy that she shall be cursed for falsehood is like a scream to herself not to do what she fears she shall. Cressida is perhaps more "divided" here than Troilus claims she is in 5.2, and to judge her actions in that difficult scene without considering her earlier, impassioned fears is to minimize the conflicting emotions she expresses as she meets Diomedes. As I shall argue shortly, and as I argue on Hamlet's "Mousetrap," the staging of such complex scenes must be considered in their full dramatic context, especially when imagining such scenes performed on the Globe's thrust stage.

Equally significant to the dramatic context of 5.2 is the lovers' parting in 4.2, a painfully ironic aubade. Troilus urges Cressida back to sleep, claiming the "busy day" calls him, but revealing also his fear of being seen with her: "dreaming night will hide our joys no longer." Cressida immediately senses his insecurity:

> Prithee, tarry. You men will never tarry.
> O foolish Cressid! I might have still held off,
> And then you would have tarried. Hark, there's one up.
>
> (4.2.17–19)

The persistent knocking, like that of 2.4 in *I Henry IV* and 2.3 in *Macbeth,* signals the intrusion that destroys the lovers' sanctuary; "Priam and the general state of Troy" have decreed that Cressida is to be traded. Troilus's initial reaction is crucial: "How my achievements mock me! / I will go meet them. And, my lord

Aeneas, / We met by chance; you did not find me here" (4.2.71–
73). Cressida is suddenly but a sexual "achievement," and he is
embarrassed to have been found with her. Troilus leaves with
Aeneas, blandly accepting Cressida's banishment as he returns
to male society.[18] Thus, when Cressida is told of her fate, she is
alone, abandoned by her lover as she was by her father. Contrary
to Troilus's selfish resignation, her response is passionate rage:

> O you gods divine!
> Make Cressid's name the very crown of falsehood
> If ever she leave Troilus! Time, force, and death,
> Do to this body what extremes you can;
> But the strong base and building of my love
> Is as the very center of the earth,
> Drawing all things to it. I'll go in and weep—
> . . . . . . . . . . . . . . . . . . .
> Tear my bright hair and scratch my praisèd cheeks,
> Crack my clear voice with sobs and break my heart
> With sounding "Troilus." I will not go from Troy.
>                                   (4.2.100–6, 108–10)

Cressida suddenly seeks to deface the beauty that Troilus desired, as if destroying that beauty could obliterate her ever having been desired and thus any occasion for her ever having
yielded. Helen, the whore, shall be kept; Cressida, who feared
the sexual indulgence that Helen flouts, shall be bartered.[19] The
"blind oblivion" that Cressida prophesied in 3.2 would swallow
cities has blindly reduced her, and her passionate love, to a mere
commodity. Cressida rightly feared sexual commitment in such
a world, and, having yielded when she most feared she should
not, her rage now turns destructively upon herself.[20]
    In 4.4, despite his claim that he loves Cressida "in so strained
a purity," Troilus expresses his fear, probably created by his
having so readily enjoyed Cressida, that she shall be untrue.
Having abandoned her when he heard she was to be traded,
he now implicitly questions *her* integrity, neither realizing his
selfishness and incipient insecurity[21] nor questioning his suddenly fleeing the morning's light and Aeneas's intrusion.
Though he protests his love throughout the scene, Troilus's simply handing her over to Diomedes with virtually no protest, as
if he were merely the emissary of the state council that has
pawned her, will be recalled by spectators in 5.2 as part of the
continuum of performance. Indeed, the many sexual innuen-
does during this exchange, as in Troilus's "I charge thee use her

well, even for my charge," and Diomedes's "When I am hence, /
I'll answer to my lust" (4.4.126, 131–32), anticipate the sordid
sexual tensions of 5.2 and clarify to Cressida and to spectators
that she is valued as only a convenient exchange for a Trojan
general so that Paris may continue to enjoy Helen.[22] In this
environment, having yielded to the man who now exchanges
her at the behest of his father's council, in which women's
value—indeed, identity—is determined solely by men's view of
them, what ought one expect Cressida to do? What—or, indeed,
who—is Cressida? The rest of this essay examines Shakespeare's
dramatization at the Globe of possible answers to these questions in 5.2.

The most extensive treatment of this scene's dramaturgy heretofore is by Douglas Sprigg.[23] In his superb analysis of this scene
at the Globe, Sprigg demonstrates how his suggested blocking
would have been integral to his perception of the scene's theatrical impact on its Elizabethan audience. He notes initially that
since Diomedes enters first and replaces Thersites, who has just
exited, and then calls to Calchas, Diomedes should remain upstage.[24] Sprigg continues:

> While the seducer [Diomedes] waits impatiently, perhaps pacing
> back and forth upstage with his flaming torch, Troilus and Ulysses
> enter and, unnoticed, move with conspiratorial swiftness downstage
> to a position "where the torch may not discover" them. They are
> followed onstage by Thersites, who also sneaks away from the flame
> to establish, unnoticed by the other two groups, yet a third position
> onstage. Cressida enters and, in the provocative manner suggested
> by her first line ("Now, my sweet guardian!"), approaches Diomedes.[25]

Sprigg's suggested blocking places Cressida and Diomedes upstage right and left, respectively, Ulysses and Troilus downstage
right, and Thersites downstage left (see Appendix A). As Sprigg
cogently argues, this blocking allows Cressida's physical movements between Diomedes and Troilus to image her ambivalent
motives, shifting loyalties, and moral uncertainties; it also juxtaposes the choric comments of Ulysses and Thersites against Troilus's growing incredulity. This staging of the scene exemplifies
the potential for complex, simultaneous stage meaning on the
Globe's thrust stage:

> By positioning a series of observers, each perceiving the situation
> with degrees of greater awareness, Shakespeare creates a complex
> scene of multiple eavesdropping. Cressida and Diomedes interact

upstage aware only of each other's responses. Troilus registers the responses of the upstage couple, but perceives this interaction within an entirely different frame of reference. Thersites' perspective is broader still. He views the upstage interaction in juxtaposition to the reactions of Troilus. The audience provides the fourth group in the chain of observers zigzagging in toward the upstage scene. By creating such a system of observed observers, Shakespeare insures that the slightest response from the upstage couple will be magnified by a chain reaction of responses from the series of eavesdroppers. In a sense, Shakespeare has created a series of mutually informing plays within plays, each with its own frame of reference, receding in depth away from the audience toward Cressida.... The scene is centrally concerned with the potential for contradictory perceptions of human behavior, and, thus, Shakespeare is at pains to create physical actions between the upstage couple that may be perceived and reacted to differently by each of the downstage observers.[26]

The perceptions of human behavior in the scene are, indeed, contradictory. Sprigg writes that Troilus is shocked by Cressida's "blatant physical familiarity" with Diomedes, whereas Ulysses sees it as merely "characteristic of [Cressida's] behavior"; Thersites meanwhile "reacts to Ulysses' reaction to Troilus's reaction to Cressida's behavior by emphasizing, for the benefit of the audience, the more indecent implications of such an interpretation.... Shakespeare insures the impact of Thersites' jaundiced point of view by having him speak directly to the spectator, who completes the linkage in the chain of eavesdroppers."[27] This blocking of the scene at the Globe would have created on stage "a physical manifestation of a moral tug-of-war":

Visually and symbolically situated on a continuum between polar opposites, Cressida is pulled stage-left by her lust for Diomedes ... and she is pulled stage-right toward the exit by her memory of the undoubting devotion of Troilus. From the audience's vantage point, every movement toward Diomedes sends her away visually from the observing Troilus, and every movement away from Diomedes brings her back visually toward Troilus. Equally important, a movement toward Diomedes is not only away from Troilus; it is also a movement in the direction of Thersites. On both a literal and symbolic level, the nature of her inner psychological struggle is given an external physical manifestation. Cressida's movement, in relation to the positioning of the other characters onstage, enacts her dilemma and creates a visual emblem of the forces warring within.[28]

Sprigg's analysis of the scene's multiple perspectives, especially of the "visual emblem" of Cressida's tortured dilemma, demonstrates convincingly Shakespeare's creative use of his flexible stage. However, Sprigg's blocking assumes, as he says, that Thersites' perspective is the broadest in the scene: Cressida and Diomedes are aware of only each other; Troilus's reactions to them are filtered through his own distraught emotions; and Thersites "views the upstage action in juxtaposition to the reactions of Troilus." Sprigg envisions an emotional chain reaction originating between Diomedes and Cressida, darting zigzag across the platform from Troilus and Ulysses to Thersites, and terminating in the central theater audience; the "mutually informing plays within plays" recede "in depth away from the audience toward Cressida."[29] Sprigg's major assumption, that the final reference point of these multiple perspectives is the downstage, or central audience, weakens his argument because he assumes a unified audience response to this scene. For all of his exemplary sensitivity to the visual experience of theater at the Globe, Sprigg's own perspective on the scene is too narrow. The "series of mutually informing plays within plays" that he so carefully analyzes is more complex than he suggests, for in his blocking the side audiences, those sitting closer to the stage right and left sections of the Globe's thrust stage, would have had contrasting perspectives. The stage-right portion of the audience sees/hears all from Cressida's perspective, whereas the stage-left audience is influenced more by Diomedes. The "zigzag" pattern Sprigg envisions (emotions from Diomedes/Cressida to Ulysses to Troilus to Thersites to central audience) is actually a web of crisscrossing lines: the stage-right spectators observe Cressida directly, and see/hear Thersites' remarks through Ulysses and Troilus; the stage-left spectators observe Diomedes more directly but may be more influenced by Thersites, depending on how far upstage he is positioned. As Cressida and Diomedes move, even these perspectives change; the entire scene becomes a kaleidoscope of constantly changing character and spectator perspectives. Shakespeare thus creates here, for and within the entire audience, an amazingly close analogue to the stage action. Spectators seated in the center of the theater observe Cressida being observed by spectators near Ulysses and Troilus, and Diomedes being observed by spectators nearer to him (and possibly) Thersites. Similar complications abound from the stage-left and -right spectators watching the central audience closer (on one side) to Ulysses and Troilus, and (on the other) to Thersites. Different portions of the theater audience relative to the several speaking eavesdroppers (and to Diomedes and Cressida) experience different angles of vision on, degrees of involvement with, and judgments about the stage action. The "meaning" of this scene, like its dramaturgy and the stage characters' emotions, is continually changing.

Sprigg's blocking raises other questions. Does not he assume that Shakespeare intended Thersites to be the scene's final arbiter for the entire theater audience, and does this assumption determine where Sprigg places Thersites on stage? Does not this blocking also prejudice most spectators' reactions to Cressida's meeting with Diomedes, assuring them that what they see/hear is only what Thersites says it is: "Lechery, lechery, still wars and lechery; nothing else holds fashion" (5.2.198–99); or that Cressida is pulled toward Diomedes only by "lust"; and that Troilus has shown her "undoubting devotion"? What might a different blocking of this scene have yielded at the Globe, and might a different staging of this scene have emphasized more of the complexities within Cressida that Shakespeare has created earlier in the play, especially in 4.2 and 4.4, just before the assignation scene?

Consider now Appendix B. Diomedes enters first, calls to Calchas, and then Ulysses and Troilus enter followed by Thersites. Ulysses's "stand where the torch may not discover us" does not place them in any particular stage position, nor does Thersites's entrance.[30] As Appendix B indicates, I suggest placing Ulysses and Troilus upstage right, about midway between the stage facade and the stage-right post, and I would then have Diomedes, after his second call to Calchas, and just after Ulysses and Troilus have positioned themselves, walk to downstage left. When Cressida enters, through the right stage door, imagine her walking downstage past the "hiding" Ulysses and Troilus, thus arousing Troilus's concern and symbolizing her imminent disavowal of him. Thersites, whose position is now radically different from Sprigg's placement, is upstage left and no longer positioned to suggest that his comments on the stage action are definitive. If Cressida and Diomedes interact on the downstage center *platea,* without either Troilus's or Thersites's exclamations interposed between them and the central spectators, then this portion of the theater audience can judge the couples' words for themselves. Furthermore, now a smaller portion of the audience, those near stage left, views the action through Thersites's eyes, and his "authority" on this spectacle is now considerably diminished. Also changed radically are Troilus's and Ulysses' positions relative to Diomedes and Cressida: in Sprigg's blocking, Troilus and Ulysses were, like Thersites, relatively close to the central audience, whereas in my blocking, they, like Thersites, are proximate to a smaller portion of the total audience—those stage right. Without Troilus's or Thersites's reactions to "guide" the central spectators' experience of this complex, enigmatic scene, these spectators can weigh more directly the frightening emotions to which Cressida can only allude.

I wish now to consider notions of "character," especially Cressida's, in relation to these two blocking options. Appendix A presumes that the principal issues *for the entire audience* are Troilus's reactions to Cressida's "betrayal" and Thersites' reaction to and comments on Troilus's dismay. Sprigg writes that Thersites "functions as a Greek Pandarus, an emblem of the potentially repulsive aspects of sexual desire," whereas Troilus "suggests the idealization" of sexual relations.[31] He adds: "All the touching becomes an excitement to trembling rage and despair from Troilus on one side of the stage and an excitement to lecherous imaginings from Thersites on the other."[32] Sprigg sees the stage sharply divided into two camps, each representing a clearly defined set of moral values:

> On the down-right side of the stage stands the naive, romantic Troilus. Even as Thersites suggests the sordid side of sexual relations, so Troilus suggests the idealization. The positioning of these two divides the stage into opposing camps of love and lechery, innocence and decadence, fidelity and venality. The stage begins to suggest the dialectics associated with the larger war of which this small skirmish is a part.[33]

Cressida moves between these poles, either toward Diomedes, and thus Thersites, or toward Troilus. The entire audience is tugged between these poles as it juxtaposes these radically opposed character reactions. Thus, in Sprigg's staging of the scene, Cressida's character is judged for the entire theater audience by Troilus and Thersites. She becomes whatever one of them says she is at the moment he is speaking: a betrayer of a sensitive, if naive, lover; or an emblem of omnipresent lechery. The stage enacts an allegorized struggle in which Cressida's motivations and actions are reduced to two men's morally opposite judgments of them.

As opposed to Sprigg, I see the stage picture as it evolves during performance as being morally far more complex and ambiguous, especially regarding Cressida's motives. If, as I suggest in Appendix B, Cressida and Diomedes are downstage center, with

Troilus/Ulysses and Thersites upstage right and left, then most, but not all, of the audience judges for itself what Cressida is, what she is doing, and why. Most of the spectators in Appendix B hear from equidistant parts of the stage disparate choric comments about Cressida the truth of which they can judge for themselves. The distance of Thersites and Troilus from the action's center and from the central audience minimizes their authority as commentators; their knowledge of what the central audience witnesses is limited and incomplete. Furthermore, because the central spectators watch Diomedes and Cressida being observed by Thersites on one side and by Troilus/Ulysses on the other, these spectators also observe one of the two side audiences being more influenced by Thersites and the other more by Troilus/Ulysses. As the central spectators attempt to judge the "validity" of these two sets of choruses, they simultaneously juggle their own theatrical experience and that of the characters onstage: one portion of the total audience sees/hears the stage action primarily through Thersites; and the other through Troilus/Ulysses. Which set of commentators is right about Cressida's "assignation"? Which set of the theater's side observers is more "correct" in its view? Is either portion of the side audiences seeing/hearing *all* stage action and dialogue correctly, and is either thus "right" about what Cressida and Diomedes are doing/saying? The very uncertainty of this brutal scene in performance, especially regarding Cressida's motives, is mirrored among all spectators' own discordant views of the *total* theatrical experience they see/hear (i.e., stage action + on-stage observers' commentary + theater spectators' reactions.) Appendix B, then, clearly places Thersites and Troilus in stage positions that suggest a seminal point of this scene: that Cressida is not necessarily at any one moment what any man here says she is. Throughout the play, Cressida is far more complex than most of the men with whom she interacts, especially Troilus. Positioning Troilus and Thersites in this scene to suggest that Cressida's "identity" is only how any man defines that identity limits her dramatic role and minimizes her character. The complexities of characters' motivations and their and theater spectators' responses inherent in this scene during performance on the Globe's thrust stage defy the abstract dichotomy into which Sprigg attempts to divide it.

Yes, Cressida betrays Troilus, but has not Troilus already betrayed Cressida by his selfishness and denial in 4.2 when he learns that she is to be traded for another commander—a male warrior—to the Greeks? Troilus can think only of how his achievements mock *him*; he never mentions the effect of his father's decree on the woman he insists he loves, despite his "cruel battle here within," which militarily disarms him in 1.1. He denies even their night of love: "And, my lord Aeneas, / We met by chance; you did not find me here." As René Girard observes, Troilus is a remarkable example of "bad faith" who "Like all of us, . . . remembers selectively. Among his sentiments and his actions, he remembers only those that consolidate his image of himself as a virtuous man, abominably wronged by others but never guilty himself. He does not remember the discontinuity in his love for Cressida."[34] Further, when Cressida steps out of Calchas's tent, she leaves a father who has defected to the Greeks and abandoned her, and whom she had renounced in 4.2 when told she must leave Troy. Thus, when Cressida says to Diomedes, "Now, my sweet guardian! Hark, a word with you," she has already been betrayed twice: once by her father, whose defection left her no protection in Troy; and once by Troilus, who left her alone to be told she was being sent to the Greeks and then virtually handed her over to Diomedes with astonishingly ambiguous language: "I charge thee use her well, even for my charge" (4.4.126). Troilus asks, "Yea, so familiar?" and Ulysses adds "She will sing any man at first sight." Thersites claims "And any man may sing her, if he can take her clef. She's noted" (5.2.10–11). But do any of these men fully understand Cressida's emotions or motives at this *moment?* Cressida's anguish is immediately evident; she pleads with Diomedes not to tempt her to folly, and not to hold her to her oath: "Bid me do anything but that, sweet Greek" (5.2.28). Diomedes then threatens to do exactly what Calchas and Troilus have previously done: abandon her: "No, no, good night. I'll be your fool no more. . . . And so, good night" (5.2.33, 46). Cressida is alone in the Greek camp; she has just left her father whom she had denied in 4.2 as she frantically tried to prevent being sent to the Greeks; and now, in a war being fought for a whore by men who callously determine a woman's worth, Cressida fears being abandoned among strangers with no immediate contact at all: "Nay, but you part in anger" (5.2.46).

"Guardian!—Why, Greek!" What is the motive for this strange outburst? Cressida asks—pleads?—again for a guardian; in the Greek camp, this is precisely what she needs at this moment. Voth and Evans argue that the one "folly" of which Cressida can justly be accused is abandoning what she knew to be the reality of her world and giving herself wholly to Troilus's romanticized, idealized love.[35] And that was within the supposedly safe walls of Troy; here, among strangers, "merry" Greeks, and a betraying father, Cressida desperately seeks a guardian, even if she knows what this "guardianship" will entail. Troilus watches her stroke Diomedes's cheek, and searches for patience; Thersites immediately abstracts and stereotypes Cressida's words and actions, completely ignoring her paralyzing fear: "How the devil Luxury, with his fat rump and potato finger, tickles these together! Fry, lechery, fry" (5.2.56–57). Diomedes asks for a token, and Cressida returns to her father's tent. If, as I have suggested, Cressida and Diomedes are downstage center, then as she walks upstage to Calchas's tent and then returns with Troilus's sleeve, she twice walks past the incredulous Troilus as she did in her initial entry into the scene, thus visually magnifying the tension on stage. Even as Thersites insists that the sleeve is Cressida's "pledge" to Diomedes and that Cressida is a "whetstone" that now "sharpens," Cressida's tumult and pain are clearly evident:

| | |
|---|---|
| *Cressida.* | You look upon that sleeve. Behold it well. |
| | He loved me—O false wench!—Give 't me again. |
| *Diomedes.* | Whose was 't? |
| *Cressida.* | It is no matter, now I ha't again. |
| | I will not meet with you tomorrow night. |
| | I prithee, Diomed, visit me no more. |
| *Thersites* | [aside]. Now she sharpens. Well said, whetstone! |
| *Diomedes.* | I shall have it. |
| *Cressida.* | What, this? |
| *Diomedes.* | Ay, that. |
| *Cressida.* | O all you gods! O pretty, pretty pledge! |
| | Thy master now lies thinking in his bed |
| | Of thee and me, and sighs, and takes my glove, |
| | And gives memorial dainty kisses to it, |
| | As I kiss thee. Nay, do not snatch it from me; |
| | He that takes that doth take my heart withal. |

(5.2.71–84)

In her anguish, Cressida suddenly adopts Troilus's romantic, almost Petrarchan imagery—"sighs, and takes my glove, / And gives memorial dainty kisses to it"—as if she could conjure an ideal, romantic world of faithful, sighing lovers away from this fearful camp and its sordid emissary. Cressida knew that "Men prize the thing ungained more than it is," and in 4.2 realized that "You men will never tarry. / O foolish Cressid! I might have still held off, / And then you would have tarried" (lines 17–19). She does not know, however, of Troilus's denial of their liaison to Aeneas, and thus even as she desperately tries to invoke this ideal world as an alternative to the real one she knows she is about to enter, spectators know that despite his fervid protests Troilus was never capable of being the selfless, supportive lover Cressida hoped he could be when she abandoned her fears for his romantic visions. In the blocking I have suggested, both the horrid reality of Cressida's situation and the pathetic discrepancy between her Petrarchan fantasy and Troilus's selfish failure to uphold it are clearly evident on stage. The central action of the scene becomes the dramatization of Cressida's desperate struggle to maintain a sense of "self," symbolized visually by the sleeve which she tries to retain with her(self) and Diomedes snatches from her. Troilus's and Thersites's remarks about this terrible moment are limited, incomplete choric comments that do not attempt to probe the causes of Cressida's anguish. To stage this scene as if these choric comments were its central point would significantly lessen its dramatic tension and spectators' role in determining its meaning.[36]

In Appendix B this scene is equally elusive and enigmatic for the stage-right and -left audiences, whose perspective is markedly different from spectators more centrally placed in the Globe. The stage-right spectators see/hear the stage action from Ulysses' and Troilus's perspectives, whereas the stage-left spectators see/hear from Thersites'. But each side audience observes the other experiencing the scene from an equally limited perspective; each is influenced by one set of commentators. For the central spectators the sets of commentators are about equally distant from them, whereas for the side audiences even this equanimity is shattered. For the stage-right spectators, Ulysses/Troilus, being closer, assume more prominence as commentators, and Thersites' remarks, which Sprigg assumes dominate this scene, are minimized; for the stage-left spectators, Thersites dominates, and the views of Troilus and Ulysses are minimized. Which set of commentators is "right"? No certainty is possible, and, I contend, none should be. This is the central point of this scene *for the entire audience.* Further, the side audiences see spectators closer to the center of the theater, observing this spectacle from a perspective that is irreconcilable with their own. Thus, Cressida may appear to be what Ulysses, Troilus, or Thersites says she is, but each side audience's view is as limited as

that of the commentators nearest to them. Perhaps, as the side
audiences watch the central audience observing Cressida and
Diomedes and juggle the eavesdroppers' comments, they realize
how limited their own perspectives are, for they mirror what
they see and hear: three men judging an abandoned young
woman trapped in horrendous circumstances, making her be,
or become, what they want her to be or become. Regardless of
the sight lines of the Globe's ca. 3000 spectators, this scene became in that theater a perfect analogue of the stage action and
thus an image of its most difficult element: discerning its characters' motives and actions, especially Cressida's.

Cressida's final speech would seem clearly to indict her as
"whore" and to justify Thersites's final, cynical judgment on the
entire scene:

> Troilus, farewell! One eye yet looks on thee,
> But with my heart the other eye doth see.
> Ah, poor our sex! This fault in us I find:
> The error of our eye directs our mind.
> What error leads must err. O, then conclude:
> Minds swayed by eyes are full of turpitude.
>
> (5.2.110–15)

Cressida is physically attracted to Diomedes; to deny this is to
deny her plain words. Nor does she deny this attraction; she is
"full of turpitude," her mind directed by Diomedes' sexual al-
lure. But her mind also recalls, as theater spectators will, but
Troilus cannot, the "merry Greeks," led by Agamemnon, greet-
ing her in their camp as a virtual whore in 4.5, and Ulysses
immediately suggesting, after Agamemnon kisses her, that
"'Twere better she were kissed in general." Despite her words,
which here may be an unrecognized self-deception, a generalized, oversimplified excuse for women's frailty masking her terrible fear, Cressida's "capitulation results from a complex of
causes: sexual attraction to Diomed, along with her need for a
protector, compounded by a change in environment from one
in which "'Words, vows, gifts, tears, and love's full sacrifice' are
offered as a prelude to exploitation, to an environment in which
such niceties are totally discarded, leaving Cressida disarmed of
even her limited powers of control."[37] Also in Cressida's mind at
this precise moment may lurk, as R. A. Yoder proposes, a fatalism
about love in time of war hinted much earlier in her remarks
when she watched the returning troops in 1.2: "Perhaps in the
sensual pleasure of the here and now, however bittersweet it

proves, Cressida has got hold of the only value her world affords. All that is left to her is a little touch of Troilus in the night—or of Diomedes, what does it matter? One or the other will be dead next evening."[38] Troilus apprehends none of this; he is, after all, among those perpetuating this war, having argued that Helen's worth, or any object's or person's, is "but as 'tis valued," and having accepted unquestioningly Cressida's "value" as barter for a fellow soldier. He recalls none of this when he asserts that "this is Diomed's Cressida," and that "If there be rule in unity itself, / This is not she" (5.2.141, 145–46). Indeed, in his frightening naïveté Troilus utterly fails to realize that the scene he observes before him shatters any notion of unity anywhere, whether in himself, Cressida, or the cause for which he fights. As René Girard observes, Troilus's memory is very selective, nowhere in the play more so than here.

Like the entire play, 5.2 of *Troilus & Cressida* is unpleasant. We usually agree with Thersites's closing evaluation: "Lechery, lechery, still wars and lechery; nothing else holds fashion. A burning devil take them!" (5.2.198–200). However, like Troilus, Thersites is but one character, and his view is often narrow; throughout the play, he is "lost in the labyrinth of [his] fury." I believe we err if we assume that *during performance* his view of 5.2 is necessarily the broadest, or that Shakespeare intended his judgment to determine all spectators' responses to the stage action. Rather, Thersites's is but one judgment of a terrifying scene in which sexuality is a pawn, and anyone failing to protect his or her interests is a fool. Cressida, rather then being simply what Ulysses, Troilus, or Thersites alternately label her, symbolizes, in the very moments that Sprigg so brilliantly analyzes, the essence of this scene; blocking so as to limit, rather than expand, this symbolism can narrow and prejudice spectators' experience of it. Furthermore, as Gayle Greene succinctly argues, the "disturbance of the hierarchical order" in the play qualifies men's judgments about her: "By showing Cressida in relation to the men and society who make her what she is, [Shakespeare] provides a context that qualifies the apparently misogynist elements of her characterization, and far from presenting a simple character type or even a complex of types, the stereotypical in her character occurs in a context that constitutes a critique of stereotyping."[39] If there is no sense of order or hierarchy in this play, upon what basis do some pretend to judge others? If all values are relative, how does one justify labeling another unfaithful, lecherous—a whore?

I would argue that at the Globe, this scene from *Troilus &
Cressida,* like Hamlet's "Mousetrap," would have been carefully
rehearsed by Shakespeare's company to establish on stage an
intrinsic link between script and performance. Sprigg's analysis
of this scene at the Globe is immensely important, urging scholars to think critically about Shakespeare's Globe plays in performance at the theater for which they were designed. But I believe
Sprigg has ignored earlier moments in the play regarding Troilus's and especially Cressida's character in designing his proposed staging. Sprigg is absolutely right when he asserts that
"Shakespeare does not merely dramatize the anxiety of Troilus's
attempt to reconcile conflicting views of Cressida, and Cressida's
attempt to reconcile conflicting views of herself; he allows the
audience to experience some part of it."[40] He also points out that
in performance at the Globe "the rapid changes of focus engage
the spectator . . . actively in the alternation of conflicting viewpoints generated by the stage." These conflicting viewpoints
"provoke incongruous responses in the spectator . . . which he
must reconcile with his personal view and evaluation of the situation."[41] But even as he intuitively grasps and superbly communicates the complexities of this scene at the Globe, Sprigg seems
to assume that certain "meanings" will emerge from a unified
audience response: "The spectator shares the confusion of a
young woman trying to satisfy contradictory needs, the pain of
a young man who actually witnesses his betrayal by the woman
he loves, and the cynicism of a nihilist who revels in the agony of
others."[42] As should be clear from my arguments and suggested
staging, I do not believe that Cressida is just betraying Troilus.
Further, his claim to "love" Cressida is seriously attenuated by
his selfishness and denial in 4.2 and his complicity in her banishment. I thus question whether one can label so simply Troilus's and Cressida's actions in this immensely unpleasant scene.
With spectators on three sides of the stage having different perspectives on the action and recalling Troilus's and Cressida's
extremely disparate words and actions earlier, and with only
portions of the audience likely to be significantly influenced by
the reactions of the three observers, my proposed staging would
have produced views of Cressida's actions very different from
Sprigg's. I would conclude that these different, and probably
irreconcilable, views of Cressida are *precisely* the dramatic point
of this scene *in a Globe performance.*[43]

The different approaches to this scene demonstrate a seminal
fact: that Shakespeare's Globe Theatre granted him a marvel-

ously fluid medium for his revels. Neither Sprigg's nor my blocking is "right"; as he asserts, "To argue that there is a 'right' way for a play to be done is to deny theater the variations that give life to the art form. It would be equally foolhardy to assert that the text provides incontrovertible evidence as to how Shakespeare's plays were in fact staged in the Globe Theatre. The text may suggest the original staging, but, obviously, we can never be certain as to how a play was first performed."[44] Sprigg adds that Shakespeare's texts contain important "suggestions" about the "range and complexity" of his visual stagecraft[45] and that from these suggestions we can speculate about the actual performance of plays at the Globe. By trying to forge a link between the characters of Troilus and Cressida as revealed in Shakespeare's script and an argument for a visual staging of 5.2, which incorporates the Globe audience's multiple perspectives, this essay has proposed but one response to the performance "suggestions" in this play. H. R. Coursen reminds us that "Shakespeare's scripts ... represent inscriptions of ongoing narratives."[46] However one reacts to my argument, or to Sprigg's, each should remind us that a scene's "meaning" finally cannot be isolated from performance, and that Shakespearean scenes were written for a unique theatrical setting.

A final point, relevant to this chapter and that on *Hamlet,* concerns Weimann's distinction between the variable authorities of the *locus* and *platea* on the Elizabethan platform stages. As I state in footnote 70 p. 228, I find Weimann's distinction convincingly argued and immensely useful in thinking about uses of the stage during Elizabethan performances. However, as my essay about staging 5.2 of *Troilus & Cressida* indicates, and the essay on staging the "Mousetrap" in *Hamlet* will argue in the final chapter, I believe the Elizabethan stage could be and often was used more creatively and symbolically than Weimann's dichotomy implies. For example, both my and Sprigg's proposed Globe blockings of 5.2 examined in this chapter, especially in our analyses of the powerful emotional reactions to the staged action among the characters themselves, create a stage "picture" dramatically much more involved and demanding of spectators than a division of the stage into competing authorities of *locus* and *platea* can accommodate. Perhaps this is simply another way of saying that the subject matter and hence the actions of most Elizabethan/Jacobean plays were far more complex than those of many medieval or early Tudor predecessors, and that thus in performance the stage of Elizabethan or Jacobean plays symbolically represented more numerous and elaborate "places" than most earlier plays demanded: e.g., an inn for fat knights in Eastcheap, a battlefield, a castle's frigid platform at midnight, a queen's chamber, a scholar's study, a Venetian courtroom, or a council room within Troy or tents outside the city's walls. As Stephen Orgel explains in his important essay "Shakespeare Imagines a Theater," the "basic fluidity" of Renaissance theater "depends for its truth upon its audience,"[47] and I can certainly believe that Elizabethan spectators readily transformed the *locus* and *platea* of the bare stage into whatever separate "locations" and separate "authorities" Renaissance playing demanded. But I am equally certain that the very fluidity of the stage, which both Orgel and especially Weimann propose in their theoretical discussions of Elizabethan staging techniques, allowed Shakespeare to construct and stage scenes that transcended the *locus/platea* dichotomy that Weimann elucidates. The presence in Shakespeare's plays of such multidimensional scenes as Cressida's assignation and Hamlet's "Mousetrap" suggest that even our most complex theories about how the Elizabethan stage and its players engaged their spectators are not necessarily comprehensive, and that our theories of Elizabethan staging and resulting theatrical meaning should be as open to "re-viewing" as were Shakespeare's most involved scenes when staged amid the multiple perspectives of the Globe's thrust stage.

# TROILUS & CRESSIDA

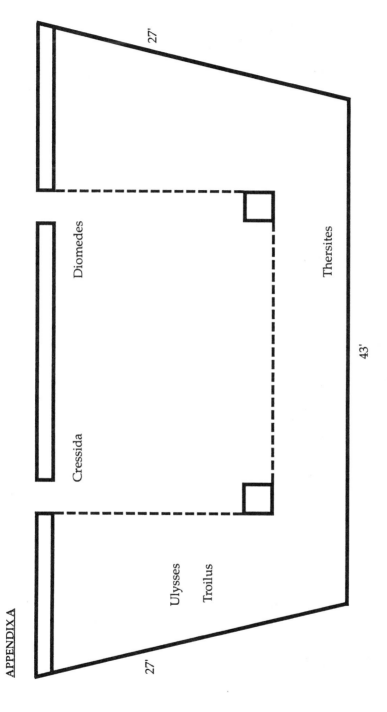

Cressida

Diomedes

Ulysses

Troilus

Thersites

27'

27'

43'

Based on Sprigg, "Shakespeare's Visual Stagecraft"

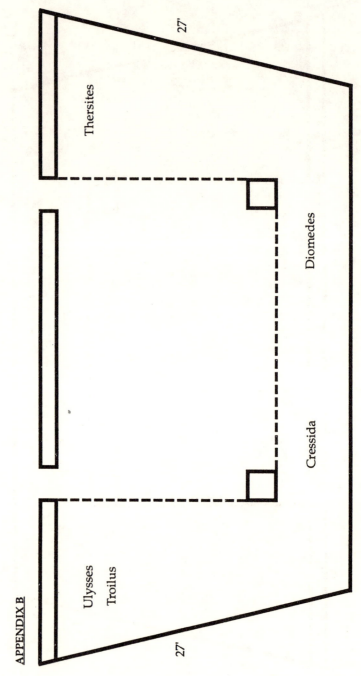

APPENDIX B

TROILUS & CRESSIDA

Thersites

27'

Diomedes

43'

Cressida

Ulysses
Troilus

27'

# 8

## "Get You a Place": Staging the "Mousetrap" at the Globe Theatre

ALTHOUGH Shakespeare probably wrote *Troilus and Cressida* after *Hamlet,* I conclude this study with the "Mousetrap," the "Murder of Gonzago," because this scene seems to me Shakespeare's most theatrically fascinating and dramatically complex use of the Globe's thrust stage. As in the previous chapter on the assignation scene in *Troilus & Cressida,* I shall contrast different options for staging the "Mousetrap" on the Globe's stage, and then argue for a particular staging of the scene. In formulating my argument about this staging, I shall rely primarily on two points about drama that are especially relevant to performance. First, all visual and aural aspects of drama convey meaning and must be considered when interpreting a script; second, a play is an organic whole, all of whose moments are interconnected. Using these principles as the foundation for this conjectural staging of the "Mousetrap," I hope to show that we can best recover this scene's place in *Hamlet* by examining it in its original theatrical setting. As I have argued in previous chapters, because of the thrust stage and surrounding audience at the Globe, the placing of characters on stage in various blockings could affect how an audience viewed characters within particular scenes, and a major part of my argument about the "Mousetrap" will rely on similar points. Although the legion of commentators on this scene have concentrated on literary "problems" within the script, such as whether or not Claudius sees the dumb show or the merits of the "second tooth" theory,[1] I wish, instead, to focus on how I believe the script of *Hamlet* up to 3.2 suggests a particular staging of the "Mousetrap" at the Globe, and then to argue that this hypothetical staging would have created an inner play intricately related to the larger play up to 3.2.

Daniel Seltzer describes the "shape of performance" assumed

by *Hamlet* in the theater in terms of the play's rhythm, the "tempo and pace of physical and verbal activity in time."[2] Seltzer divides the play into fifteen "episodes," the "Mousetrap" being the tenth. The rhythm of these episodes (i.e., Hamlet's stage experience) up to the entry of the players fluctuates wildly; Hamlet is alternately pensive and distraught, social and withdrawn, perfectly explicable and utterly inexplicable. As he moves Hamlet toward the "Mousetrap," Shakespeare compresses the rapidly shifting beats of the play's tempo, creating precisely the impression necessary for understanding what is happening to Hamlet before the inner play and what will happen to him during it: Hamlet is on a roller-coaster of emotions and moods that will finally overwhelm his attempt to gain the self-control he knows he needs to defeat his adversary.

Hamlet's "roller-coaster" is most evident in the moments just before the "Mousetrap" sequence begins. Hamlet's advice to the players reveals his ability to sustain enormously difficult and rapid mood changes.[3] His final, scathing line to Ophelia, "To a nunnery, go" (3.1.151–52), is followed just forty lines later by his "Speak the speech, I pray you, as I pronounced it to you." Hamlet's major concerns throughout his advice to the players are decorum and dignity: "Suit the action to the word, the word to the action, with this special observance, that you o'erstep not the modesty of nature" (3.2.17–19). Forty lines after viciously attacking Ophelia, Hamlet seems here quite composed. Especially relevant is his worry about actors who will "tear a passion to tatters, to very rags" (3.2.10). Considering Hamlet's own actions during the "Mousetrap," this concern is ironic, but one must observe that just before the inner play begins, Hamlet is most concerned lest an explosive passion cause someone in this carefully orchestrated entertainment to overplay his role.

Hamlet's last speech before the players enter is to Horatio, whom Hamlet admires because he is not "passion's slave": "for thou hast been / As one, in suffering all, that suffers nothing"; "and blest are those / Whose blood and judgment are so well commeddled / That they are not a pipe for fortune's finger / To sound what stop she please" (3.2.64–65, 67–70). Surrounded and pursued by people he can neither believe nor trust, Hamlet seeks refuge in Horatio's calm, supportive nature immediately after learning from Polonius that the King and Queen will "hear this piece of work . . . and that presently" and ordering Polonius and then Rosencrantz and Guildenstern to "Bid the players make haste" and "hasten them" (3.2.46–48, 49–50). Hamlet gives orders, demands haste; he is resolute but anxious; and, in his remarks to Horatio, he seems to anticipate his·inability to play properly his own vital role as careful observer. Hamlet is to "rivet" his eyes to Claudius's face, and asks Horatio to observe his uncle also "even with the very comment of thy soul" (3.2.78). Horatio's keen observation and dispassionate judgment endear him to Hamlet at this crucial moment. As the trumpets and kettle drums announce the court, Hamlet leaves his trusted companion: "They are coming to the play. I must be idle. / Get you a place" (3.2.89–90). On the Globe's thrust stage, where was Horatio's place, and where was Hamlet's?

When proposing questions about possible stagings of the "Mousetrap" at the Globe, one must approach this inner play exactly as it is: a unique Shakespearean scene[4] designed to be played before an audience in a particular Elizabethan theater. Because of its three-sided shape, and because of the physical relationships with its audience created by this shape, the Globe's thrust stage embodied precisely an image of the multiple perspectives central to the "Mousetrap" scene. Most of the fascinating questions about this scene involve "seeing": did Claudius "see" the dumb show? Did Gertrude? Was Claudius unable to see either or both the dumb show and the actual "Murder of Gonzago" because of his position on stage, or because he was talking to Gertrude and Polonius? Is a steely Claudius able to sit through *both* the dumb show and the actual murder, and, if so, why does he suddenly rise, call for lights, and leave without speaking to *anyone?* Hamlet is ecstatic immediately after the royal family leaves, but how much has Hamlet seen, and how reliable is his judgment about the inner play? What has Horatio actually seen? And did he see exactly what Hamlet saw? These are not new questions, and I do not propose here radically new answers. I suggest only that thinking about this scene in its original theatrical setting—the setting in which Shakespeare initially intended it to be played—may help us to understand how the script of *Hamlet* may have influenced the actual staging of the scene, and how this staging may then help us appreciate how dramatically central to the "Mousetrap," and to *Hamlet,* are this scene's continually fascinating riddles.

Recall here D. A. Latter's arguments, to which I refer in my Introduction, that the sight lines in typical Elizabethan public playhouses were probably adequate for all spectators. Latter concludes that spectators in all sections of an Elizabethan playhouse probably could have seen clearly all parts of the stage, and that the theaters certainly would have been built to maximize spectators' involvement in the performances. Thus, as I argued in my Introduction, despite our having precious little specific information about the actual dimensions of Elizabethan theaters, including the Globe, nonetheless speculations about the actual staging of plays at the Globe can safely assume two propositions: first, that the Globe permitted maximum visibility for most spectators, especially those buying the most expensive tickets; and, second, that this visibility allowed the actors to stage their plays with the greatest possible attention to the intrinsic relationships between script and performance. Given these assumptions, which I contend remain reasonably defensible, one can discuss the staging of the "Mousetrap" at the Globe assuming that the entire stage would have been available to the actors to present their scene to their spectators surrounding and above the stage.

Any discussion of staging the "Mousetrap" should begin with the use of space on the Globe stage. As Claudius, Gertrude, and the others enter, the bare platform becomes Claudius's court, and one must immediately begin placing characters about the stage. J. L. Styan divides the participants into four essential groups: the King and Queen; Hamlet and Ophelia; the "Player King and Queen"; and Horatio and the other courtiers.[5] Styan locates Claudius and Gertrude upstage center. This seems a logical blocking because it places the King and Queen where they could easily be seen by both the on-stage and Globe audiences, and because at the Globe this seems the likely positioning of Claudius and Gertrude in the opening court scene of 1.2.[6] The back of the stage, near the facade, what throughout this book following Weimann I have termed the *locus,* thus becomes the "throne" of the court of Denmark, the place of political power, perhaps signified by swiftly placing two chairs as the court assembles to hear the play. The positioning of the remaining characters is more problematic. Both Styan and C. Walter Hodges, in his staging diagrams for The New Cambridge *Hamlet,*[7] place Hamlet downstage right, near the base of the stage-right post, once the inner play has begun (see Appendix A). Styan argues that downstage positions, in what Weimann terms the *platea,* were the most authoritative on the Elizabethan thrust stage,[8] and although most contemporary directors and actors would agree that downstage positions are usually prominent, in a scene as *visually* complex as the "Mousetrap" on the Globe's thrust stage, is this assumption valid? Because Hamlet is the play's title character, and because this inner play is his planned entertainment/trap for his uncle (and perhaps his mother also), must we then assume that his place *at this moment* must be in what Styan asserts is the dominant stage position? Indeed, does the "Mousetrap" even have a "dominant" stage position; and, if not, might this fact be one of the scene's salient dramatic points? Might an alternative blocking at the beginning of this scene appear more compatible with Hamlet's "pulsating rhythm" up to this stage moment? With this latter blocking, might one be able to argue that the lack of a dominant stage position suggests a more symbolic use of space on the Globe stage than either Styan or Hodges envisions? As with my essay on *Troilus & Cressida,* I would argue here that even Weimann's careful distinction between *locus* and *platea,* which is immensely helpful for understanding the staging of most Elizabethan plays, does not necessarily apply as readily to the "Mousetrap" as it may generally to other Shakespearean plays I have examined. This is not to say that this distinction suddenly disappeared when spectators walked into the Globe to see *Hamlet.* It is rather to argue that although Weimann's distinction between the performance authorities of the *locus* and *platea* is useful for scholarly examination of Elizabethan staging, one ought not limit one's conception of such staging to a formula, especially when examining a unique scene such as the "Mousetrap."

I suggest then that Hamlet be placed not downstage near the post but rather further upstage and, as Styan and Hodges indicate, on stage right. This placement, near the "throne," suggests his "place" within the royal family; recall that he has been named heir by Claudius. This position would also put him relatively near Gertrude and Claudius, to whom he speaks during the inner play and whom he wishes to observe. Further, and most important, this stage position would suggest Hamlet's intense involvement in and uncertainty about this scene as it opens. Recall that just before the King and Queen enter, Hamlet praises Horatio as one whose "blood and judgment are so well commeddled." Hamlet respects Horatio's judgment and so wishes Horatio to scrutinize the inner play, especially as it approaches those circumstances of his father's death which Hamlet has told Horatio. Where, then, was Horatio's "place" for the "Mousetrap," and how would this place symbolize Hamlet's desire that Horatio mark the performance so that his balanced, dispassionate judgment might be most useful to Hamlet? Hamlet tells Horatio to give Claudius "heedful note," while he will "rivet" his eyes on Claudius's face; afterward, Hamlet insists, "we will

both our judgments join / in censure of his seeming" (3.2.85–
86). Hamlet says he "must be idle"; not so Horatio.

I would argue that the significant differences between Hamlet
and Horatio, not only in Hamlet's own view, but also for the
theater audience, should be indicated in the blocking. (The dramatic illusion pretends that Horatio and Hamlet choose their
own places; my argument is about where I believe Shakespeare's
*script,* as employed by his actors, would have placed them for
maximum dramatic and symbolic meaning in performance of
this scene.) Although Styan places both Hamlet and Horatio
downstage, one right, the other left, to indicate that they must
be physically separated so they can view the King from different
stage vantages, I propose that placing them nearly opposite and
parallel each other in what Styan assumes are stage positions
of equal authority obscures the significant differences in their
emotional states and in how these differences will be demonstrated during the ensuing moments. I suggest instead placing
Horatio very far down on stage left, near the front of the stage,
and thus the furthest from the throne.

What follows from this being Horatio's "place" for the "Mousetrap"? First, theater spectators would see Hamlet much closer
to, and thus very involved with, the court party and Horatio
physically distanced from it. Presumably then, Horatio's position would leave unimpaired, both emotionally and physically,
the judgment that Hamlet believes may be superior to his own,
especially during these intense, eagerly anticipated moments.
From this suggestion follows the second, ironic point that theater spectators would see that Horatio, who is further from the
anticipated focus of the scene—the "Murder of Gonzago" and
Claudius's reaction to it—is yet in a position that Hamlet, and
perhaps Horatio himself, believes will enable him to judge
clearly what transpires during the inner play, especially regarding Claudius. The stage positions I propose not only indicate
the significant temperamental differences between Horatio and
Hamlet, but also symbolize initially the complex scene we are
about to see, in which multiple and conflicting perspectives are
not only enacted but also experienced by both the on-stage and
theater audiences. Although Beckerman argues that relatively
little time was spent by Shakespeare's company on blocking and
stage movements,[9] given the uniqueness and complexity of this
scene, I am convinced that in dramatizing it Shakespeare as
director and his extraordinary actors, by 1600–1601 remarkably
polished *ensemble* players, would have seized every conceivable

symbolic and visual feature of this scene to stimulate the "imaginary forces"[10]of their spectators.

The dialogue initiating the "Mousetrap," then, quickly places people about the stage. Claudius and Gertrude are upstage center; Gertrude invites Hamlet to sit by her; he declines in favor of Ophelia, near whom Hamlet must sit. Hamlet and Ophelia are stage right, close to Claudius and Gertrude, placed thus between the King and Queen and on the opposite side from Horatio, who is far down stage left (see Appendix B). Two features of this suggested staging are crucial. First, *Hamlet's physical position on stage mirrors his emotional involvement in this scene.* He is in its midst, not an objective, external judge of it. As the inner play unfolds, and Hamlet becomes increasingly impatient and unnerved, his inability to control himself, to "play his part," in his own scripted entertainment will be symbolized visually by his stage position until the scene's final, frenzied moment. Second, the Globe's thrust stage enabled Shakespeare's actors to create a visual analogue of what the spectators themselves experience. Horatio is "outside" the court, farther away from Claudius than Hamlet is, and thus Horatio's vision of the inner play and of the King's reaction may differ significantly from Hamlet's. Horatio's vision shall differ significantly from the King's. The different positions of the stage characters, suggesting their different perspectives on and relative comprehension of what they see, reverberate throughout the theater itself. No one portion of the audience has exactly the same perspective as any other; spectators on either side of the thrust stage have differing perspectives from each other, and from those facing downstage center. The initial stage picture, therefore, mirrors the audience's own multiple perspectives. Hamlet, the ostensible focus of the audience's attention as the scene opens, images in his "place" not only his own intense immersion in the action but also a seminal fact about this scene at the Globe: that by its completion, no one in the theater, on stage or in the audience, will have "seen" its action completely—nor, as I shall argue, authoritatively.

The fourth group of characters is the players, whose logical position, I believe, as images of the player king and queen now on the Danish throne, is the large space between Claudius and Gertrude upstage and Horatio downstage. The players who enact the "Murder of Gonzago" are thus physically and symbolically "central" to this scene, but closer to Hamlet than to Horatio, and approximately equidistant from Claudius and Gertrude and

Hamlet and Ophelia.[11] Just before the dumb show itself, Hamlet debates with Ophelia the duration of woman's love, and ironically (one assumes) conflates rather brutally the time since his father's death to merely two hours. Ophelia's correction—"nay, 'tis twice two months, my lord" (3.2.126)—only exacerbates Hamlet, whose rising tension and anticipation are also evident in his reply: "O heavens! Die two months ago, and not forgotten yet? Then there's hope a great man's memory may outlive his life half a year" (3.2.128–30). Hamlet conflates time, probably for his mother's hearing, and then readily, but without explanation, accepts a major correction of his arithmetic with increasingly ironic and biting remarks about mourning and memory, churches and hobby horses. As the players enter, Hamlet's excitement rises quickly.

Following the dumb show, which I assume the King and Queen saw, Hamlet again insults Ophelia, who becomes here an easy target for Hamlet's intense anxiety and his unwillingness yet to speak to either Claudius or Gertrude. Note that no one else on stage speaks besides Ophelia and Hamlet between Hamlet's "Lady, shall I lie in your lap?" and the entrance of the Player King and Queen. Nothing in the text indicates that Claudius and Gertrude did not see the dumb show, and Hamlet's responses to the bewildered and embarrassed Ophelia, who innocently asks questions about the play, twist her words into bawdy images prompted by his growing cynicism about female sexuality and the fragility of love. Evident in Hamlet's words before the Player King and Queen enter is the initial stage of another of his emotional outbursts, this one terribly compressed and lethal to his own design.

One must note first that Ophelia's question after the dumb show, "What means this, my lord?" (3.2.134) is not surprising, because dumb shows in Elizabethan plays did not necessarily indicate what sort of play was to follow.[12] Ophelia's response to Hamlet's assertion of "miching malicho" prompts his choric response to the prologue's entry: "We shall know by this fellow. The players cannot keep counsel; they'll tell all" (3.2.139–40). Hamlet insists on talking after the prologue enters and again after the prologue begs his audience's "hearing patiently." Yet this is precisely what Hamlet cannot do; his tension is obvious as, actor himself, he begins participating in the scene during which his main purpose was to observe the King. While Horatio is silently observing, Hamlet is actively intervening. Hamlet's and Horatio's extremely different situations here, just as the

Player King and Queen enter, are symbolized by the blocking I have proposed and would have been clearly evident on the Globe stage. As the "Mousetrap" unfolds, Hamlet's frenzied responses will further distance him emotionally from Horatio and clearly indict him as Claudius's unstable and dangerous enemy.

From Claudius's question at 3.2.91, "How fares our cousin Hamlet?" to the beginning of the actual inner play there are (in Bevington's 4th ed.) 62 lines, excluding those of the dumb show; from the first line of the Player King's speech ("Full thirty times" [3.2.153]) to Hamlet's question to Gertrude, "Madam, how like you this play?" (3.2.227) there are 74 lines. Thus, with the exception of two brief remarks ("Wormwood, wormwood" [line 179]; "If she should break it now!" [line 222]), Hamlet is silent for a unit, or beat, of stage time (136 lines) at least as long, and in performance probably longer, as that which immediately precedes it. Yet Hamlet's emotions are active; consider what he, and the court, now experience. The Player King and Queen recite 74 lines of didactic, tedious heroic couplets that, we are to presume, are part of the "Murder of Gonzago" as Hamlet remembers it, plus his own "some dozen or sixteen lines" which he has asked the first player to add and that may be directed exclusively at Gertrude. (Indeed, the blocking I have proposed, with Hamlet "in the court" and thus close to Gertrude, supports the suggestion that Hamlet's purposes in the "Mousetrap" include embarrassing and shaming Gertrude as well as exposing Claudius's regicide.) No one else in the court (i.e., on stage) besides Hamlet has any reason to be affected by what is said during this dialogue; everyone else, including Horatio, hears the Player King and Queen speak lines that they assume are part of the play. Although Gertrude may be annoyed by some of the Player Queen's remarks, she has no reason at this point to think them anything other than traditional sentiments about marriage vows. But Hamlet, whose additions may be among the most didactic and redundant in this scene,[13] rapidly shows his extreme impatience. To Claudius's critical questions (3.2.230–31) "Have you heard the argument? Is there no offense in 't?"[14] Hamlet responds by speaking of what has not yet actually happened in the "Murder of Gonzago" but only in the preceding dumb show: "No, no, they do but jest, poison in jest" (3.2.232). Hamlet is confusing, or rather conflating (as he did earlier with the time since his father's death) the past and the future of his entertainment, his "play," already indicating his rapidly declining control. Yet Claudius's next question, "What do you call the play?"

(3.2.234) still indicates no particular fear of either Hamlet or the play itself; whatever Claudius may be thinking at this moment, he certainly has not revealed the "occulted guilt" Hamlet seeks.

Hamlet's answer to Claudius's questions, and his subsequent "introduction" of Lucianus as "Nephew to the King"[15] reveal fully his inability to play the role of observer. From Ophelia's "You are as good as a chorus, my lord" (3.2.243) to her "The King rises" (3.2.263) is but twenty lines, but during this beat Hamlet's emotions surge. He mixes egregious sexual insults to Ophelia with a choric cry for revenge from Lucianus, whose part Hamlet virtually usurps on stage. After Lucianus completes only six lines, and pours the poison into the Player King's ears, Hamlet explodes:

> 'A poisons him i' the garden for his estate. His name's
> Gonzago. The story is extant, and written in very
> choice Italian. You shall see anon how the murderer
> gets the love of Gonzago's wife.
>
> (3.2. 259–62)

M. R. Woodhead asserts that one must realize exactly what has happened at this precise moment to understand Claudius's sudden rising, and his previous inaction regarding what he has seen and heard. Woodhead explains that the King rises on Hamlet's talk of poisoning, not Lucianus's, and that it is "Hamlet's commentary, quite extraneous to the original plot, that terrifies Claudius. The King was unmoved by the dumb-show because he was unmoved by the play itself."[16] Hamlet is the culprit, then, in his own plot. During the "Murder of Gonzago" Hamlet violently "o'erstep[s] . . . the modesty of nature," violates his own advice to the players, and threatens not only Claudius but also implicitly the entire court. Hamlet, not Lucianus, speaks of murder and "bellows" for revenge. As Seltzer suggests, Hamlet's antics here are consistent with his theatrical energy during the final moments of act 2 and the early moments of act 3: "the shape . . . is one of high energy alternating with low, emotional fury or intellectual aggressiveness chained in—and then unleashed."[17]

Let me return now to my suggested blocking. Hamlet is now certain of the King's guilt, yet achieving certitude has been costly: the entire court has heard him threaten the King and insult the Queen. Thus, Hamlet's position on stage should reflect his crucial errors during the entire inner play, for he has clearly been "passion's slave" and not the rational, scrutinizing observer he claimed he would be: "For I mine eyes will rivet to his face" (3.2.84). A striking visual symbolism emerges from my suggested blocking. Envision the area of the stage covered by the canopy and framed by the posts as symbolizing the "space" of the Danish throne, and Hamlet occupying a definite place *within* this royal space for the inner play; or, perhaps to emphasize his uncontrolled, erratic state, moving around but still within this space[18] during the scene's final moments. Then Hamlet's indiscretions during the "Mousetrap" are what disrupt this "royal" space, which, with Polonius's "Give o'er the play" (3.2.266), becomes chaotic: two poisoners, one real, the other fictive; two kings, one real, the other fictive, but both "players"; an adulterous queen, shamed perhaps by the Player Queen's moralizing, yet confused and terrified by her son; and several equally frightened guards and courtiers, who have just seen the noble Hamlet, Claudius's announced heir, hideously threaten the King in an utterly bizarre play—all scatter off the stage, much as the guests do after the mutilated banquet in *Macbeth*. Hamlet himself is thus part of the chaos that his own destructive rage creates. As Hamlet now stands center stage, the "place" used by the players, singing about "strucken deer" and getting a "fellowship in a cry of players" (3.2.269–76), his own rage during the inner play seems just one more image of the misrule plaguing this diseased kingdom. The "real" figures of this court, from Claudius to Hamlet, cannot properly execute their roles; ironically, the only good actors in this kingdom are the traveling players, whose "play," requested, and altered, by a prince, has been treated rudely by him, despite his proclaiming them his "good friends." Hamlet certainly would not get a "fellowship" in a cry of players were he to act as he has here. He simply does not realize that at this moment he is no better an actor than his despised uncle.

Horatio's "place" in this scene, I have suggested, is initially far downstage left, closest to the central audience. He is thus symbolically outside the throne space framed by the Globe's canopy and posts, and immune to its intrigues.[19] He has had a wider, more objective view of the events; as a careful observer rather than an hysterical participant, he is presumably better able than Hamlet to judge exactly what he has seen. Yet consider what he and Hamlet say after the King's party exits. Horatio's responses to Hamlet's questions are curious:

> *Hamlet.* O good Horatio, I'll take the ghost's word for a thousand pound. Didst perceive?

> *Horatio.*   Very well, my lord.
> *Hamlet.*    Upon the talk of poisoning?
> *Horatio.*   I did very well note him.
>
>                                               (3.2.284–88)

Horatio says that he did "very well" note the King's reaction. But to what? Horatio does not indicate whether or not he perceived that the "talk of poisoning" was Hamlet's, not Lucianus's.[20] Thus, one cannot know definitely whether Horatio realizes that what has frightened the King is both an enactment of his crime and a regicidal threat from his nephew. Nor need Horatio's words imply that he entirely agrees with Hamlet about the King's guilt. If Horatio realizes that it was Hamlet's frenzied assumption of Lucianus's murderous role that terrified Claudius, Horatio does not say so. All Horatio says is that he noted well Claudius's response. Hamlet cries "Ah ha!" He assumes that Horatio's words have confirmed his own view and applauded his usurping Lucianus's role, whereupon he calls for the recorders and immediately engages in more word games with his favorite victims, Rosencrantz and Guildenstern.

Horatio's remarks return my argument to a major, earlier point. Dramatized on the Globe's thrust stage, the "Mousetrap" would be an immensely complex scene of multiple perspectives. Just as on stage no one has completely understood what has happened, so no one in the Globe theater audience, surrounding the stage on three sides, can have understood the scene completely. For at the Globe no two sets of spectators would have had the same perspective on the action: those facing center stage would have seen the action primarily from Horatio's position; those sitting stage right, closest to Hamlet (and Ophelia), would have seen the action from his perspective; and spectators sitting directly opposite them, stage left, would have had yet a different view.

Thus, the total experience of spectators at a Globe staging of the "Mousetrap" would have virtually mirrored what they have seen. Stephen Booth asserts that *Hamlet* is a play in which audience members cannot make up their minds,[21] and this phenomenon is visually central to the Globe staging I have proposed here, for it treats staging as an integral component of, and complement to, the script. The visual experience of the "Mousetrap" for Hamlet and the theater audience exemplifies a central dramatic feature of the entire play:

It has been seen as an essential characteristic of *Hamlet*—and a matter for adverse criticism—that the various points of view in the play are not subordinated to a single synoptic vision. But what if this was the dramatist's purpose? If so, perplexities about the conduct of the action may be as misguided as objections, by champions of academic perspective, to Cubism.[22]

As the center piece of his tragedy, Shakespeare has created a scene of multiple perspectives and shifting angles of vision in which no one "place" on stage—neither Claudius's nor Hamlet's nor Horatio's—is finally authoritative, regardless of how it may have appeared to the characters themselves, especially Hamlet. Indeed, Hamlet is the most deceived. Similarly, no one "place" for the Globe spectators would have yielded an authoritative view of Hamlet's chaotic attempt to catch the King's conscience. Like a cubist painting, the "Mousetrap" at the Globe yields numerous perspectives—each valid yet incomplete, and each striking yet inconclusive. Just as to "see" all of a cubist painting one would have to collate every perspective of it, so would one have to collate every one of the different, seemingly conflicting visions of the "Mousetrap" on stage and in the theater to grasp its dramatic and visual complexity. In the very impossibility of so doing lies the enduring mystery of this scene in performance, especially in the theater for which Shakespeare initially designed it.

Despite prodigious scholarly efforts, our knowledge of how Shakespeare's actors actually used the Globe stage is still limited, and we will never know whether the staging I have proposed here was ever actually employed. This staging is only a conjecture, based on my sense of how the *Hamlet* script up to 3.2 suggests this particular interpretation of the "Mousetrap." Certainly other interpretations, such as Styan's, merit consideration. The goal of performance criticism ought to be continual elucidation of how Shakespeare's scripts create meaning in the theater, and many arguments about Globe stagings (such as whether the actors rehearsed blockings) or approaches (such as Weimann's about whether certain areas of the stage assumed symbolic importance) will necessarily contain much supposition and speculation. But examining Shakespeare's plays with their initial theatrical settings in mind can immensely benefit our sense of him as a dramatist, and although many of the salient features of the "Mousetrap" I have examined here are evident in modern productions of *Hamlet,* I believe that only by imagining production of this scene at the Globe can we fully appreciate its central place in Shakespeare's play.

# HAMLET

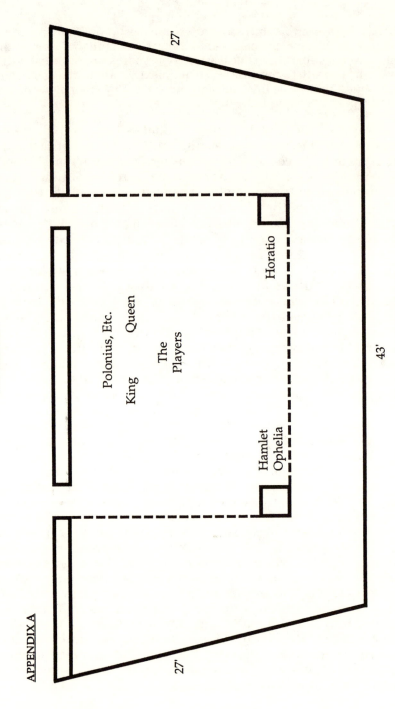

Polonius, Etc.

King        Queen

The
Players

Horatio

Hamlet
Ophelia

27'

27'

43'

Based on Styan, _Shakespeare's Stagecraft_

# HAMLET

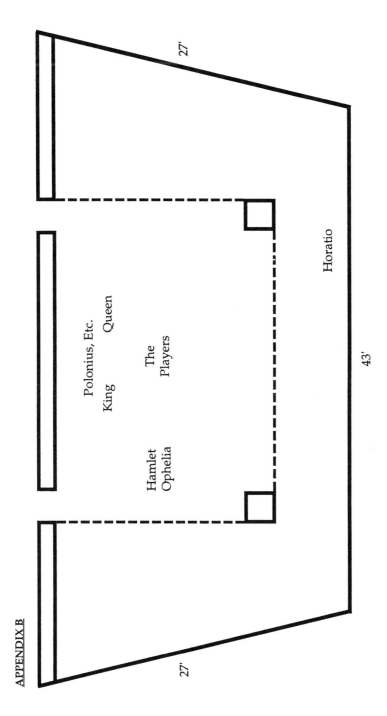

Polonius, Etc.    Queen

King

The
Players

Hamlet
Ophelia

Horatio

27'

27'

43'

# Notes

## Chapter 1. Introduction

1. My approach is best summarized by the first of the six characteristics which Marvin and Ruth Thompson attribute to performance criticism: "Performance criticism is an approach by which the text of a play is closely related to what can be known or considered about the conditions of the stage" (Marvin and Ruth Thompson, eds. *Shakespeare and the Sense of Performance.* [Newark: University of Delaware Press, 1989], 13). For a superb history of the development of performance criticism, see J. L. Styan, *The Shakespeare Revolution* (Cambridge: Cambridge University Press, 1977). An important review of performance criticism is Michael Shapiro's "Role-Playing, Reflexivity, and Metadrama in Recent Shakespeare Criticism," *Renaissance Drama* n.s. 12, edited by Alan C. Dessen (Evanston: Northwestern University Press, 1981), 145–61.

2. Bernard Beckerman, *Dynamics of Drama* (1970; reprint, New York: Drama Book Publishers, 1979), 20.

3. Philip C. McGuire, "Introduction," in Philip C. McGuire and David A. Samuelson, eds., *Shakespeare: The Theatrical Dimension* (New York: AMS Press, 1979), xix–xx. Kent Cartwright, *Shakespearean Tragedy and Its Double: The Rhythms of Audience Response* (University Park: The Pennsylvania State University Press, 1991), writes that "Performance-orientated criticism assumes that dramatic language is to be performed, that it takes on different valences and nuances in spoken dialogue than in reading, that the challenges of performance define and animate the experience of the play, that signals to performative choices and to spectatorial responses inhere in the text itself, and that the transaction between audience and actor-as-character develops its own special and intense 'energies.' Performance-oriented criticism focuses on process, the 'how' often displacing or subsuming the 'why'" (8). J. I. M. Stewart, *Character and Motive in Shakespeare* (New York: Barnes and Noble, 1949), asserts that "The awareness of an audience settled in a theatre is not that of a reader over his book. It is substantially a group awareness; there is a merging of consciousness; doors are thrown open which even the practiced reader can never hope to do more than push slightly ajar" (39). Richard David's statement in *Shakespeare in the Theatre* (Cambridge: Cambridge University Press, 1978), that "only in the theatre [do Shakespeare's plays] develop their full *impact*" (emphasis added) (1) describes the plays' impact on live spectators. In the "Introduction" to his study *Speechless Dialect: Shakespeare's Open Silences* (Berkeley: University of California Press, 1985), McGuire writes: "Those who utilize [the literary] approach . . . seek to understand Shakespeare's plays by treating the words that Shakespeare wrote as if they were elements of a literary text rather than parts of a dramatic script. They take assumptions, concepts, and processes of analysis developed for and apropriate to works written to be

read by individuals in silent solitude and apply them to works designed to be heard and seen by people who have come together as a group and in public in order to see and hear a play" (xviii). McGuire brilliantly elucidates places in Shakespeare's scripts where questions of meaning would only be evident—and could only be answered—in performance. On the dangers of pushing either performance criticism or close reading too far or to the exclusion of the other, see Richard Levin's sobering essay, "Performance-Critics vs. Close Readers in the Study of English Renaissance Drama," *Modern Language Review* 81, no. 3 (July 1986): 545–59. In his article "The Rhetoric of Performance Criticism," *Shakespeare Quarterly* 40 (winter 1989): 441–55, W. B. Worthen argues that the "justifying critical agenda" of performance criticism should be to "locate the space and practice of criticism in relation to the practices of performance" (442). Worthen argues that all performances of a Shakespearean play are "interpretations" and that the "true nature" of a Shakespearean text remains elusive, as the play text is always subject to the prevailing conditions and conventions of acting and production.

4. Homer Swander, "Shakespeare and Beckett: What the Words Know," in *Shakespeare and the Sense of Performance,* 64.

5. Ibid.

6. Michael Goldman, *Shakespeare and the Energies of Drama* (Princeton: Princeton University Press, 1972), 3. Goldman adds that "in the theater a play happens not to you or me but to us. It is our bodily presence, en masse, which completes the actor's being and sustains him in his quality, our heightened receptiveness as part of the peculiar community of silent strangers that constitutes an audience. . . . All kinds of aesthetic distance may be established in the theater, but it will always manifest itself with a special tension because the interplay between live actor and bodily sensitive audience is constantly breaking the distance down" (5, 6).

7. McGuire, *Dialect,* 135.

8. Ibid., 138.

9. Because no performance of a play is ever definitive, and its meaning is thus constantly evolving, we can speak of the "stages" of our developing knowledge of a play, as perhaps one specific performance, on a particular stage causes us to "see" or "hear" a facet of the script we had not especially noticed before. These multiple meanings of "stages" all suggest both the fluidity of a "script" and the evolving nature of our encounters with it as it assumes new dimensions through theatrical performance.

10. Norman Rabkin, *Shakespeare and the Problem of Meaning* (Chicago: University of Chicago Press, 1981), 27. Rabkin's arguments first appeared as "Shakespeare and Meaning," in J. M. R. Margeson and Clifford Leech, eds., *Shakespeare: 1971* (Toronto: University of Toronto Press, 1972), 89–106.

11. Homer Swander, "In Our Time: Such Audiences We Wish Him," *Shakespeare Quarterly* 35, no. 5 (summer 1984), 538–39. In his essay "Performing at the Frontiers of Representation: Epilogue and Post-Scriptural Future in Shakespeare's Plays," in Murray Biggs et al., eds., *The Arts of Performance in Elizabethan and Early Stuart Drama* (Edinburgh: Edinburgh University Press, 1991), 96–112, Robert Weimann writes, "As dramatic writing and theatrical production in several vital respects appear to condition one another, the cultural uses of performance in their turn must not be studied in isolation from either the dramatic text or the stage and its potentiality" (98). J. L. Styan points out that "most of . . . Shakespeare's plays were not first performed at a

single theatre of fixed design." *Shakespeare's Stagecraft* (Cambridge: Cambridge University Press, 1967), 7. This is probably true, but one can reasonably assume that the stage and size of the Theatre and Globe were similar, and we do not know certainly how many, if any at all, of Shakespeare's plays opened, or ever played at, the Curtain. Roslyn Lander Knutson, in *The Repertory of Shakespeare's Company: 1594–1613* (Fayetteville: University of Arkansas Press, 1991), writes that "The Chamberlain's men were themselves without a playhouse sometime in 1596–97 because the Burbages' ground lease on the Theatre was to expire in the spring of 1597. Presumably, the company moved to the Curtain until the Globe was ready for occupancy in early summer 1599" (58). We know nothing about the Curtain's physical structure and can only assume that it generally resembled the Theatre.

12. In "Teaching the Theatre of Imagination: The Example of *I Henry IV*," *Shakespeare Quarterly* 35, no. 5 (summer 1984): 517–27, Sherman Hawkins writes: "Many of these specifics [of performance] Shakespeare doubtless envisaged as he wrote the plays, but they can be performed in any of a dozen ways— so long as we remain true to the central conceptions which inform them. It is these that Shakespeare strove to embody and enact, and it is these that we must strive to recapture and make real" (520). In these essays I do not intend to be overly prescriptive about too many specifics of Elizabethan performance, but I shall argue that by thinking about performances in Elizabethan playhouses we can grasp how those performances would have generated spectators' reactions and thus dramatic meanings that I believe Shakespeare's scripts suggest he intended in his theatres. In *The Shakespeare Revolution,* J. L. Styan praises directors, such as Tyrone Guthrie and Barry Jackson, who "sought repeatedly to give their audiences what they took to be the stuff of the Shakespeare experience. As far as it could be reclaimed three centuries later, they tried to capture and translate the temper of the original. Each man's search was for an authentic balance between the freedom a Shakespeare script grants the actor and the responsibility of recharging the play's first meaning" (5). As Andrew Gurr explains (see n. 33), the play's "first meaning" is permanently lost, but we can nonetheless attempt to appreciate some of Shakespeare's theatrical intentions.

13. Stephen Orgel, *The Illusion of Power* (Berkeley: University of California Press, 1975), 1. Glynne Wickham emphasizes the importance of the Globe: "The first Globe was the first playhouse built in England exclusively by professional actors and for their own exclusive use." *Early English Stages,* vol. 2, pt. 2. (London: Routledge & Kegan Paul, 1972), 116.

14. Orgel, *Illusion,* 2.

15. Harry Berger Jr. "Theater, Drama, and the Second World: A Prologue to Shakespeare," *Comparative Drama* 2 (spring 1968): 16.

16. Stephen Orgel, "Shakespeare Imagines a Theater," in Kenneth Muir, Jay L. Halio, and D. J. Palmer, eds., *Shakespeare, Man of the Theater* (Newark: University of Delaware Press, 1983), 44. In *The Theater and the Dream: From Metaphor to Form in Renaissance Drama* (Baltimore: Johns Hopkins University Press, 1973), Jackson I. Cope cites the importance of José Ortega y Gassett's essay *El espectador* and his lecture *Idea del teatro* in formulating a modern theory of "perspectivism," which emphasizes theater as essentially an epistemological experience. Cope defines perspectivism as "the seeing of that which is without but which can only be validated as real by the confluence of viewpoints" (5). Viewed this way, theater as an aesthetic experience is validated

only by the viewers' *combined* perspectives on the performed script. Michael E. Mooney, *Shakespeare's Dramatic Transactions* (Durham: Duke University Press, 1990), develops this approach further in his analysis of how Shakespeare's drama invites and directs audience participation (5–6). Mooney also draws on Antonin Artaud's *The Theater and its Double,* translated by Mary C. Richards (New York: Grove Press, 1958).

17. Marco De Marinis, "Dramaturgy of the Spectator," translated by Paul Dwyer. *TDR* 31, no. 2 (summer 1987), 101, 102.

18. See Styan's instructive diagrams of the significantly different sightlines and actor/audience relationships in Elizabethan and Victorian playhouses in *Shakespeare's Stagecraft,* 15. C. Walter Hodges's drawing of the second Globe in Hardin Craig and David Bevington, eds. *The Complete Works of Shakespeare,* rev. ed. (Glenview, Ill.: Scott Foresman, 1973), 68–69, illustrates these differences and shows clearly that one cannot assume a unified theatrical experience for spectators in a thrust-stage theater. In his introduction, Cartwright argues that "while Elizabethan responses may have varied in intensity . . . Shakespeare largely appears to have sought a coalescent audience. . . . With dramatic performance, auditors are present to each other, recognize their own and others' reactions, respond univocally as a community, and make noises that express and reinforce recognition and unanimity" (25). Robert Hapgood, *Shakespeare the Theatre-Poet* (Oxford: Clarendon Press, 1988), argues in several essays that Shakespeare generally "guides [playgoers'] direct involvements" in his plays, while creating performance options that "not only allow the performers to make certain interpretative emphases but also allow for individual differences among the spectators" (3, 218). Cartwright's and Hapgood's arguments are compelling, but neither considers actual performance in Shakespeare's thrust-stage theaters, which is what I attempt to do in these essays. For a review of some of the practical and aesthetic aspects of playing before a thrust-stage audience, see Derek Peat's fascinating and challenging article "Looking Up and Looking Down: Shakespeare's Vertical Audience," *Shakespeare Quarterly* 35, no. 5 (summer 1984): 563–70, esp. 564.

19. Alvin B. Kernan, "Shakespeare's Stage Audiences: The Playwright's Reflections and Control of Audience Response," in Philip H. Highfill, ed., *Shakespeare's Craft* (Carbondale: Southern Illinois University Press, 1982), 151.

20. Louis Adrian Montrose succinctly examines the dialectical and reflexive nature of Shakespearean drama in "The Purpose of Playing: Reflections on A Shakespearean Anthropology," *Helios* n.s. 7, no. 2 (1979–80), 53–74. Montrose argues that the many features of *As You Like It* (1599–1600) that exploit the *theatrum mundi* metaphor, especially the conscious role playing, many disguises and "poses" of the characters, rites of "fraternal and social communion," and an "ingratiating epilogue" all made this play a likely and "appropriate consecration rite for the new theatre, a celebration of the collective social enterprise—indissolubly spiritual and commercial—of professional playwright and players with their public audience. The metaphorical identification of the world and the stage is not an incidental commonplace; it is one of the reflexive dramatic and theatrical strategies by which Shakespeare asserts a reciprocal relationship between his work and his world" (51–52). Montrose stresses Robert Weimann's point that "Shakespeare's theater and his society were interrelated in the sense that the Elizabethan stage, even when it reflected the tensions and compromises of sixteenth-century England, was also a potent force that helped to create the specific character and transitional

nature of that society" Robert Schwartz, ed. *Shakespeare and the Popular Tradition in the Theater* [Baltimore: Johns Hopkins University Press, 1978], xii. Earlier studies of the theatrical metaphor in Shakespeare's plays include Anne Righter (Barton), *Shakespeare and the Idea of the Play* (London: Chatto and Windus, 1962); and S. L. Bethell, *Shakespeare and the Popular Dramatic Tradition* (London: P. S. King and Staples, 1944).

21. I use the term "explore" here in the spirit of Ralph Berry's "explorations" into Shakespeare's plays in his book *Shakespeare and the Awareness of the Audience* (London: MacMillan, 1985). Like Berry, I do not offer a sustained argument about every Shakespearean play I discuss, nor will I attempt the same kind of interpretation about every scene or play. My essays are separate explorations into some of the ways I believe Shakespeare's scenes and plays created meaning when played on the thrust stages of the Theatre and Globe playhouses.

22. On the discovered remains of the Rose and Globe, and the consequences thereof for students of the old (and new) Globe, see esp.: Simon Blatherwick and Andrew Gurr, "Shakespeare's Factory: Archaeological evaluations on the site of the Globe Theatre at 1/15 Anchor Terrace, Southwark Bridge Road, Southwark," *Antiquity* 6 (June 1992): 315–33; John Orrell, "The Accuracy of Hollar's Sketch of the Globe," *Shakespeare Bulletin* 5 (spring 1993): 5–9, which argues convincingly for a Globe Theatre diameter of 100 feet, thus with room for a very large stage; essays in Franklin J. Hildy Jr., ed. *New Issues in the Reconstruction of Shakespeare's Theatre* (New York: Peter Lang, 1990); two important articles by Paul Nelsen in *Shakespeare Bulletin:* "Reinventing Shakespeare's Globe? A Report of Design Choices for the ISGC Globe," 10 (fall 1992), 5–7; and "Sizing up the Globe: Proposed Revisions to the ISGC Reconstruction," 11 (fall 1993), 5–13; and, finally, Andrew Gurr and John Orrell, *Building Shakespeare's Globe* (New York: Routledge, 1989).

23. Richard Hosley, "The Playhouses and the Stage," in Kenneth Muir and S. Schoenbaum, eds. *A New Companion to Shakespeare Studies* (Cambridge: Cambridge University Press, 1971), 26.

24. Andrew Gurr, "The Rose Repertory: What the Plays Might Tell Us About the Stage," in Hildy, ed., *New Issues,* 133.

25. D. A. Latter, "Sight Lines in a Conjectural Reconstruction of an Elizabethan Playhouse," *Shakespeare Survey,* vol. 28, edited by Kenneth Muir (Cambridge: Cambridge University Press, 1975), 125–35.

26. J. L. Styan, "In Search of the Real Shakespeare; or, Shakespeare's Shows and Shadows," in Hildy, ed., *New Issues,* 198.

27. Peter Thompson, *Shakespeare's Theatre,* 2d ed. (London: Routledge and Kegan Paul, 1992), 60.

28. Michael Hattaway, *Elizabethan Popular Theatre: Plays in Performance* (London: Routledge and Kegan Paul, 1982), 54.

29. Styan, in chapters 4 and 5 of *Shakespeare's Stagecraft,* examines stage groupings as part of Shakespeare's "visual craft."

30. E. A. J. Honigmann asserts that "Shakespeare wrote his tragedies for an audience that had to exert itself to keep up with new impressions in every scene—an audience that he asked to respond creatively, at the very highest level of participation." *Shakespeare: Seven Tragedies* (London: MacMillan, 1976), 29. Although I do not wish to argue that all of Shakespeare's plays are as demanding of their audiences as the great tragedies, I do believe that all of his plays demand active audiences. Certainly his mature comedies, such as

*The Merchant of Venice* and *Twelfth Night,* create new impressions in nearly every scene.

31. Emrys Jones, *Scenic Form in Shakespeare* (Oxford: Clarendon Press, 1971), 50.

32. Andrew Gurr, "The 'State' of Shakespeare's Audiences," in Thompson, *Shakespeare and the Sense of Performance,* 174. One must also realize another limitation outlined by Kent Cartwright: "Studying Shakespeare with an interest in effect . . . draws us to the audience 'implied' in the text, not a real audience but a fictional and abstract one. . . . Thus, the theatrically orientated critic explores the text as a blueprint for performance (independent of any particular performances), viewing the audience as an entity the playwright sets out to construct with each play" (29). Moving from "script" (which I strongly prefer over "text") to this "fictional and abstract" audience is difficult because the contemporary critic tries to recreate the spectator reactions he thinks Shakespeare intended, while simultaneously having to admit that "no textual analysis can guarantee the historical Elizabethan response" (Cartwright, *Shakespearean Tragedy,* 28).

33. Gurr, "Shakespeare's Audiences," 178.

## CHAPTER 2. FROM FICTION TO REALITY: CHARACTER AND STAGECRAFT IN *THE TAMING OF THE SHREW*

1. H. J. Oliver, ed., *The Taming of the Shrew* The Oxford Shakespeare (Oxford: Clarendon Press, 1982), writes that "*The Taming of the Shrew* cannot be later, in its original Shakespearean form, than 1592" (32).

2. Sir Arthur Quiller-Couch, ed. *The Taming of the Shrew* (Cambridge: Cambridge University Press, 1953), xxv.

3. I use the term "reading" here in the spirit of Richard L. Levin's discussion (and dissection) of "readings" in *New Readings vs. Old Plays* (Chicago: University of Chicago Press, 1979).

4. John Russell Brown, "The Theatrical Element of Shakespeare Criticism," in Norman Rabkin, ed. *Reinterpretations of Elizabethan Drama* (New York: Columbia University Press, 1969), 177–95; 188. Brown writes: "Shakespeare wrote for the theater—that is his medium, the element in which his art is designed to live—and therefore, for all its difficulties, theatrical reality is also *the* element of Shakespeare criticism" (189).

5. J. L. Styan, *Shakespeare's Stagecraft* (Cambridge: Cambridge University Press, 1967), 196.

6. When writing about Shakespeare's plays, the critic should remember Peter Brook's simple but succinct remark: "A play is play." *The Empty Space* (New York: Atheneum, 1978), 141.

7. Larry S. Champion, *The Evolution of Shakespeare's Comedy* (Cambridge, Mass.: Harvard University Press, 1970), 40.

8. M. C. Bradbrook, *The Growth and Structure of Elizabethan Comedy* (London: Chatto & Windus, 1955), 76.

9. Bradbrook, 79.

10. Alexander Leggatt, *Shakespeare's Comedy of Love* (London: Methuen, 1974), 49.

11. The folk backgrounds of the shrew-taming story are examined by Jan Harold Brunvand, "The Folk-Tale Origin of *The Taming of the Shrew,*" *Shake-*

*speare Quarterly* 17 (autumn 1966): 345–69; and by Michael West, "The Folk Background of Petruchio's Wooing Dance: Male Supremacy in *The Taming of the Shrew*," *Shakespeare Studies* 7 (1974): 65–73. Other probable sources, including a colloquy by Erasmus and an anonymous verse tale, are suggested by Richard Hosley, "Sources and Analogues of *The Taming of the Shrew*," *Huntington Library Quarterly* 27 (1963–64): 289–308.

12. J. Dennis Huston, *Shakespeare's Comedies of Play* (New York: Columbia University Press, 1981), 64.

13. Oliver, Oxford *Shrew*, 42. Oliver argues that "Shakespeare was already too good a dramatist for the material he was dramatizing: characterization and farce are, finally, incompatible" (52). I shall argue that Shakespeare's characterization of Katharina and Petruchio must indeed be taken seriously.

14. Regarding the element of "play" in the Induction, and its "halls of mirrors," which continually reflect even deeper levels of play, see Huston, *Comedies of Play*, 67–68. David Daniell, "The Good Marriage of Katherine and Petruchio," *Shakespeare Survey* 37 (1984): 23–31, also examines the theatricality in the Induction and its relation to the rest of the play. Daniell writes: "By the time Lucentio and Tranio enter to start the specially mounted play some quite large areas of the capability of theatre to create illusion have been coloured in" (24).

15. Some similarities between Sly's and Kate's situations are suggested by Robert B. Heilman, ed., *The Taming of the Shrew* Signet Shakespeare (New York: The New American Library, 1966), xxvi.

16. Oliver, Oxford *Shrew*, 34–43, discusses Sly's disappearance.

17. Bevington, 4th ed., glosses "paint" at 1.1.65 as "make red with scratches"; in context, this seems a perfect interpretation of Kate's threat.

18. Eric Bentley, *The Life of the Drama* (New York: Atheneum, 1970), writes that a fictitious character, in a novel or play, is primarily a "force in a story" (45).

19. Coppélia Kahn, "*The Taming of the Shrew*: Shakespeare's Mirror of Marriage," *Modern Language Studies* 5 (spring 1975): 88–102, writes that "Though [Katharina] commits four acts of physical violence onstage . . . in each instance the dramatic context suggests that she strikes out because of provocation or intimidation resulting from her status as a woman" (93). Professor Kahn's essay is reprinted with revisions in *Man's Estate: Masculine Identity in Shakespeare* (Berkeley: University of California Press, 1981), 104–18.

20. H. B. Charlton, *Shakespearian Comedy* (London: Methuen, 1938), 96.

21. The social backgrounds of the play, including marriage customs, are examined by George R. Hibbard, "*The Taming of the Shrew*: A Social Comedy," in *Shakespearean Essays*, eds. Alwin Thaler and Norman Sanders (Knoxville: University of Tennessee Press, 1964), 15–28.

22. Hortensio is the "straight man" for Katharina in 1.1 and Petruchio in 2.1. Thus, Hortensio's appearance with them together on the road to Padua in 4.5 suggests visually the end of Petruchio's and Katharina's hostilities.

23. Kahn, "Mirror of Marriage," writes that "Petruchio's confident references to 'great ordnance in the field' and the 'Loud 'larums, neighing steeds, trumpets' clang' of battle bespeak a lifelong acquaintance with organized violence as a masculine vocation. . . . In its volume and vigor, his speech also suggests a robust manliness that would make him attractive to the woman who desires a master" (93). These statements naively assume that Petruchio's bragging about battle etc. should be taken seriously, and ignore completely his tendency towards hyperbolic speech and action. He is a nobleman's son, not a soldier.

As Daniell, "Good Marriage," notes, Petruchio "sets out to play a part," and "He has only just left home by his own confession, apparently setting off for the first time" (1.2.49–57; Bevington 4th ed.) (28, 29). What is evident in Petruchio's developing relationship with Katharina is not mastery, but evolving hyperbolic play.

24. Huston, *Comedies of Play,* neatly summarizes the hypocrisy in Baptista's actions: "Baptista *thinks* he loves his daughter and tries to treat her fairly. But in fact he does not. Instead of love he gives Kate only the conventional responses of a loving father. . . . However pure Baptista's motives . . . may be, the results are disastrous. He makes a public disgrace of Kate because she has no suitors. . . . With no concern for Kate's feelings, he is hastily disposing of her, like faulty merchandise, to the first bidder he finds in the marketplace" (70).

25. Kahn, for example, writes in "Mirror of Marriage": "Those critics who maintain that [Petruchio's force] is acceptable because it has only the limited, immediate purpose of making Kate reject an 'unbecoming' mode of behavior miss the real point of the taming. The overt force Petruchio wields over Kate by marrying her against her will in the first place and then by denying her every wish and comfort, by stamping, shouting, reducing her to exhaustion, etc., is but a farcical representation of the psychological realities of marriage in Elizabethan England, in which the husband's will constantly, silently, and invisibly, through custom and conformity, suppressed the wife's" (94). One must ask, however, whether the process we witness in the theater leads to Kate's being "suppressed"? Katharina's voice suddenly dominates the whole theater at the end of the play. I would argue that the sense of mutuality evident in Kate's final speech indicates a marriage that is *not* typical of those in Elizabethan England, whatever the social literature may indicate. Why must art imitate life, or life as it is assumed to have been? Why assume that Kate is every early modern English woman? She is *a character in a play!* Further, Kahn completely misses the crucial role of play within Petruchio's mock-tyranny; as Robert Weimann cogently explains, "Terror, playfully experienced, acts as a charm against real terror, or at least reduces some of its more formidable dimensions. The comic version of tyranny has a liberating effect: exaggerated authority becomes laughable. The mighty man appears comic when terrible threats and wrath, once they are subjected to irreverent imitation, are turned into burlesque" *(Shakespeare and the Popular Tradition in the Theater,* edited by Robert Schwartz [Baltimore: Johns Hopkins University Press, 1978], 72).

26. William Hazlitt, *Characters of Shakespeare's Plays* (1817; reprint, London: Oxford University Press, 1959), 245.

27. On the theatrical function of this anxiety and uncertainty among spectators, see J. L. Styan, *Drama, Stage, and Audience* (Cambridge: Cambridge University Press, 1975), 229–30.

28. Huston, *Comedies of Play,* 72–73, discusses how the Induction and acts 1 and 2 create—and demand—active audience participation in the play, and how Petruchio uses "play" to master his world.

29. Bernard Beckerman, "Shakespeare and the Life of the Scene," in *English Renaissance Drama: Essays in Honor of Madeleine Doran and Mark Eccles,* edited by Standish Henning, Robert Kimbrough, Richard Knowles (Carbondale: Southern Illinois University Press, 1976), 36–45, describes the "subsegments" of a Shakespearean scene as "the dialectic of the thrust of one energy— usually expressed by one person—against some sort of resistance." This dialec-

tic assumes a shape when "accumulated energies break the tenuous balance between thrust and resistance" (38). Petruchio's soliloquy takes the audience to the threshold of one such moment. Beckerman expands this concept in a later essay, "Shakespeare's Industrious Scenes," *Shakespeare Quarterly* 30 (spring 1979): 138–50.

30. In my analysis of this scene, I am indebted to John Russell Brown, *Shakespeare's Dramatic Style* (London: Heinemann, 1970): 16–28; esp. 24.

31. By saying "wooers," Petruchio both flatters and annoys Kate, implying she has had many conventional suitors of the kind she presumably detests (i.e., Hortensio).

32. Petruchio's use of the word "conformable" begs its own question: does Katharina sound "conformable" (i.e. "compliant") at the end of the play? She is hardly the often idealized "silent woman." Petruchio's word here, in dramatic context, like his deliberately annoying use of "Kate" several times when she prefers Katharina, is part of his hyperbolic play.

33. One must assume that Petruchio is serious about Katharina's physical beauty, despite his Petrarchan posing. If Petruchio is not at all attracted to her, then he does marry her only for her dowry. Besides, we have Hortensio's word that Katharina is "beauteous" (1.2.85).

34. In an Elizabethan playhouse the large, unlocalized stage around which Petruchio and Katharina romp in 2.1 would reinforce visually for spectators surrounding the stage what the dialogue suggests about these two people: their need for ample space between them, lest they prove lethal to each other. This realization would be far less evident in a proscenium theater, and spectators would be far less engaged with the actors than they would have been in an Elizabethan playhouse.

35. Peter Saccio, "Shrewd and Kindly Farce," *Shakespeare Survey* 37 (1984): 33–40; 37, 38. Saccio adds "Dramatic rhythm is a matter largely neglected by recent commentary on the play. . . . But dramatic events exist within a structure and rhythm of episodes, and that rhythm governs our apprehension of them" (37). Throughout his fine essay, Saccio emphasizes the necessity of our remembering that *The Shrew* is a play meant for a theater.

36. In the First Folio, the stage direction following Petruchio's "And kisse me Kate, we will be married o' Sunday" reads simply: "Exit Petruchio and Katherine." But Theobald's emendation "[severally]," in Bevington's text "[separately]," adopted by modern editors, is theatrically perfect; seeing Katharina and Petruchio exit severally reinforces visually their comically disparate attitudes: Petruchio leaves confidently predicting their marriage, whereas Katharina declares flatly, "I'll see thee hanged on Sunday first."

37. Marianne Novy, "Patriarchy and Play in *The Taming of the Shrew*" *ELR* 9 (spring 1979): 264–80, writes, "This speech again shows the coalescence of the role of player and patriarch, for the terms in which he declares ownership—the objects into which he transforms her—are extravagant enough to be a parody of patriarchal attitudes. The climactic phrase—'my anything'—declares the infinite malleability of identity within his world" (276). Professor Novy's insight into Petruchio's sense of verbal and physical "play" is essential to understanding his actions in this *play*. Her essay is reprinted in *Love's Argument: Gender Relations in Shakespeare* (Chapel Hill: University of North Carolina Press, 1984), 45–62.

38. The wedding, as Gremio explains, was a bizarre anticeremony, during which Katharina "Trembled and shook" (3.2.167). Petruchio struck the priest

and threw sops in the sexton's face "Having no other reason / But that his beard grew thin and hungerly / And seemed to ask him sops as he was drinking" (3.2.174–76). Petruchio's unreasonable sop-throwing anticipates his antics during their journey to his estate.

39. Huston, *Comedies of Play,* argues that one way to view Petruchio in the play is as the "questing hero" who rescues Katharina from a convention-bound existence and from her own prison of limited, almost wooden reactions (75–84). Huston argues that while at Petruchio's estate he acts out Kate's fear of being alone with "the monster of her anxieties," but even there he never completely abandons his sense of play. Huston locates the inception of this form of Petruchio's "play" in his absurd, histrionic, but necessary "rescue" of Katharina from Baptista's house.

40. Hugh M. Richmond, *Shakespeare's Sexual Comedy* (New York: Bobbs-Merrill, 1971), 91, discusses Katharina's growing awareness of others at the end of act 3.

41. John C. Bean, "Comic Structure and the Humanizing of Kate in *The Taming of the Shrew,*" in *The Woman's Part: Feminist Criticism of Shakespeare,* edited by Carolyn R. S. Lenz, Gayle Greene, and Carol Thomas Neely (Urbana: University of Illinois Press, 1983), 65–78; 72.

42. Bean, "Comic Structure," 72–75.

43. Regarding this soliloquy, Kahn, "Mirror of Marriage," writes:

I suppose Kate is actually being elevated in this speech, in view of previous references to her as her husband's horse, ox, and ass, for a falcon was the appurtenance of a nobleman, and a valued animal. But the blandness of Petruchio's confidential tone, the sweep of his easy assumption that Kate is not merely an animal, but *his* animal, who lives or dies at his command, has a dramatic irony similar to that of his exit speech at the wedding scene. Both utterances unashamedly present the status of woman in marriage as degrading in the extreme, plainly declaring her a sub-human being who exists solely for the purposes of her husband. (95–96)

Kahn misses completely Novy's sense of the absurd in Petruchio's earlier catalog of patriarchal authority (3.2.229–32; Novy, n. 37), and thus assumes that Petruchio's falcon imagery merely continues the reduction of Katharina to the status of a trained possession. If one misses the spontaneous, histrionic playfulness of much of Petruchio's relationship with Kate and assumes, as Kahn does, that Petruchio's "taming" of Kate is but one more element in his "lifelong acquaintance with organized violence as a masculine vocation" (93), then one misses completely the liberating sense of play which is fundamental to their mutual development during the play. H. R. Coursen, *Shakespearean Performance as Interpretation* (Newark: University of Delaware Press, 1992), writes "An examination of the woman-falcon equation . . . suggests that it need not be read as a degradation of Kate and of women" (51). Coursen quotes Margaret Loftus Ranald's observation on this soliloquy: "The falcon must be taught obedience to her master, but at the same time her wild and soaring nature must be preserved. This is a cardinal principle of hawk-taming. The bird must retain her hunting instinct: otherwise she is useless." ("The Manning of the Haggard: or *The Taming of the Shrew." Essays in Literature* 1, n. 2 [1974]: 149). Coursen adds: "I would go further and suggest that Petruchio's soliloquy . . . represents the taming of Petruchio. In falconry he discerns his metaphor for his relationship with Kate, for the transformation he is achieving in her and in himself, and for their relationship" (51). Coursen refers to Edmund Burt's seventeenth century work *An Approved Treatise of Hawkes and Hawking* (reprint, London, 1891), for references to mutuality in hawking exercises (51).

44. 1.2.106–7. Note also that Grumio specifically says that Petruchio will "woo" Katharina with words, what he calls "rope tricks." Even though Grumio has had his ears wrung by Petruchio, he predicts that Petruchio will use only rhetorical "figures" in wooing Kate, not any physical violence. Apparently Petruchio's love of rhetorical "figures" is well established.

45. Saccio, "Kindly Farce," superbly examines the accelerating rhythm of the second half of the play, and notes that "The accelerating pace of scenes is matched on the local, verbal level, by rhetorical schemes of repetition leading to climax—anaphora, epistrophe, ploce—schemes that Katherine adopts from Petruchio and uses increasingly. Of particular importance in reinforcing this pace is the sense of improvisation" (38). Sensing this increasing rhythm can only happen in the theater, not in the library, and it is part of spectators' experience of the play as a play, not as a social document.

46. Regarding Kate's reactions in this scene with the tailor, Huston, *Comedies of Play,* writes that Petruchio wants to free Katharina from "her woodenness of response" (71).

47. Novy, "Patriarchy and Play," scrutinizes Petruchio's several games with clothes: "Petruchio . . . is not interested in using clothes as signs of a playful or serious rise in the social hierarchy. Instead, his choice of clothes for the roles he plays dramatizes his independence of the status concerns usually coded by Elizabethan clothing. . . . Thus, although characters in all plots play games with clothing, Petruchio's games challenge rather than pay tribute to the social hierarchy" (270).

48. Although one ought not make too much of Petruchio's insights into clothing, his insistence that "honor peereth in the meanest habit" anticipates some of Lear's ravings about the hypocrisy of clothing: To choose only one small example: "Through tattered clothes small vices do appear; / Robes and furred gowns hide all" (4.6.164–65; Bevington 4th ed.).

49. As Bean cogently observes, "Kate is tamed not by Petruchio's whip but by the discovery of her own imagination, for when she learns to recognize the sun for the moon and the moon for the dazzling sun she is discovering the liberating power of laughter and play" ("Comic Structure," 72). Bean adds that Kate's remark that she is "so bedazzled with the sun" that all she looks on "seemeth green" suggests that "When Kate discovers laughter, the weather turns springtime, for Shakespeare sees in Kate not a taming but a renewal and a rebirth. When she is liberated from shrewishness, she perceives the world with new eyes and everything 'seemeth green'" (73). Regarding this entire sun/moon exchange between Petruchio and Katharina, Paola Dionisotti, who played Katharina for the RSC in 1978, writes:

Kate picks up all those images of sun and moon and intensifies them. She *dances* with it. The beauty of the speech becomes like an escape from the situation. The images are warm and the meshing of the lines gives the feeling that they're writing a love poem together, or playing a game. She has finally discovered that it *is* a game, and they can play it together. (20)

See "Kate: Interpreting the Silence," in Carol Rutter, ed., *Clamorous Voices: Shakespeare's Women Today* (London: The Women's Press, 1988), 1–25.

50. Saccio, "Kindly Farce," 38.

51. Ibid., 39.

52. Bevington, 4th ed., glosses 5.2.56 as "turns on you like a cornered animal and holds you at a distance." Oliver, Oxford edition, glosses the line: "Tranio is carrying on the image of the hound hunting the deer; the deer now stands at bay, ready to defend itself against attack" (224). That the other *men* describe Petruchio's marriage in animal metaphors shows that they have no idea what has transpired between Petruchio and Katharina. This ignorance of their relationship is also evident in the final lines of the play spoken by Hortensio and Lucentio. Each insists that Petruchio has tamed a "curst shrew," without sensing what has happened *within* Katharina: the liberation from convention and the consequent "renewal and rebirth" as Bean describes the process which spectators have seen and understood, but Hortensio, Lucentio, and Baptista have not. This complete misunderstanding of the Petruchio-Katharina relationship by those outside it stresses the couple's reliance only on each other. Consider the end of *Much Ado*, often considered Shakespeare's later version of Petruchio and Katharina; Benedick says to Claudio "Come, come, we are friends," and they and Beatrice and Hero mutually celebrate their weddings. At the end of *Shrew*, Petruchio and Katharina are off-stage, alone, and others are left only to wonder at what they have accomplished for and by themselves. Those who speak of their marriage in animal terms represent the patriarchal society which, at play's end, Petruchio and Kate have— literally and rapidly—left! Shirley Nelson Garner, "*The Taming of the Shrew*: Inside or Outside the Joke?" in *Bad Shakespeare,* edited by Maurice Charney (Rutherford: Fairleigh Dickinson University Press, 1988), 105–19, writes:

> Underlying the notion of heterosexual relationships in *Taming,* especially marriage, is that one partner must dominate. There can be no mutuality. The male fantasy that the play defends against is the fear that a man will not be able to control his woman.... In taming Kate, Petruchio seems to give comfort to all the other men in the play. (108)

This argument collapses all the men in the play into one dominating sexual stereotype and sees no difference between Kate's marriage and those of Bianca and the widow. Petruchio gives no comfort at all to Hortensio or Lucentio; they are "sped," not because their wives are apparently now disobedient, but because there is neither mutuality nor "play" in their marriages.

53. In their word games with Vincentio, Petruchio and Kate brilliantly display their complete independence of the normal Elizabethan importance assigned to clothing. In their witty and deliberate play, they pretend to be able to see through clothing, or to make it disappear: the "young budding virgin" needs no clothes to define her sex and age, as if clothes were a barrier to one's identity within the couple's totally imaginary world.

54. Novy, "Patriarchy and Play," 268.

55. Saccio, "Kindly Farce," makes a crucial point about the placing of Kate's final speech and its resulting dramatic importance: "Long doctrinal speeches in Shakespeare—the fable of the belly in *Coriolanus,* the divine-right speeches of *Richard II*—are often subject to ironic examination by the events of the play, but Katherine's speech is the only such sermon in Shakespeare occurring so late in its play that no further event can challenge it" (39).

56. Bean, "Comic Structure," 69–70, summarizes the major points of the humanist marriage reformers.

57. Ibid., 70.

58. Daniell, "Good Marriage," perceives the double purpose and theatrical importance of Katharina's speech here, specifically in her political metaphor: "Her final deed is to act a big theatrical set-piece . . . its length totally disrupting the rhythms presented by the other plot. 'Women', she says—that is, the conventionally married in front of her—are to be submissive. But she has been hunting with Petruchio as a couple for some time now, and she sends him, inside the speech, a message about themselves, Katherine and Petruchio, in the language of dramatized civil war. The play would founder—which it doesn't—if Katherine had merely surrendered to a generalization about 'women', and said nothing intensely personal about herself and Petruchio" (30).

59. Novy, "Patriarchy and Play," 277. She adds: "When Kate reprimands the other wives, she confirms her uniqueness as the only Shakespearean comic heroine without a female friend at any point in the play. For all the patriarchal approval, the character distribution gives her and Petruchio exclusive dependence on each other; it presents their marriage as a private world, a joke that the rest of the characters miss, a game that excludes all but the two of them" (277). Carol Thomas Neely, *Broken Nuptials in Shakespeare's Plays* (New Haven: Yale University Press, 1985), sees in Kate's final speech "a celebration of reciprocity": "In it she deftly draws on a number of male/female stereotypes to reconcile patriarchal marriage with romantic love and mutual desire. She defines marriage not just as a hierarchical social institution in which an obedient wife dutifully serves her lord but, conversely, as a playful Petrarchan romance in which an ardent lover courageously serves a beautiful woman. . . . As Petruchio transforms Kate's shrewishness into spirited devotion, she redefines his bullying as service, 'painful labor by sea and land,' which will leave her in peace. Following this joyous reassertion of her marriage vows and the recelebrated wedding feast, the couple can go off to bed for the belated consummation of their marriage" (30, 31). Neely stresses, as does Novy, the mutuality and play in Katharina's speech, and I would differ from her analysis only in finding more irony and "play" in Kate's describing Petruchio as one who will "labor" on sea and land. In a long note, Neely speaks thoughtfully of the "conflicting impulses," which many feminist critics feel about *Shrew,* expressing, on the one hand, their abhorrence of male dominance and female submission and, on the other, their "equally profound pleasure" at the play's end (218). I do not pretend to offer a solution to this deeply felt dilemma, which I certainly recognize. However, I do believe that increased attention to the play in performance, and especially to its shared comic rhythms between Petruchio and Katharina; to their developing and mutual sense of play and improvisation; and to the sheer verbal power, rhetorical sophistication, and physical dominance of Katharina *on stage in the theatre* in the final scene indicate that she exits, *as a character in this play,* as a powerful woman.

60. Karen Newman, "Renaissance Family Politics and Shakespeare's *The Taming of the Shrew,*" *ELR* 16 (winter 1986): 86–100, specifies another important way in which the ending of *Shrew* is unique among Shakespeare's comedies:

Unlike any other of Shakespeare's comedies, we have here [in Kate's last speech] represented not simply marriage, with the final curtain a veiled mystification of the sexual and social results of that ritual, but a view, however brief and condensed, of that marriage over time. And what we see is not a quiet and submissive Kate, but the same energetic and linguistically powerful Kate with which the play began. We know, then, in a way we never know about the other comedies . . . that Kate has continued to speak. . . . Kate's having the last word contradicts the very sentiments she speaks; rather than resolve the play's action, her monologue simply displays the fundamental contradiction presented by a female dramatic protagonist, between woman as a sexually desirable, silent object and women of words, women with power over language who disrupt, or at least italicize, women's place and part in culture. (97–98, 99)

Newman stresses theatre spectators' hearing and seeing (i.e., the *physical, theatrical experiencing*) of the strength of Kate's pronouncement. Coppélia Kahn claims that Kate's speech "sets the seal on a complete reversal of character, a push-button change from rebel to conformist which is . . . part of the mechanism of farce. Here as elsewhere in the play, farce has two purposes: it completes the fantasy of male dominance, but also mocks it as mere fantasy" (99). This interpretation obliterates the process by which Kate regains her voice and suddenly reduces her to a captive, paid performer advocating her own enslavement. This approach also enervates Kate's energy and her playful improvisation, and asserts that her well-educated, rhetorically brilliant mind has suddenly been emptied of all sense. In short, Kahn's argument ignores the verbal energy of Kate's communication with Petruchio and makes him into an idiot who said, "'Tis the mind that makes the body rich" having absolutely no idea what the words meant. Kahn's interpretation of Petruchio would also completely delete from the play his profound sense of the importance of "play" and its crucial role in his relationship with Kate.

61. Ann Thompson, ed., *The Taming of the Shrew.* New Cambridge Shakespeare (Cambridge: Cambridge University Press, 1984), glosses Kate's question about "goodly speech" thus: "Katherina's sarcastic enquiry reminds us that Petruchio's speech is indeed a calculated performance" (90). Oliver, Oxford, glosses "goodly" as "fair, elegant" (149).

62. Styan, *Shakespeare's Stagecraft,* 196.

63. Ralph Berry, *Shakespeare's Comedies: Explorations in Form* (Princeton: Princeton University Press, 1972), 69.

64. While it is easy for a male critic to write about what and how he thinks Katharina's final speech communicates, the testimony of Sinead Cusack supports my contentions. Cusack, who played Kate in the 1982 RSC production, writes in *Clamorous Voices* that Kate's final speech is "a declaration of independence":

At the end of the play I was determined that Kate and Petruchio were rebels and would remain rebels for ever, so her speech was not predictable. Having invited her to speak, he couldn't know what form her rebellion was going to take. He [Alun Armstrong, Petruchio] was very shaky indeed in the scene, not knowing what was coming. This so-called "submission" speech isn't a submission speech at all: it's a speech about how her spirit has been allowed to soar free. She is not attached to him. He hasn't laid down the rules for her, she has made her own rules, and what he's managed to do is to allow her to have her own vision. It *happens* that her vision coincides with his. There's a privately shared joke in the speech. And irony. And some blackness. The play is dark, savage sometimes. But I enjoyed the last speech. They're going to go on to a very interesting marriage. Petruchio was on his knees. I was standing. (21–22)

65. "Scolding Brides and Bridling Scolds: Taming the Woman's Unruly Member," *Shakespeare Quarterly* 42 (summer 1991): 179.

66. Boose, "Scolding Brides" 200.

67. On his production of *Shrew,* especially in relation to Michael Bogdanov's, see Graham Holderness, *The Taming of the Shrew* Shakespeare in Performance (Manchester: Manchester University Press, 1989), 73–94.

68. Robert Weimann, "Bifold Authority in Shakespeare's Theatre," *Shakespeare Quarterly* 39 (winter 1988): 402, 409.

69. Weimann, "Bifold Authority," 405.

70. Weimann develops thoroughly the distinction between *locus* and *platea* in *Shakespeare and the Popular Tradition in the Theater,* ed. Robert Schwartz (Baltimore: Johns Hopkins University Press, 1978), 73–85. Weimann's distinction is convincingly argued, is certainly present in medieval theatrical traditions, and is immensely useful for thinking about where certain scenes probably would have been performed on the large Elizabethan stages and how such performances would have conveyed different senses of "authority" to spectators. In later chapters, I shall use this distinction frequently, as I find it beneficial in thinking about how Elizabethan productions created meanings in performance. However, I am not convinced that this distinction necessarily holds *exactly* as Weimann describes it for *all* scenes in *all* of Shakespeare's plays. As I shall argue in the final two chapters, I believe the playing "space" on the Elizabethan stages was, or could be, more flexible than Weimann's discussion allows, and that Shakespeare came to use the platform stage in more complex ways than the strict *locus*/*platea* dichotomy prescribes.

71. During a lecture at a NEH Institute at James Madison University on July 28, 1995, Andrew Gurr speculated that double doors may have existed behind the central arras of Elizabethan playhouses and that these doors may have been used for "special entrances," such as royalty, or perhaps symbolically, such as a communal "exeunt" of the formerly warring families at the end of *Romeo and Juliet.* A similarly symbolic exit would occur in *Shrew* if Petruchio and Katharina left together through these central doors, thus contrasting vividly their final, unified exit with their earlier, individual exits through separate doors at the end of their first meeting in 2.1.

## CHAPTER 3. INNER PLAYS AND MIXED RESPONSES IN *LOVE'S LABOR'S LOST* AND *A MIDSUMMER NIGHT'S DREAM*

1. Bevington, 4th. ed., suggests that "Possibly [*LLL*] was first written in about 1588–89 for a boys' company and revised for Shakespeare's company in about 1596–97," and dates *Dream* ca. 1594–95 (31–32; 147). G. R. Hibbard, ed., *Love's Labor's Lost* The Oxford Shakespeare (Oxford: Clarendon Press, 1990), writes that *LLL* "could well have been one of the first plays [Shakespeare] wrote for his new company; and the date 1594–95 the likeliest for its composition" (45). Harold F. Brooks, ed., *A Midsummer Night's Dream* The Arden Shakespeare (London: Methuen, 1979), writes that "The hypothesis which fits the largest number of facts and probabilities—though it must remain a hypothesis—is that [*Dream*] was composed in the winter of 1595–96, for the [Elizabeth] Carey wedding on 19 February [to Thomas, the son of Henry, Lord Berkeley]" (lvii). While *Dream* may have been written for a specific occasion, possibly a wedding, as Brooks says, this is still an hypothesis, and I shall assume that whenever or for whatever reason Shakespeare wrote *Dream,* he did so with staging at the Theatre in mind. We still do not know that the play was not first performed at the Theatre and then requested afterward for a

private wedding performance. What is relevant to my purposes is that each play dramatizes an onstage audience, and the probable dates of composition suggest that with the formation of the Chamberlain's Men in late 1594, Shakespeare wrote soon thereafter two plays with the metatheatrical element of inner plays. The nature of spectator response apparently interested Shakespeare greatly at this crucial point, and obviously later, in his career.

2. On Shakespeare's use of Lylian structural techniques and patterns, see G. K. Hunter, *John Lyly: The Humanist as Courtier* (London: Routledge and Kegan Paul, 1962), 298–349, esp. 326–49.

3. Ronald Watkins and Jeremy Lemmon, *In Shakespeare's Playhouse: A Midsummer Night's Dream* (Totowa, N.J., Rowman and Littlefield, 1974), accept T. W. Baldwin's casting of Burbage as Demetrius (20). This is certainly possible, especially if Burbage played Berowne in *LLL*. But I think Burbage, having already played a young lover in *LLL*, would have played Theseus in *Dream* to increase his range of roles as the Chamberlain's Men (and Shakespeare himself) experimented with his talents.

4. J. L. Styan suggests this placement in *Shakespeare's Stagecraft* (Cambridge: Cambridge University Press, 1967), 104.

5. We know that actors occasionally used the gallery above the back of the stage, the "lords' room," for an acting area. It is possible that Berowne's line "Like a demigod here sit I in the sky" (4.3.75), would have been spoken from this gallery, but 4.3.147, "Now step I forth to whip hypocrisy" suggests that his previous line is to be taken metaphorically.

6. Styan, *Shakespeare's Stagecraft*, 104.

7. Marco De Marinis, "Dramaturgy of the Spectator," translated by Paul Dwyer *TDR* 31, no. 2 (1987), 102.

8. One assumes that the men and women would be placed together on stage in pairs, especially the King and Princess. However, an alternative placement, with the men on one side of the stage and the women on the other, would signal clearly the remaining and possibly future division within each of the couples.

9. De Marinis,"Dramaturgy," 100–6.

10. John Russell Brown, *Shakespeare and His Comedies* (London: Methuen, 1957), 94

11. Alvin B. Kernan, *The Playwright as Magician* (New Haven: Yale University Press, 1979), writes perceptively on this moment in the play:

> Since all of life is play-acting, the play seems to be saying, and since all men are such awkward and o'erparted players, it behooves members of an audience to treat even inept actors and foolish plays with the good manners and sympathy which should be born out of an awareness of their own deficiencies as fellow players. Such tolerance will help a play create the illusion needed to bring about the ends toward which the internal plays in *Love's Labour's Lost* aim: the triumph of love, the reconciliation of opposites, and the expression of good will and the desire to please. (72–73)

12. For a superb general discussion of *LLL* on the Elizabethan stage, see Miriam Gilbert, *Love's Labour's Lost* Shakespeare in Performance (Manchester: Manchester University Press, 1993), 1–20.

13. On the men's "neglect" and "waste" in the play, see John Dixon Hunt, "Grace, Art and the Neglect of Time in *Love's Labour's Lost*," in David Palmer and Malcolm Bradbury, eds., *Shakespearian Comedy* Stratford-upon-Avon Studies, no. 14 (London: Edward Arnold, 1971), 75–96.

14. Styan, *Shakespeare's Stagecraft,* 125.

15. Ibid., 127.

16. Ibid., 128. Styan places Oberon and Puck upstage center; Titania and Bottom midcenter; and Hermia and Lysander downstage left and Helena and Demetrius downstage right. Thus all three groups occupy clearly distinct sections of the large platform stage.

17. Philip C. McGuire, "Hippolyta's Silence and the Poet's Pen," in *Speechless Dialect: Shakespeare's Open Silences* (Berkeley: University of California Press, 1985), 1–18; and "Egeus and the Implications of Silence," in Marvin and Ruth Thompson, eds., *Shakespeare and the Sense of Performance* (Newark: University of Delaware Press, 1989), 103–15.

18. Robert Weimann, "Bifold Authority in Shakespeare's Theatre," *Shakespeare Quarterly* 39 (winter 1988): 402.

19. This blocking is suggested by Ronald Watkins and Jeremy Lemmon, *In Shakespeare's Playhouse,* 124–25. I examine this staging later in this chapter.

20. Jay Halio, *A Midsummer Night's Dream* Shakespeare in Performance (Manchester: Manchester University Press, 1994), reminds us that the greater intimacy in Shakespeare's theater was an essential feature in a performance of the mechanicals' play:

> We need to remember that Shakespeare's theatre, besides being mechanically less sophisticated than ours, also allowed for greater intimacy: aristocrats in the audience might sit upon the stage as well as in the 'lords' room' immediately above it and comment aloud on performances. Shakespeare's view of this sort of kibbutzing may be reflected in the remarks of the aristocrats attending 'Pyramus and Thisbe' and the reactions of the actors attempting to deal with such interruptions. Lacking this intimacy, at least in larger theatres, recent productions have found the interplay pointless or at any rate so prolonged as to slow down the pace and tempo of the concluding episode, now reaching for a final climax, and so cut many of the comments. (7)

Halio's remarks emphasize how important the actual stage and theatre structures are to appreciating that Shakespeare's plays were written for a specific kind of setting.

21. Brown, *Shakespeare and His Comedies,* 94.

22. McGuire, *Speechless Dialect,* xx.

23. James L. Calderwood, *Shakespearean Metadrama* (Minneapolis: University of Minnesota Press, 1971), observes that in the lovers' escape into the Athenian woods, into, that is, their "dream" from which they awaken in 4.1, "the breakdown of sexual relationships . . . becomes part of a general dissolving of past identities" (131).

24. Ibid., 137.

25. Joseph H. Summers, *Dreams of Love and Power* (Oxford: Clarendon Press, 1984), 11, argues for this distancing:

> The crew's ludicrous version of Pyramus and Thisbe, lovers fated like Romeo and Juliet, who find only death when they flee from opposing parental authority, distances the young Athenian lovers who have also fled to the woods even more decisively from tragic possibilities than Titania's and Oberon's metaphysical discord and reachieved harmony distance them from the possibilities of ordinary sour marriages.

26. Watkins and Lemmon, *In Shakespeare's Playhouse,* 124.

## CHAPTER 4. SHYLOCK, ANTONIO, AND *THE MERCHANT OF VENICE* IN PERFORMANCE

1. Norman Rabkin, "Meaning and *The Merchant of Venice*," in *Shakespeare and the Problem of Meaning* (Chicago: University of Chicago Press, 1981), 27.

2. Ibid., 22–23.

3. Ibid., 19.

4. Homer Swander, "Shakespeare & Beckett: What the Words Know," in *Shakespeare and the Sense of Performance,* edited by Marvin and Ruth Thompson (Newark: University of Delaware Press, 1989), 77.

5. Stanley Cavell, "A Matter of Meaning It," in *Must We Mean What We Say?* (New York: Charles Scribners Sons, 1969), 236–37; quoted in Rabkin, "Meaning," 14–15.

6. John Russell Brown, ed., *The Merchant of Venice* The Arden Shakespeare (1961; reprint, New York: Routledge, 1989), xi.

7. Patrick Stewart, "Shylock in *The Merchant of Venice*," in *Players of Shakespeare* vol. 1, edited by Philip Brockbank (Cambridge: Cambridge University Press, 1989), 19.

8. Ibid., 17.

9. Douglas Cole, *Suffering and Evil in the Plays of Christopher Marlowe* (Princeton: Princeton University Press, 1962), 132; quoted in Alan C. Dessen, "The Elizabethan Stage Jew and Christian Example," *MLQ* 35, no. 3 (September 1974), 233.

10. M. M. Mahood, ed., *The Merchant of Venice,* The Cambridge Shakespeare (Cambridge: Cambridge University Press, 1987), 19.

11. Mahood, 15–16, discusses the protection Jews experienced in Venice.

12. On usury and Shylock's use of the Jacob and Laban story to justify it, see Lawrence Danson, *The Harmonies of The Merchant of Venice* (New Haven: Yale University Press, 1978), 148–50. Danson writes: "Shylock's point . . . is that if Jacob 'was blest' despite the artificial manner in which he had influenced the ostensibly 'natural' process of breeding, the moneylender may similarly thrive through *his* artificial means of breeding" (149).

13. 1.3.127; Danson, *Harmonies,* 150–57.

14. Ruth Nevo, *Comic Transformations in Shakespeare* (New York: Methuen, 1980), 130.

15. On the symbolic importance of Gobbo's gift to Shylock, see my essay "Gobbo's Gift and the 'Muddy Vesture of Decay' in *The Merchant of Venice*," *Essays in Literature* 10 (fall 1983): 139–48.

16. Bevington, 4th ed., discusses this aspect of Shylock in his Introduction to *Merchant,* 181.

17. Mahood, 30–31, discusses Gratiano's speech that includes this image, and calls Gratiano's "the play's most haunting lines" (30). Rabkin, "Meaning," notes that Lorenzo is a poor witness to Shylock's hatred of music, since "'treasons, stratagems [sic], and spoils' characterizes [sic] his exploits at least as accurately as it [sic] does those of Shylock" (18).

18. Ibid., 31.

19. John R. Cooper, "Shylock's Humanity," *Shakespeare Quarterly* 21 (spring 1970): 117–24, writes: "There is no reason to take their [Salerio's and Solanio's] view of Shylock, or of anyone else, as correct. They find Shylock

ridiculous, but they also find Antonio's melancholy amusing, and they are even able to discuss Antonio's losses lightly. Moreover [they] . . . are slightly absurd because there are two of them and they cannot be told apart" (119).

20. D. M. Cohen, "The Jew and Shylock," *Shakespeare Quarterly* 31 (spring 1980): 53–63, argues stridently that *Merchant* is a racist play. Cohen writes: "The symbol of evil in *The Merchant of Venice* is Jewishness, and Jewishness is represented by the Jew" (58). Cohen argues that any sympathy for Shylock, especially in 3.1.50–69, is completely misplaced: "[Shylock] is abused chiefly because he is a devil. The fact of his Jewishness only offers his abusers an explanation for his diabolical nature; it does not offer them the pretext to torment an innocent man" (60).

21. Dessen, "Elizabethan Stage Jew," asserts flatly "There will be no final solution to the Shylock problem" (231). Danson, *Harmonies,* 126–70, thoroughly reviews the "Shylock problem" and examines Shylock's deceptive rhetoric on 106 ff.

22. Cooper, "Shylock's Humanity," 120.

23. Graham Holderness distills the dichotomy between "similarity" and "difference" in Shylock's appeal: "Certainly the common humanity to which Shylock lays claim is a simple concept: human beings are biologically virtually identical to one another despite the differences and barriers of race, religion, and culture. . . . On the other hand, Shylock is launching his demand for equality of rights and dignity specifically from a position of difference" (34–35). See *Shakespeare: The Merchant of Venice* Penguin Critical Studies (London: Penguin Books, 1993).

24. Holderness writes: "[T]here is on the one hand the Utopian ideal of a universal equality: a fundamental biological kinship between all human beings, which should prescribe parallel values of social, cultural and political equality. Running quite counter to this is a contrary idea: a reductive diminution of all human existence to the lowest possible level" (35). Nevo writes that at the speech's end, Shylock "consolidates his disintegrated, fragmented self upon the will to revenge. . . . If we do not see the weight Shakespeare is giving the birth and growth of this obsession in Shylock we will lose a large part of the dramatic agon of the trial scene" (132).

25. Cohen, "The Jew and Shylock," 61.

26. Holderness, *The Merchant of Venice,* 37.

27. Nevo argues that "if Shylock is seen as craftily, and stereotypically, planning the death of Antonio from the start it will be easier to assimilate the play to its fairy tale pole." Nevo believes that "it is the father's grief that is presented as engendering the thirst for revenge, the determination to *seek* revenge" (130).

28. Cohen, "The Jew and Shylock," 56–57.

29. Anthony Brennan, *Shakespeare's Dramatic Structures* (New York: Routledge, 1986), 39–51, esp. 45–48.

30. Consider C. Walter Hodges's drawing of a suggested staging of 4.1 in Mahood's Cambridge ed., 38.

31. Cooper, "Shylock's Humanity," 122.

32. Spectators have also heard Bassanio praise Antonio as "the kindest man, / The best-conditioned and unwearied spirit / In doing courtesies, and one in whom / The ancient Roman honor more appears / Than any that draws breath in Italy" (3.2.292–96). Certainly Bassanio is welcome to his view of Antonio, and at this moment in the play Bassanio is suddenly destitute and needs Portia's help. But like Salerio's praise of Antonio in 2.8. 35 ff. ("A kinder

gentleman treads not the earth"), Bassanio's praise of Antonio omits his abuse of Shylock, as if abusing a Jew, and thus an alien, as the trial will label Shylock, does not soil one's record of "Christian" kindness.

33. *The Merchant of Venice*, 50–51. Holderness writes, "The Christian culture of Venice is not . . . prepared to embrace Shylock's otherness, to concede true equality to his alien status; it will accept him only as a Christianized Jew who is prepared to renounce his race, religion and beliefs along with his legal action against Antonio" (51).

34. As a gloss not only on this scene, but also on the entire theatrical *process* of Shylock's interactions with Venetian Christian society, consider Luke 6: 41–42, which reads in *The Geneva Bible* (1560): "And why seest thou a mote in thy brothers eye, and considerest not the beame, that is in thine owne eye? . . . Hypocrite, cast out the beame out of thine owne eye first, & then shalt thou se perfectly, to pul out the mote that is in thy brothers eye." The gloss for this verse reads: "He [Christ] reproueth the hypocrisie of suche as winke at their owne horrible fautes [*sic*], & yet are to curious to spie out ye least faute in their brother." In their dealings with Shylock, the Christians presume the right to judge him. In performance, especially in a nominally Christian culture, spectators ought to recognize this unchristian assumption among the Venetians, and see themselves as perhaps, at the end of the trial, caught up in the same assumptions about the right to judge as the Venetians they see on stage.

35. Nevo, *Comic Transformations*, 131.

36. Laurence Olivier, *On Acting* (New York: Simon and Schuster, 1986), 179–80, explains that for his performance of Shylock at Old Vic Theatre in 1970, the loss of Jessica was crucial:

> My performance remained contained in uprightness and civility until Jessica was stolen away, and then, with justification, slowly went demented. To take the daughter was like carving the heart out of Shylock, and this I tried to emphasize in the role. The departure of his daughter turned his brain. Once this happened, he was prepared to sue, to destroy. Once she had gone off with a Gentile, as far as he was concerned she was dead. The pound of flesh was nothing compared with the abduction. He had been raped by pack of Christian dogs. From that moment onwards I let the fury and the rages come.

37. Although Shylock's knife is only visible during the trial itself (it is mentioned first by Gratiano at l.121, while Nerissa presents the letters from Bellario, and Shylock probably [l.344—"Tarry Jew!"] drops or surrenders the knife well before being ordered off stage by the Duke at l. 395), I suggest that it is visually quite significant in performance. Alan Dessen, in *Elizabethan Drama and the Viewer's Eye* (Chapel Hill: University of North Carolina Press, 1977), speaking of Hamlet's sword, asserts:

> The usual *reading* of [*Hamlet*] concerned largely with verbal effects will not establish the sword as a crucial element either poetically or structurally. Although weapons continually may be called to our attention . . . there is no famous speech, no purple passage, to make Hamlet's sword part of our cultural arsenal. But regardless of any lack of emphasis for the reader, Hamlet's sword does play a highly significant role for any viewer of the play and for that reader conscious of presentational as well as verbal effects. (91)

Certainly Shylock's knife is not nearly as prominent visually as Hamlet's sword; however, during the trial in performance, as Shylock not only whets the knife but also carries it across the *platea* to Antonio's place on stage, the "presentational effect" of the weapon is clear: the knife embodies the severity of the hatred and rage in this court. As late as l. 302 (Shylock: "Most learned judge! A sentence! Come, prepare"), everyone, except Portia, expects Shylock to cut Antonio to death before the entire court. Scholarly, reductive "readings" of this play ignore the dramatic effect Shakespeare created with the visible knife for Elizabethan *spectators* of this play who had not read it in English Literature 101.

38. Alexander Leggatt, *Shakespeare's Comedy of Love* (New York: Methuen, 1974), 142.

39. Holderness, *The Merchant of Venice,* asserts that the "other statues," which Portia produces, "unlike the law protecting the cosmopolitan freedom of commercial exchange, are fundamentally racist in character, since they are designed to protect the Venetian citizen against the competitive actions of racial or cultural outsiders" (52). Steven Mullaney asserts that the greatest irony of the trial scene is that "Shylock's possessions and life are forfeit, not if he spills a drop of blood unspecified in his bond or takes more or less than a pound of flesh, but because he is what he always claimed to be—an alien in Venice . . . . The case was never in question; the verdict against Shylock was always there, from the time he first proposed his bond to Antonio. More discomfiting for Shylock than the decision against him is his alienation, at this moment, from precisely what he has embraced as a cultural identity distinct from Christian Venice" (83–84). See "Brothers and Others, or The Art of Alienation," in *Cannibals, Witches, and Divorce: Estranging the Renaissance* Selected Papers from The English Institute, 1985, edited by Marjorie Garber (Baltimore: Johns Hopkins University Press, 1987), 67–89.

40. The disparity between Jewish Law and Christian Love in *Merchant* is thoroughly examined by John S. Coolidge, "Law and Love in *The Merchant of Venice,*" *Shakespeare Quarterly* 27, no. 3 (summer 1976): 243–63.

41. Rabkin, "Meaning," 14.

42. Cooper's remarks here are seminal to grasping the dramatic significance of this moment:

> While the distinction of the Law and Christian mercy is made emphatically by the play, the distinction between Jew and Christian is blurred by the behavior of the actual Christians. . . . Salarino [sic] and Salanio as well as Shakespeare's Christian audience ought to have been disturbed by Shylock's saying, "If a Jew wrong a Christian, what is his humility: Revenge." This is too true an observation of actual behavior to be dismissed as Shylock's deceitful rhetoric. The point is not simply the difference between Christian profession and Christian behavior. Rather, it is that Christians fail on precisely that point which is supposed to provide the superiority of Christian ethic to the old Law. ("Shylock's Humanity," 122)

43. Dessen, "Elizabethan Stage Jew," says of Gratiano: "in his vindictiveness [he] . . . calls attention to the persistence of values previously identified with Shylock and serves as a foil to set off the Christian example provided by the Duke and Antonio" (243). Yet Antonio's "Christian example" is also seriously qualified in the play, beginning with his first meeting with Shylock in 1.3.

44. Ejner Jensen, *Shakespeare and the Ends of Comedy.* (Bloomington and Indianapolis: Indiana University Press, 1991), 16–17.

45. This is the argument made by Leggatt, *Shakespeare's Comedy of Love*, 143–44.

46. Ralph Berry, "Discomfort in *The Merchant of Venice*," in *Shakespeare and the Awareness of the Audience* (London: MacMillan, 1985), 61. Berry writes: "In all the meanings generated by *The Merchant of Venice*, Jessica's silence is the representative of the undefined, incurable malaise that haunts the action. She is the dark fringe on the final scene which, in so much critical and theatrical folklore, is a paean to harmony, reconciliation and intimations of celestial accords" (61).

47. Bevington, 4th ed., glosses "respect" as "comparison, context" (213); Mahood refers to *Hamlet*, 2.2.249: "there is nothing either good or bad but thinking makes it so," and to Donne's "The Progess [*sic*] of the Soul": "There's nothing simply good, nor ill alone, / Of every quality comparison / The only measure is, and judge, opinion" (159).


CHAPTER 5. FALSTAFF AND THE THEATER OF SUBVERSION: THE AUDIENCE AS THIEVES IN *I HENRY IV*

1. Sherman Hawkins, "*Henry IV*: The Structural Problem Revisited," *Shakespeare Quarterly* 33 (autumn 1982): 278–301; 301.

2. Ibid., 298.

3. David Bevington, introduction to *II Henry IV, The Complete Works of Shakespeare,* 4th ed. (New York: Harper Collins, 1992), 804. A. R. Humphreys, ed., *The First Part of King Henry IV,* The Arden Shakespeare (1960; reprint, London: Methuen, 1974), xi–xii, discusses the popularity of the play and Falstaff ca. 1598.

4. Scott McMillin, *Henry IV, Part One* Shakespeare in Performance (Manchester: Manchester University Press, 1991), 5.

5. Humphreys, Arden *I Henry IV,* xiii–xiv, dates *I Henry IV* in late 1596 and production in the 1596–1597 winter season.

6. On Will Kempe's playing Falstaff, see J. A. Bryant, "Shakespeare's Falstaff and the Mantle of Dick Tarlton," *Studies in Philology* 51 (April 1954): 149–62. David Wiles, *Shakespeare's Clown: Actor and Text in the Elizabethan Playhouse* (Cambridge: Cambridge University Press, 1987), 116–35, argues convincingly that Falstaff was Kempe's role. In his review of Wiles's book in *Shakespeare Quarterly* 39 (winter 1988): 518–19, T. J. King writes: "[I]t was customary for the leading actor to play the largest role in any given play. For example, external evidence identifies Richard Burbage in the roles of Richard the Third, Hamlet, King Lear, and Othello. It therefore seems likely that Burbage, the leading actor of the Chamberlain's Men, played Falstaff, the largest role in *I Henry IV*" (519). King's objections to Wiles's argument are logically flawed. Just because Burbage played leading tragic roles does not mean he played Falstaff just because that is the largest role in *I Henry IV*. Further, if Hawkins is right that Shakespeare did plan two parts of *Henry IV,* why would Shakespeare want Burbage to play a character who is dismissed at the end of part 2, and who does not appear in *Henry V*, which we may also suppose Shakespeare planned much sooner than he wrote it? It makes much more *theatrical* sense to imagine Shakespeare wanting Burbage to play Hal in *I* and *II Henry IV,* and then the king in *Henry V*. Certainly this identification of Burbage with the Hal/Henry V role would have encouraged spectators' presence

at a third play (i.e., *Henry V*) featuring Burbage playing the role of the former prodigal turned military victor. Having Burbage play Falstaff twice and then Henry V in the third play in the historical progression seems a bad casting choice.

7. Steven Mullaney, *The Place of the Stage* (Chicago: University of Chicago Press, 1988), 8.

8. Ibid., 8. See also Jonas Barish, *The Antitheatrical Prejudice* (Berkeley: University of California Press, 1981), 80–132.

9. John Stockwood, *A Sermon Preached at Paules Crosse.* (London, 1578), 134; quoted in Mullaney, *Place of the Stage,* 27.

10. "The Lord Mayor and Aldermen to the Privy Council," 28 July, 1597. In E. K. Chambers, *The Elizabethan Stage,* 4 vols. (Oxford: Clarendon Press, 1923), 4, 321–22.

11. On the religious authorities' opposition to the stage, see Russell Fraser, *The War Against Poetry* (Princeton: Princeton University Press, 1970); Barish, *Antitheatrical Prejudice;* and Patrick Crutwell, *The Shakespearean Moment* (New York: Vintage Books, 1960), chapt. 5, 138–61.

12. Michael D. Bristol, *Carnival and Theater* (New York: Methuen, 1985), 108.

13. Ibid., 110.

14. Ibid., 113–14.

15. Ibid., 138.

16. Ibid.

17. Ibid., 155.

18. On the history of Bolingbroke's reign, see Peter Saccio, *Shakespeare's English Kings* (London: Oxford University Press, 1977), chapt. 3, 37–63.

19. Chambers, *Elizabethan Stage,* 4, 322.

20. For the wild Prince Hal stories, see Humphreys, Arden *I Henry IV,* xxix–xxxi. For the popularity of the prodigal figure in Elizabethan literature, see Richard Helgerson, *The Elizabethan Prodigals* (Berkeley: University of California Press, 1976).

21. Thomas McFarland develops this line of argument in *Shakespeare's Pastoral Comedy* (Chapel Hill: University of North Carolina Press, 1972), 191.

22. Humphreys, Arden *I Henry IV,* analyzes Falstaff's parody of Puritan rhetoric (18).

23. Humphreys explains that Gad's Hill was "notorious for robberies" (17). The extent and ease of thievery are stressed by having robbery "as secure as sleep" even in well known places. By using a contemporary Elizabethan location, Shakespeare questions the efficacy of Elizabethan law and authority, which the theaters openly flaunted.

24. James Winny, *The Player King* (London: Chatto & Windus, 1968), writes "[I]f Hal can prove his credentials by taking part in a highway robbery, that is because he has a master-thief as a father" (139).

25. Winny thoroughly examines Falstaff as a "substitute father" in *Player King,* 105–31.

26. On the Shylock "problem," see Alan Dessen, "The Elizabethan Stage Jew and Christian Example," *Modern Language Quarterly* 35 (September 1974), 231–45.

27. Hawkins, "Structural Problem," 285–86, points out that Hal does not mention Falstaff in his soliloquy; indeed, "[Hal] does not yet clearly envisage the banishment of Falstaff" (285).

28. Chambers, *Elizabethan Stage*, 4, 322.

29. As Winny, *Player King*, writes: "A noble and virtuous young man deliberately masquerading as a dissolute prodigal, Hal is not likely to overlook the
deep moral blemishes in his father which he attacks so viciously in Falstaff,
who reproduces them in comic form; nor not to have noticed the moral hypocrisy of Bolingbroke's assumption of right. . . . As though taking his lead from
the King, who hides his dishonorable record behind a front of kingly authority,
the Prince masks his holiday and respect for law by putting on the appearance
of contempt for order and justice, so inverting the moral paradox presented
by his father" (136–37).

30. Speaking of this soliloquy, Jonas Barish, "The Turning Away of Prince
Hal," *Shakespeare Studies* I (1965), 9–17, observes that: "Even his most expansive moments, it may be urged, such as that with the drawers, are tinged with
calculation; Hal is practising sounding the base string so as to be able later to
play the whole gamut of the viol of state. But the more we insist on the element
of planning in the Eastcheap truancy, the more we turn Hal into a cardboard
prince, incapable from the outset of responding to the vitality of Falstaff. Under
these conditions, the sojourn in the tavern becomes little better than an empty
masquerade . . . (14). Mullaney, *Place of the Stage* writes of this soliloquy:
"Moving forward to deliver his opening soliloquy, he moves beyond the confines of audience expectation to reveal a strange and unfamiliar visage: not a
prodigal youth given over to vile participation but a prince who plays at prodigality, and means to translate his rather full performance into the profession
of power" (81).

31. Humphreys, Arden *I Henry IV*, quotes Samuel Johnson's keen insight
into Hal's incomplete understanding of himself and his motives at this moment: "This speech is very artfully introduced to keep the prince from appearing vile in the opinion of the audience: it prepares them for his future
reformation, and, what is yet more valuable, exhibits a natural picture of a
great mind offering excuses to itself, and palliating those follies which it can
neither justify nor forsake" (20).

32. On the individuality of Hotspur's speech in the play, see G. R. Hibbard,
*The Making of Shakespeare's Dramatic Poetry* (Toronto: University of Toronto
Press, 1981), 174–80.

33. Stephen Greenblatt, "Invisible Bullets: Renaissance Authority and its
Subversion, *Henry IV* and *Henry V*," in Jonathan Dollimore and Alan Sinfield,
eds., *Political Shakespeare* (Ithaca: Cornell University Press, 1985), 18–47,
writes: "It is precisely because of the English form of absolutist theatricality
that Shakespeare's drama, written for a theatre subject to State censorship,
can be so relentlessly subversive: the form itself, as a primary expression of
Renaissance power, contains the radical doubts it continually provokes" (45).
Laughing at authority is perhaps the most potent form of subversion, and in
Falstaff Shakespeare ridicules the very powers which continually threatened
to destroy his and his company's theatrical enterprise.

34. A. C. Bradley, "The Rejection of Falstaff," in *Oxford Lectures on Poetry*
(1909; reprint, London: Macmillan, 1965), 269.

35. Chambers, *Elizabethan Stage*, 4, 322.

36. Maurice Morgann defends Falstaff at Gad's Hill as having been "surprised
with fear in this single instance, . . . off his guard" (253), and argues that we
should not accuse Falstaff of cowardice from just this one instance (253–59).
However Falstaff's cowardice here is blatant; what matters is how this repro-

bate activity is transformed into a carnival disregard for not only valor, but also history. What matters to Falstaff is survival in the present moment, regardless of the means employed. See "Essay on the Dramatic Character of Sir John Falstaff," in D. Nichol Smith, ed., *Eighteenth Century Essays on Shakespeare* (Oxford: Clarendon Press, 1963), 203–83.

37. Mark Rose, *Shakespearean Design* (Cambridge: Harvard University Press, 1972), 50–59.

38. Greenblatt, "Invisible Bullets," details Hal's role, as a member of the nobility, in producing the "oppressive order" to which Francis is bound.

39. Rose, *Shakespearean Design,* 51.

40. Ibid.

41. Ibid., 53. Hibbard, *Dramatic Poetry,* 181–82, stresses the vividness and spontaneity of Falstaff's creative imagination.

42. Bradley, "Rejection of Falstaff," writes: "Shakespeare was not writing a mere farce. It is preposterous to suppose that a man of Falstaff's intelligence would utter these gross, palpable, open lies with the serious intention to deceive, or forget that, if it was too dark for him to see his own hand, he could hardly see that the three misbegotten knaves were wearing Kendall green. No doubt, if he *had* been believed, he would have been hugely tickled at it, but he no more expected to be believed than when he claimed to have killed Hotspur" (265). Bradley's logic is sound, but it diminishes Falstaff's gall, wit, and disdain for historical fact, the latter crucial to understanding his subversiveness in a "history play." In performance, especially if Falstaff plays the beginning of this scene totally seriously, spectators are not sure what he intends, thus markedly increasing his theatrical influence. The more entertaining Falstaff is, the more dangerous he is to Hal's history play.

43. In his essay "Laughter," in *Comedy,* ed. Wylie Sypher (Garden City, N.Y.: Doubleday, 1956), 61–190, Henri Bergson describes one of the comic situations as "The snow-ball" in which, like a snowball rolling downhill, a comic effect "grows by arithmetical progression, so that the cause, insignificant at the outset, culminates by a necessary evolution in a result as important as it is unexpected" (113). Bergson also describes this comic situation as the proverbial "house of cards," in which the slight movement of one card eventually causes "the work of destruction, gathering momentum as it goes on, rushes headlong to the final collapse" (113). Falstaff's "combat report" from Gad's Hill builds expectations of this kind of collapse, only to yield exactly the opposite: an irresistible challenge to his mental dexterity.

44. Harry Berger Jr. "Theater, Drama, and the Second World: A Prologue to Shakespeare," *Comparative Drama* 2 (spring 1968): 16.

45. Humphreys notes that here, Falstaff "invents a morality character representing aged respectability" (72).

46. James L. Calderwood, *Metadrama in Shakespeare's Henriad* (Berkeley: University of California Press, 1979), 46. Winny, *Player King,* writes: "This farcically disrespectful imposture by Falstaff gives visible form to the moral reality of Bolingbroke's kingship, and supplies in advance a satirical commentary on the gravely serious scene between Hal and his father" (107).

47. Berger, "Prologue to Shakespeare," 16.

48. Winny, *Player King,* discerns that "[I]t seems ... likely that Falstaff's satirical function is to counterpoise the forgetfulness that allows Bolingbroke to give so plausible a performance as king. Falstaff's comically distorted allusions to wrongs committed by Bolingbroke against Richard, his own support-

ers, and the laws of which he is now supreme protector, keep the audience awake to the irrevocable dishonour which the King has incurred, and frustrate his attempts to pass himself off as the authentic figure of God's deputy-elect" (109).

49. See J. L. Styan, *Shakespeare's Stagecraft* (Cambridge: Cambridge University Press, 1967), 15.

50. J. Dover Wilson, *The Fortunes of Falstaff* (Cambridge: Cambridge University Press, 1944), esp. chapt. 2.

51. Speaking of these lines, C. L. Barber, *Shakespeare's Festive Comedy* (Princeton: Princeton University Press, 1959), writes: "they embody an effort at a kind of magical naming. Each repetition of 'sweet Jack Falstaff, kind Jack Falstaff' aggrandizes an identity which the serial clauses caress and cherish. At the very end, in 'plump Jack,' the disreputable belly is glorified" (212).

52. Hawkins, "Structural Problem," writes: "The slower evolution of the comic plot and the postponement of its decisive turn suggest [that] . . . Shakespeare knows he has twice as long to develop this plot. And this is because the rejection of Falstaff is the proper conclusion to Part 2, just as the defeat of Hotspur is the proper conclusion of Part 1" (287). Hawkins is probably right that Shakespeare knew he had until the end of Part 2 to dismiss Falstaff. What I wish to stress is that in the Theatre, during this play considered as an artistic unity, Hal does not and cannot dismiss Falstaff; Hal can only play at doing so. And he gilds Falstaff's "up-so-doun" version of Shrewsbury history with a lie in 5.4.

53. When Falstaff hides behind the arras, Elizabethan spectators would have seen the play's most obviously "theatrical" character receiving royal "protection" from the Prince of Wales. One wonders whether London authorities would have seen this moment as an emblem of the protection against civic complaints that Shakespeare's company received from the Court.

54. McFarland, *Pastoral Comedy,* 190. McFarland's central thesis about Falstaff is that he is an "outcast from a pastoral realm," who "seems to draw his inexhaustibly antisocial energies from an order outside the reality in which he moves" (179).

55. Bradley, "Rejection of Falstaff," 266.

56. Barish, *Antitheatrical Prejudice,* writes: "Falstaff embodies the vitality of life lived on the level of improvisation. Without a trade, without a family, without plans or projects, without a past or a future, contemptuous of consistency, he lives exclusively in the present by a chameleon like adjustment to the needs of the moment. Past and future, plans and projects imply a part in a regular pattern, a submission, in some measure, to a restriction of one's identity. Falstaff bows to no rule other than that of his pleasure and appetite" (128).

57. McMillin, *Henry IV, Part One,* writes of this scene: "What I have called the confidence of the writing is actually the confidence in a theatre company. I take this scene as a sign that Shakespeare's company was very certain of itself and its audience by the later 1590's" (8).

58. On Shakespeare's use of the historical material from his sources in the two Henry plays, see Hawkins, "Structural Problem," esp. 288–94.

59. Winny, *Player King,* 96–97, discusses Bolingbroke's self-incrimination.

60. Hawkins, "Structural Problem," 287.

61. Humphreys, *Arden Henry IV,* n. to 3.2.1.12, p. 128.

62. Hawkins, "Structural Problem," writes that Falstaff's role becomes "di-

minished" in act 4 because the "distinctive comic subplot" is now over; in act 4 Shakespeare elaborates "his depiction of the rebels as he did his portrayal of the robbers in Act II. This is not change of plan but deliberate balance, opposing Falstaff's world in the first two acts to Hotspur's in the final two" (288). Because *I Henry IV* is not about Hotspur or Falstaff, but about the Prince, then "the line of Hal's development requires that the Falstaff and Hotspur subplots occur sequentially . . . as the Prince moves from the tavern to the battlefield, . . . from Falstaff's world of pleasure to Hotspur's world of honor" (288). Although Hotspur and the preparation for war certainly dominate act 4, the structure of acts 4 and 5 indicates that Falstaff's role is hardly diminished. Falstaff's four remaining appearances in the play, though relatively brief, are strategically placed. Just when the history of the play—of this individual play, not this play considered with part 2—demands serious attention from its audience, Shakespeare interjects Falstaff's astonishing ability to ridicule. Rather than a "diminished" role, Falstaff's comic energy reduces to virtual absurdity every heroic ideal of the remaining two acts.

63. McFarland, *Pastoral Comedy*, 190. Humphreys, Arden *Henry IV,* 128, documents this wide spread abuse in Elizabethan England.

64. Winny, *Player King,* 118.

65. This is the context that makes perfect sense of Michael Goldman's remark that Falstaff "has no politics; that is why he is central to these [*I* and *II Henry IV*] most political of plays." *Shakespeare and the Energies of Drama* (Princeton: Princeton University Press, 1972), 46.

66. Humphreys, Arden *Henry IV,* 151.

67. Winny, *Player King,* 119.

68. Morgann, "Dramatic Character of Falstaff," 245.

69. Stockwood, *A Sermon Preached at Paules Crosse,* quoted in Mullaney, *Place of the Stage,* 27.

70. Bolingbroke suggests this possibility in 3.2.121–28: e.g. "Why, Harry, do I tell thee of my foes, / Which art my nearest and dearest enemy?" (lines 122–23).

71. Leo Salingar, "Falstaff and the Life of Shadows," in *Dramatic Form in Shakespeare and the Jacobeans* (Cambridge: Cambridge University Press, 1986), 32–52, discusses the Falstaff/Douglas fight as a dumb show, 45.

72. Bristol, *Carnival and Theater,* writes: "By treating honorable death as a joke, Falstaff speaks to a plebeian consciousness that maintains itself despite sacrifices demanded in the name of the nation-state" (183). Bristol's remark reminds us that this play was written for a popular Elizabethan audience perilously situated in opposition to that very same nation-state when seated within the Theatre/Globe.

73. *Metadrama in Henriad,* pp. 80, 82. Calderwood reviews several interpretations of Hal's developing character vis-à-vis Hotspur and Falstaff as symbolized in this scene.

74. Mullaney, *Place of the Stage,* 58. Of Barabas's "rising" outside the walls of Malta, when "the domain outside the city walls is itself brought on stage," Mullaney observes: "Rising from his double death, standing in a place twice-removed from the city—once in representation, again in actuality—Barabas stands before us as the master of an incontinent vitality. And standing where he does, he situates that vitality, ambivalent and recreative and theatrical as it is, in the place where it most emphatically belongs: at the heart of the Elizabethan stage" (58). Falstaff, "rising" and defying death at the Theatre in

the midst of a crucial historical battle, represents exactly this kind of danger-ous vitality that *completely* disregards circumstances. Richard Hillman, *Shake-spearean Subversions: The Trickster and the Play-Text* (New York: Routledge, 1992), says that here Falstaff's subversiveness "is enriched by a blasphemous parody of Christ, as well as by an allusion to 'atheistic' denigrations of religious miracles of fakery. Such larger-than-life identification with life incorporates the trickster's darker side, his link with death" (120).

75. Robert Hapgood, *Shakespeare the Theatre Poet* (Oxford: Clarendon Press, 1988), 40.

76. Calderwood, *Metadrama in Henriad,* imagines Falstaff here giving the theatre audience "an enormous conspiratorial wink" (71).

77. Ibid., 80.

78. Stephen Gosson, *Plays Confuted in Five Actions* (London, 1582); quoted in Mullaney, *Place of the Stage,* 142.

79. Barbara Hodgdon, *The End Crowns All* (Princeton: Princeton University Press, 1991), 12.

80. In his essay "Ambivalence: The Dialectic of the Histories," A. P. Rossiter, *Angel With Horns,* edited by Graham Storey (1961; reprint, New York: Theatre Arts Books, 1974), 40–64, eloquently argues the necessity for the comic in the midst of history: "Shakespeare's intuitive way of thinking about History . . . is *dialectical.* The old eristic-argumentative system which he used is static, changeless; but *his* thought is dynamic, alterative, not tied to its age. . . . In History Shakespeare felt that men were constrained to be much less than their full selves. He knew the burden of princehood: the Ceremony lines alone would proclaim it. All the Lancasters are less than full men. . . . Now Comedy is the field of human shortcoming; and therefore Shakespeare's History, at its great-est, *had* to be comic. What isn't Comic History in the Histories is what I can only call 'Obscure Tragedy'" (62–63).

## CHAPTER 6. DISABLING JOY: DRAMATIC STRUCTURE AND AUDIENCE RESPONSE IN *TWELFTH NIGHT*

1. Peter G. Phialas, *Shakespeare's Romantic Comedies* (Chapel Hill: Uni-versity of North Carolina Press, 1965), examines structural links between the romantic and "secondary action[s]" of Shakespeare's comedies; for a broader approach to Shakespeare's structural use of analogy, see Joan Hartwig, *Shake-speare's Analogical Scene* (Lincoln: University of Nebraska Press, 1983). Thad Jenkins Logan, "*Twelfth Night*: The Limits of Festivity," *Studies in English Literature* 22 (spring 1982): 223–38, writes that "*Twelfth Night* . . . is an anat-omy of festivity which focuses in the main plot on sexuality and in the sub-plot on revelry" (224).

2. See the interview of Miller in Tim Hallinan, "Jonathan Miller on *The Shakespeare Plays,*" *Shakespeare Quarterly* 32 (summer 1981): 134–45.

3. Bevington, 4th ed., dates *Twelfth Night* 1600 or 1601; Elizabeth Story Donno, ed., *Twelfth Night* The New Cambridge Shakespeare (Cambridge: Cam-bridge University Press, 1985),1–4, dates the play sometime after January, 1601.

4. I assume here that no cuts were made in the play's script in initial productions at the Globe. As I say in my Introduction, I don't agree with Michael Hattaway's arguments about cuts in playscripts.

5. This "sequence" is reinterpreted every time *Twelfth Night* is produced. Audiences will never see the exact same interpretation but, barring transpositions and major cuts, will always see the same sequence, or structure, performed on stage. Interpretations—costumes, casting, directors' "concepts"—will differ; the received script remains constant. Recall here Philip C. McGuire's reminder that an audience's response to a play is sequential and limited to "theatre time"; spectators cannot return to a previous scene for another look, as one can in a study. See McGuire's "Introduction," to *Shakespeare: The Theatrical Dimension,* eds. Philip C. McGuire and David A. Samuelson (New York: AMS Press, 1979), xix–xx. When analyzing an audience's theatrical experience of a play, one must abandon looking *both* backward *and* forward. Avoiding such peripheral vision is crucial to my argument.

6. 2.5, Malvolio's letter reading, concludes act 2; however, because it is structurally different from both 1.5 and 2.4, I treat it separately.

7. Logan, "Limits of Festivity," counts twenty-nine references to madness in the play (236).

8. Thomas Van Laan, *Role Playing in Shakespeare* (Toronto: University of Toronto Press, 1978), 78. Joseph H. Summers writes that "Every character has his [sic] mask, for the assumption of the play is that no one is without a mask in the seriocomic business of the pursuit of happiness. . . . At the opening of the play Orsino and Olivia accept the aristocratic (and literary) ideas of the romantic lover and the grief-stricken lady as realities rather than as ideas." "The Masks of *Twelfth Night,*" *The University Review* 22 (1955): 25–32; reprinted in Walter N. King, ed., *Twentieth Century Interpretations of Twelfth Night* (Upper Saddle River, N.J.: Prentice Hall, 1968), 16. Joseph Westlund, *Shakespeare's Reparative Comedies* (Chicago & London: University of Chicago Press, 1984), examines Orsino's and Olivia's narcissism, 98–107.

9. Stephen Booth, "*Twelfth Night* 1.1: The Audience as Malvolio," in Peter Erickson and Coppélia Kahn, eds. *Shakespeare's "Rough Magic"* (Newark: University of Delaware Press, 1985), 149–67, brilliantly analyzes the utter nonsense of Orsino's opening lines and the audience's mental gymnastics involved in deciphering meaning from them.

10. Ruth Nevo, *Comic Transformations in Shakespeare* (New York: Methuen, 1980), 205.

11. L. G. Salingar, "The Design of *Twelfth Night,*" *Shakespeare Quarterly* 9 (spring 1958): 117–39; reprinted in Stanley Wells, ed., *Twelfth Night: Critical Essays* (New York: Garland Publishing, 1986), 193. Salingar's extensive analysis of the play's sources and design is immensely helpful, but as a scholarly "overview" does not address the audience's sequential experience of the play in theatre time.

12. Jean E. Howard, *Shakespeare's Art of Orchestration* (Urbana: University of Illinois Press, 1984), writes that by "stringing these three scenes together" to begin the play, Shakespeare focuses audience attention "not upon plot, but upon tonal and kinetic contrasts that illuminate some of the differing attitudes toward life and some of the different ways in which energy is expended in Illyria" (182). Although I disagree with Howard's conclusions about the end of the play, I thoroughly admire her essay as an account of *Twelfth Night* in performance.

13. Judd D. Hubert discusses Viola's "script" and her "complete lack of involvement in her message" in *Metatheater: The Example of Shakespeare* (Lincoln: University of Nebraska Press, 1991), 46–47.

14. Westlund, *Shakespeare's Reparative Comedies,* 106.

15. Ibid., 107.

16. Bertrand Evans's claim, in *Shakespeare's Comedies* (Oxford: Clarendon Press, 1960) that Shakespeare introduces Sebastian in 2.1 to assure us that "all is well and will end well" (122) is simply not the audience's experience at this juncture; rather, Sebastian appears as one more confused figure in Illyria, an impression heightened by his strange, unexplained assuming of the name Rodorigo. Evans, like many critics, has forgotten the *sequential* nature of theatrical experience.

17. Ralph Berry, "*Twelfth Night:* The Experience of the Audience," in *Shakespeare and the Awareness of the Audience* (London: MacMillan, 1985), 63–74, notes that Sir Toby is "gripped by that ennui which is the condition of the unemployed, at all social levels. More, to base any dramatic system of festive values on Sir Toby is self-evidently absurd, for 'holiday' is a meaningless concept save to those who work. Sir Toby does not work, and therefore usurps the values of 'play'" (66).

18. Howard, 187–88, superbly examines the shifts in tone and atmosphere experienced by the audience from 2.3 to 2.4.

19. D. J. Palmer, "*Twelfth Night* and the Myth of Echo and Narcissus," *Shakespeare Survey* 32 (1979), 73–78, asserts that this "is a moment of true emotional consonance, and as Orsino recognizes by Viola's answer that his page knows what it is to be in love, the two are drawn closer together" (76). Theater spectators must decide whether or not this moment in act 2 makes Orsino's sudden expression of love for Viola later in act 5 convincing. That this dialogue is the only pretext for Orsino's offer, and that Viola's love is clearly a version of the conventional "love at first sight" stresses my point about the play's lack of romantic closure in act 5.

20. In describing Orsino's speeches in this scene, Nevo, *Comic Transformations,* summarizes both his and Olivia's self-delusion: "Olivia represents to him the sonneteer's lady he believes himself in love with, while what his nature truly needs and responds to is the youthful, dependent, and devoted femininity of Viola which is scarcely veiled by the page disguise. What we are thus invited to perceive in each of these protagonists is not merely illusion, posture or attitudinizing. They are each in a state of disequilibrium regarding masculine and feminine roles and impulses which they themselves misassess" (209).

21. Viola's pathos at this moment is heightened by the fact that she committed to "time" what she herself has admitted she cannot untangle: "It is too hard a knot for me t' untie" (2.2.41). Orsino's obtuseness only exacerbates Viola's helplessness, a conviction heightened among spectators when Toby's unruly "plot" pits Andrew against Viola in 3.4.

22. On the letter scene, Karen Greif, "Plays and Playing in *Twelfth Night,*" *Shakespeare Survey* 34 (1981), 120–30, writes: "Malvolio's private playlet of revenge and his discovery of the letter are staged in a deliberately theatrical manner, played before the unruly audience of Sir Toby, Sir Andrew, and Fabian. His play-acting exposes Malvolio's folly to comic perfection; but it also, in its own topsy-turvy fashion, holds the mirror up to nature for both the spectators in the box-tree and the audience beyond the stage. It is a glass more like a fun house mirror than the symmetry of a 'natural perspective,' but in Malvolio's absurd performance the pranksters are presented with a comically distorted image of their own follies and delusions" (127).

23. Walter N. King, "Introduction" to *Twentieth Century Interpretations of Twelfth Night,* writes that Toby scorns that which Malvolio worships: order (8).

24. Olivia's employees are somewhat unpleasant people, perhaps driven by competition for power within her household, and apparently hostile towards strangers who have suddenly gained private audience with her. Richard A. Levin, *Love and Society in Shakespearean Comedy* (Newark: University of Delaware Press, 1985), interprets the pursuit of power as the primary motivation of everyone in Olivia's household. See esp. 141–45.

25. Salingar, "Design of *Twelfth Night,*" 202, 204. As I indicated above (n. 11), Salingar's approach to *Twelfth Night* is immensely helpful, but it is a scholarly overview that sees the play as a literary device, not as a script experienced *sequentially* in theater time and without explanatory footnotes.

26. Ibid., 202.

27. Robert Weimann, "Bifold Authority in Shakespeare's Theatre," *Shakespeare Quarterly* 39 (winter 1988): 402.

28. Toby's motivations for his "fun" can be seen as quite malicious. Levin, *Love and Society,* stresses Toby's drive for power in Olivia's household, and his fear that Cesario, who Toby knows is determined and articulate (cf. 3.1.69–91), may become Olivia's preferred company and thus ruin Toby's ruse that Olivia loves Andrew, whose money Toby is imbibing. Berry, "Experience of the Audience," suggests Toby is "obsessively addicted to making sport out of others" (67).

29. 3.2.75–76. The expected violence of this revenge should not be ignored: Maria says "I can hardly forbear hurling things at him. I know my lady will strike him" (3.2.79–80). Maria also says "I have dogged him like his murderer" (3.2.74–75). Logan, "Limits of Festivity," finds Malvolio's plight, here and in 4. 2, "too close to our own nightmare fears . . . for us to feel quite comfortable laughing at him" (228).

30. Westlund, *Shakespeare's Reparative Comedies,* 114–15, discusses Malvolio's narcissism and the ambiguity about him which this narcissism creates. Maria's plot "works so brilliantly because she plays on his desire to be the absolute center of attention. . . . If he is merely conceited, then the trick might be good for him, take him down a bit—or at least be deserved ridicule. Yet if he lacks self-esteem, then he is pitiful and sad, and the characters and the play treat him cruelly" (115).

31. In the second half of *Twelfth Night,* Shakespeare allows the audience no interlude or "breathing room" to assimilate events on stage, such as the "willow scene" in *Othello.* See Jean Howard's superb analysis of this "space" in *Othello* in *Art of Orchestration,* 12–13.

32. Van Laan, *Role Playing,* 83.

33. Howard, *Art of Orchestration,* writes that in 3.4 "a genuine sense of climax begins to build as action increasingly takes precedence over talk and as character after character begins to reap the fruit of his or her unnatural or affected posture. As each exposes his folly in its most extreme form, the audience is set free to laugh at a world gone utterly mad, until the laughter becomes strained by our growing awareness that things are spinning out of control" (194).

34. The other possible Globe location for Malvolio's "prison" was of course the trap door beneath the stage, but as I explain I think the upstage location theatrically far more effective.

35. This point is made by Summers, "Masks of *Twelfth Night*," in King, ed., 15.

36. Logan, "Limits of Festivity," 26.

37. Regarding spectators' response to Feste's treatment of Malvolio, Logan writes:

> [Malvolio's] imprisonment is a striking emblem of the psychic reversal that underlies Saturnalian festivity: impulses that are normally repressed are liberated, while the controls of the super-ego are temporarily held in check. What gives Illyria its distinctive atmosphere is our sense that in this world such a reversal is a way of life. . . . The sorts of things we learn about the night-world of the psyche are profoundly disturbing. Festivity turns out to be fraught with dangers and complications: Eros mocks the individual; Dionysus is a god of pain as well as a god of pleasure. (226–27)

38. Harold Jenkins, "Shakespeare's *Twelfth Night*," *Rice Institute Pamphlet* 45 (January 1959): 19–42; reprinted in Wells, ed., *Critical Essays,* 188.

39. Greif, "Plays and Playing," 129. C. L. Barber, *Shakespeare's Festive Comedy* (Princeton: Princeton University Press, 1959), sees Malvolio's imprisonment differently: "To play the dark house scene for pathos, instead of making fun out of the pathos, or at any rate out of most of the pathos, is to ignore the dry comic light which shows up Malvolio's virtuousness as a self-limiting automatism" (256). Barber's view of Malvolio is part of his larger view of *Twelfth Night* as "Shakespeare's last free and easy festive comedy" (257). I disagree completely with Barber's view that *Twelfth Night* is a "free and easy festive comedy."

40. Donald Sinden, who played Malvolio in John Barton's RSC *Twelfth Night* in 1969, reminds us that Malvolio's "prison scene" should be examined in the context of Elizabethans' fondness for very cruel "sports":

> Apart from the almost incidental 'We'll have him in a dark room and bound' Shakespeare in no way prepares his audience for the shock of Malvolio's next appearance. The play was written when bull-and bear-baiting were common sports, the pillory entertained jeering crowds, idiots were part of "the public stock of harmless pleasure" and the populace thronged to public executions. (63)

For Sinden's essay, see "Malvolio in *Twelfth Night*," in Philip Brockbank, ed., *Players of Shakespeare,* vol. 1 (Cambridge: Cambridge University Press, 1985), 41–66.

41. Summers, "Masks of *Twelfth Night*," 19.

42. J. L. Styan, *Shakespeare's Stagecraft* (Cambridge: Cambridge University Press, 1967), 196.

43. Ibid.

44. Howard writes that by the end of act four spectators "are reeling from the pace of events and sensitive—because of the repeated undermining of each character's fix on reality and because wished-for events have snowballed almost beyond the point at which we can take pleasure in them—to our dependence upon the dramatist for the *security of our perceptions* and the control of our pleasure and pain" (198; emphasis added). It is exactly here that I disagree with Howard; rather than securing our perceptions of the play and its characters, act 5 undermines that security just as we expect it. J. L. Styan writes that "the sequence of impressions projected to the audience can be violently reorientated by the arrival of characters on the stage" (*Stagecraft*, 112). The sequence of character arrivals and their parting words in act five

produce just such frequent and violent reorientations which collectively produce a profound and, with Feste's final song, lasting anxiety about the stage action. Shakespeare refuses to grant his spectators any security at the end of this play.

45. Shakespeare radically alters one of his probable sources here. In Barnabe Riche's tale "Apolonius and Silla," Apolonius threatens Silla with death because he believes she is Silvio, who has impregnated and then abandoned Juliana: "How canst thou, arrant theefe, shewe thy self so cruell and carelesse to suche as doe thee honour? Hast thou so little regard of suche a noble ladie as humbleth herself to suche a villaine as thou art, who, without any respecte either of her renowne or noble estate, canst be content to seeke the wracke and utter ruine of her honour?" Geoffrey Bullough, *Narrative and Dramatic Sources of Shakespeare,* vol. 2 (London: Routledge & Kegan Paul, 1958), 360. Riche's Duke, nobler than Shakespeare's, shows just rather than selfish rage. Salingar, "Design of *Twelfth Night,*" 195–96, further discusses Shakespeare's probable use of Riche's novel.

46. Alexander Leggatt, *Shakespeare's Comedy of Love* (London: Methuen, 1974), writes of the play's final moments: "The pairing of the lovers in the final scene is . . . beyond considerations of individual temperament. It is, like the meeting of the twins, a generalized image of love" (250). This view of the ending ignores the individualization of the lovers and their conflicts and the tension between dramatic convention and utter realism in act five.

47. Donno, Cambridge *Twelfth Night,* 137. One might respond that the significant differences between Orsino's "moods" at the beginning and end of the play only point to a very instable "character." Other than his narcissism and self-delusion, what character traits does one hear of Orsino? Olivia praises him highly in 1.5 to Viola, but we do not see these "qualities" during the play. By contrast, Orlando in *As You Like It* displays selflessness and bravery in rescuing his brother, and this quality obviously endears him to Rosalind and suggests to the audience a sound basis for Rosalind's deep love for him.

48. Logan, "Limits of Festivity," writes of the play's destructive festive energy: "The play discovers to us the fact that festive revelry is likely to unleash psychic forces that are not easily controlled. In the metaphoric language of stage action, the wounded revellers function both in terms of myth and in terms of quotidian experience: in one sense, they are suffering the predictable consequences of a drunken brawl; in another, they remind us that the rites of Bacchus culminate in bloodshed" (228–29).

49. Styan, *Shakespeare's Stagecraft,* 112.

50. Act 5 again demonstrates Shakespeare's careful, purposeful organization. Exclusive of Feste's song, 5.1 is (in Bevington's text) 388 lines long. Olivia's line "Get him [Toby] to bed, and let his hurt be looked to," line 207, ends the first half of the scene; Orsino ends the second half of the scene by trying to create harmony after Malvolio's exit line "I'll be revenged on the whole pack of you!" (line 378). Both halves of 5.1 end with images of physical or verbal violence, followed immediately by attempts to mollify the discomfort obviously present on stage. Like his characters, Shakespeare's audience cannot focus on the reputed joy of this "romantic" comedy.

51. Philip C. McGuire, *Speechless Dialect: Shakespeare's Open Silences* (Berkeley: University of California Press, 1985), 19–37, discusses the similarities between Antonio's and Andrew's silences near the end of act five and how

these "open silences" can affect the tone and meaning of the play's final moments.

52. Unlike Rosalind in *As You Like It,* we never see Viola in her woman's attire. She remains "cross-dressed" for all but her opening scene on stage. Regarding the 1983 RSC *Twelfth Night,* in which she played Viola, Zoë Wanamaker writes:

> I always thought it difficult for Orsino to make this sudden change from his obsession with Olivia, however carefully we had tried to prepare for it in the "patience on a monument" dialogue. Viola . . . is denied her "woman's weeds"; there is no marriage ceremony, not even a formal offer from Orsino. . . . The scene is a difficult one to make work, a director's nightmare . . . and I do not think that our production ever really found it, though we worked hard at it and discussed and argued about it for two years! (90)

See "Viola in *Twelfth Night,*" in Russell Jackson and Robert Smallwood, eds., *Players of Shakespeare,* vol. 2 (Cambridge: Cambridge University Press, 1988), 81–91. I would argue that Ms. Wanamaker's sense that she and her company never "found" the final scene is precisely the dramatic point: there is no center or focus there to be found; it is relentlessly mercurial, as much for actors as for spectators.

53. Anne Barton, "*As You Like It* and *Twelfth Night:* Shakespeare's Sense of an Ending," in David Palmer and Malcolm Bradbury, eds., *Shakespearian Comedy* Stratford-upon-Avon Studies 14 (London: Edward Arnold, 1971), 175, 176. Barton's theatrical point here is significant: "In the theatre, the fact that an audience will always be more struck by the *dissimilarity* in appearance of the actors playing Viola and Sebastian than by that marvelous identity hailed so ecstatically by the other characters, also serves to drive a wedge between fact and literary invention. We are dealing here, Shakespeare seems to announce, with a heightened, an essentially implausible world" (176). Logan, "Limits of Festivity," makes a similarly important point about this scene in the Elizabethan theater: "Only in myth and ritual are twins the same person, and while the stage world is, in part, a mythic realm, theater—and Shakespeare's theater in particular—is closely bound to the empirical, naturalistic world the audience inhabits. In that frame of reference, Olivia abandons her vow of chastity to pursue the first new man she meets, marries his (her) twin brother by mistake, and seems willing to transfer her affections to a man she does not know because he looks like the one she fell in love with" (235).

54. Ralph Berry, *Shakespeare's Comedies: Explorations in Form* (Princeton: Princeton University Press, 1972), writes of the ending: "[F]or Orsino and Olivia, the ending is illusion condoned. To speak of 'unmasking' is surely misleading, for they have begun neither to understand nor confront their problems; not need they. The cynicism of *Twelfth Night* lies in its acceptance of the truths that fantasy need not bring unhappiness, nor exposure to reality happiness" (211–12).

55. Berry, "Experience of the Audience," 72–74, argues that attempts to minimize Malvolio's fury in production deny Shakespeare's intentions about the end of the play. "Where is it laid down that a dramatist may not build into his design a threat to its own mood?" (73).

56. Ibid., 73.

57. Clifford Leech, *Twelfth Night and Shakespearian Comedy* (Toronto:

University of Toronto Press, 1965), speaks of the "effort ... needed for the contrivance of harmony" (42) that the ending of *Twelfth Night* evokes.

58. Joan Hartwig's distinction between the "larger benevolence" and "human revenge" operating simultaneously in the play is certainly valid. This scholarly overview, however, ignores what I have stressed throughout: the sequential, theatrical experience of *Twelfth Night* produced by its structure and its effects on viewers, rather than readers, of the play. See "Feste's 'Whirligig' and the Comic Providence of *Twelfth Night*," *ELH* 40 (1973): 501–13; reprinted as "*Twelfth Night* and Parodic Subplot," in *Shakespeare's Analogical Scene*, 135–52.

59. H. R. Coursen, *Shakespearean Performance as Interpretation* (Newark: University of Delaware Press, 1992), writes of the play's ending:

> Irony complicates response and, if we are alert to it, helps individuate response. It validates dramatic experience by allowing us to recognize that Shakespeare doesn't "cheat" with his endings. Even Feste's final song can be interpreted as a pointing back over the shoulder at the sunlit, unchanging, and "resolved" world of Illyria, and as a pointing out at the afternoon darkening above the Thames and the city across the river, the city where "comic endings" are more difficult than they have seemed in "our play." (24)

Coursen is absolutely right about the Janus-like function of Feste's song; I would add only that I think the ending of *Twelfth Night* is no more "resolved" than the endings of human affairs often are across the Thames or any other river.

## Chapter 7. Seeing and Believing: Audience Perception and the Character of Cressida in Performance

1. Homer Swander, "In Our Time: Such Audiences We Wish Him," *Shakespeare Quarterly* 35, no. 5 (summer 1984): 539. See Introduction, p. 14.

2. Philip C. McGuire, "Introduction," *Shakespeare: The Theatrical Dimension* eds. Philip C. McGuire and David A. Samuelson (New York: AMS Press, 1979), xx.

3. J. L. Styan, *Shakespeare's Stagecraft* (Cambridge: Cambridge University Press, 1967),103.

4. Ibid. Styan remarks that "A player's position on the stage add[s] a dimension of meaning to his performance even when he remain[s] silent" (82).

5. Ibid.,15.

6. Throughout this essay and the one on *Hamlet*, the division of the Globe audience into central and side portions is central to my arguments. As I explain in n. 18, p. 216, C. Walter Hodges's diagram of the second Globe in the Craig/Bevington, 2d ed., clearly shows that the experience of a play, especially of a complex scene such as the "Mousetrap," would have been significantly affected by spectators' viewing position in a thrust-stage playhouse such as the Globe.

7. Stephen Orgel, "Shakespeare Imagines a Theater," in Kenneth Muir, Jay L. Halio, and D. J. Palmer, eds., *Shakespeare, Man of the Theater* (Newark: University of Delaware Press, 1983), 44. Regarding the Elizabethan companies' resistance to printing their plays, Orgel writes: "I would think that the English resistance to print goes ... to characteristic assumptions about the nature of

theater itself: that the script is *essentially* unstable and changes as the performers decide to change it; that it is the property of the performers, not of playwrights, audiences, or readers; that the *real* play is the performance, not the text; that to fix the text, transform it into a book, is to defeat it" (43).

8. The stage history of *Troilus & Cressida* is quite uncertain. Kenneth Palmer, ed., *Troilus and Cressida,* The Arden Shakespeare (New York: Methuen, 1982), 1–17, thoroughly examines the textual history of the play, from the entry in the *Stationers' Register* of 7 February 1602–3, which claims the play was "acted by my lo: Chamberlens Men" to the Epistle in the 1609 Quarto which claims the play was "neuer stal'd with the Stage" (95). As with so many of Shakespeare's plays, we have little specific evidence of this play's actual theater history. But this uncertainty ought not preclude our examining the play as a performance script.

9. R. A. Yoder, "'Sons and Daughters of the Game': An Essay on Shakespeare's *Troilus and Cressida,*" *Shakespeare Survey* 25 (1972), 15.

10. Gayle Greene, "Shakespeare's Cressida: 'A kind of self,'" in Carolyn R. S. Lenz, Gayle Greene, and Carol Thomas Neely, eds., *The Woman's Part* (Urbana: University of Illinois Press, 1983), 137.

11. Yoder, "Sons and Daughters," 15–19, superbly examines the debate over values in the play. See also W. R. Elton, "Shakespeare's Ulysses and the Problem of Value," *Shakespeare Studies* 2 (1966): 95–111.

12. Regarding Troilus's imagery here, Greene, "Shakespeare's Cressida," writes, "The too-precise naming of her 'bed' as his goal and himself as 'the merchant' impugns his lofty idealism, but the contradiction revealed is a familiar one; exalting woman as goddess, reducing her to object, what he omits is the person" (138). Derek Traversi, *An Approach to Shakespeare,* 3d ed. (Garden City, N.Y.: Doubleday and Company, 1969), writes that Troilus's "conventional imagery is transformed, as it were, from within in a manner so closely bound up with the convention that it acts as a corrupting agent, intimately related to the surface sentiment. By giving deep sensuous value to the Petrarchan images, it conveys simultaneously an impression of intense feeling and an underlying lack of content" (328).

13. On Cressida's ability to defend herself with her ironic wit, see Stephen J. Lynch, "Shakespeare's Cressida: 'A Woman of Quick Sense,'" *Philological Quarterly* 63 (summer 1984): 357–68.

14. This idea, to which I refer later, is argued by Yoder, "Sons and Daughters," 23.

15. Janet Adelman, *Suffocating Mothers* (New York: Routledge, 1992), carefully analyzes Cressida's situation and imagery here, and argues that "whatever we may feel about the self thus revealed, we feel that it *is* a self: the very structure of the scene—ending in her soliloquy—establishes in us a keen sense both of Cressida's inwardness and of our own privileged position as the recipient of her revelations" (47).

16. Adelman, 47–48, develops this argument.

17. Grant L. Voth and Oliver H. Evans, "Cressida and the World of the Play," *Shakespeare Studies* 8 (1975): 231–39, write, "Throughout the trysting scene, part of the drama lies in the conflict between Troilus' attempt to seduce Cressida to his idealistic vision and Cressida's attempt to act on the basis of what she knows the world to be like. All her attempts to point out the truth to Troilus fail" (235).

18. Yoder, "Sons and Daughters," writes that Troilus "naively accepts the

courtly code he has inherited, [and] is frightened that the demands of sexual love will conflict with honor. . . . Troilus departs with Aeneas to join the very council that has dealt the blow" (20).

19. Robert Ornstein, *The Moral Vision of Jacobean Tragedy* (Madison: University of Wisconsin Press, 1960), asserts, "What are women but as they are valued *by men?* Troy would not sell Helen, its theme of honor, for the price of survival, but it barters Cressida for a single prisoner. The noble Hector uses Andromache's beauty and chastity as the subject of his marital brag but when she begs him to avoid the final battle, he rudely thrusts her away and orders her into the palace. When his honor is at pawn, he owes a higher obligation to his enemy than to his wife" (245).

20. As indicative of the callous attitude towards women in the play, when Pandarus hears that Cressida is to be sent to the Greeks, he can only think about Troilus's feelings: "'Twill be his death, / 'twill be his bane; he cannot bear it" (4.2.93–94). Pandarus never considers the effects of the bartering on Cressida, who is being sent to an enemy camp in war.

21. Gayle Greene's suggestion about Troilus at this moment seems quite plausible: "It may be Troilus's awareness of his own inauthenticity that accounts for his obsession with hers: his view of her is, again, determined by projection, though not now of desire, but fear" ("Shakespeare's Cressida," 143).

22. In his introduction to the play (444–47), Bevington, 4th ed., discusses how matters of state and war dwarf private concerns. But ironically, these matters of "state," including Cressida's trade for Antenor, allow Paris to pursue his lust for Helen.

23. Douglas Sprigg, "Shakespeare's Visual Stagecraft: The Seduction of Cressida," in *Shakespeare: The Theatrical Dimension,* 149–64.

24. Sprigg eloquently describes the symbolic significance of Diomedes's brief solo presence on stage:

> [Diomedes's] torch reminds the audience that it is night, and, even in the actual daylight of the Globe stage, the flame would add the suggestion of a lambent texture to the fluctuations in Cressida's responses and the resulting fluctuations in the other characters around the stage. . . . He is visually attractive, and he is dangerous. The visual image of the man and the torch is striking. Cressida, moving toward him and away, will become the fluttering moth. (150)

25. Ibid., 151.

26. Ibid., 151–52.

27. Ibid., 153.

28. Ibid., 153–54. Styan, *Stagecraft,* observes that this "three dimensional scene of double perspective could only have been conceived for the Elizabethan platform" (130).

29. Sprigg, "Visual Stagecraft," 152.

30. Following Thersites' "All incontinent varlets," which in modern editions ends 5.1, the Folio prints "Exeunt," which modern editors, following Hanmer, amend to "exit." Although the Folio s.d. is obviously an error for "exit," why does Thersites have to leave the stage after 5.1? Wouldn't the continuity among scenes on the Elizabethan stage have been emphasized by having Thersites simply slink quietly to a corner, I suggest upstage left, as Diomedes enters? Further, with his continued presence on stage from the end of 5.1 to the end of 5.2, Thersites's monologue about Diomedes's being a "false-hearted rogue" and "Nothing but lechery! All incontinent varlets," and his epilogue to 5.2

claiming "Lechery, lechery, still wars and lechery; nothing else holds fashion" would frame all of 5.2 with his bestial view of the assignation scene.

31. Sprigg, "Visual Stagecraft," 153.

32. Ibid., 157.

33. Ibid., 153.

34. René Girard, "The politics of desire in *Troilus and Cressida,*" in Patricia Parker and Geoffrey Hartman, eds. *Shakespeare and the Question of Theory* (New York: Methuen, 1985), 197.

35. Voth and Evans, "Cressida and the World of the Play," 235, 237

36. Marianne Novy, *Love's Argument* (Chapel Hill: University of North Carolina Press, 1985), is absolutely right when she asserts that the bond of Troilus and Cressida, "something like those forged in a bed trick in the other problem plays, is a bond chiefly of unintegrated sexuality" (115). Troilus's Petrarchan imagery and immense selfishness indicate just this lack of integration, and it is *exactly* what Cressida fears in him: "You men will never tarry."

37. Lynch, "Shakespeare's Cressida," 365–66.

38. Yoder, "Sons and Daughters," 23. Traversi, *Approach to Shakespeare,* argues that "the spirit in which Shakespeare created [Cressida] made it impossible for her to be shown as really responsible for her actions; and without responsibility there can be no moral evaluation" (330). I cannot agree with Traversi; Cressida is surely a victim of horrible circumstances, but I believe the seminal *theatrical* point is that Shakespeare meant to dramatize her enormous difficulty in choosing an action and meant his spectators at the Globe to sense *in the very playing of the scene* her multifaceted dilemma. Cressida is not simply to be dismissed as a victim of time or men's twisted values. She is surely a victim of both; however, she is also a complex figure whose moral *choices* are staged so compellingly in 5.2.

39. Greene, "Shakespeare's Cressida," 145.

40. Sprigg, "Visual Stagecraft," 157.

41. Ibid., 156–57.

42. Ibid., 157.

43. Sprigg does recognize that many images of Cressida emerge in staging this scene:

> the idealized Cressida seen through the eyes of a naive Troilus, a sluttish Cressida seen through the eyes of a depraved Thersites, and a calculatingly coy and flirtatious Cressida seen through the eyes of an aroused Diomedes and a cynical Ulysses. The final image of Cressida becomes a composite view created and expressed in good part by a staging that reflects the contradictions within her personality and the multiple frames of reference within which those contradictions may be viewed. The labyrinthian complexities of human behavior are made to appear even more inaccessible to understanding by the inherent prejudice of any single point of view. (162)

My principal point of disagreement with Sprigg is that he assumes a unified audience response to Cressida's and Troilus's emotions and actions in the scene, and does not consider that even within the Globe Theatre the positions of spectators will affect their interpretation and understanding of this scene which itself stages so many different levels of awareness.

44. Ibid., 149.

45. Ibid., 150.

46. H. R. Coursen, *Shakespearean Performance as Interpretation* (Newark: University of Delaware Press, 1992), 11.

47. Orgel, "Shakespeare Imagines a Theater," 44.

## CHAPTER 8. "GET YOU A PLACE": STAGING THE "MOUSETRAP" AT THE GLOBE THEATRE

1. For a survey of these and related questions about this scene, see W. W. Robson, *Did the King See the Dumb Show?* (Edinburgh: Edinburgh University Press, 1975).

2. Daniel Seltzer, "The Shape of *Hamlet* in the Theater," in William C. Holzberger and Peter W. Waldeck, eds. *Perspectives on Hamlet* (Lewisburg: Bucknell University Press, 1975), 167.

3. Michael Pennington, "*Hamlet*," in Philip Brockbank, ed. *Players of Shakespeare,* vol. 1 (Cambridge: Cambridge University Press, 1985), 115–28, writes: "Hamlet has a kind of sweet optimism, bitterly disappointed; and the struggle to *overcome* the maelstrom inside him seems truer, and potentially more moving, than a continual public display of his demons" (123).

4. Bernard Beckerman, *Shakespeare at the Globe* (New York: MacMillan, 1962), Appendix C, indicates that 2.2 and 3.2 of *Hamlet* are the only play-within-play scenes in Shakespeare's Globe plays which require more than five characters. Rehearsal and careful design of such scenes thus seems likely, given their theatrical complexity.

5. J. L. Styan, *Shakespeare's Stagecraft* (Cambridge: Cambridge University Press, 1967), 130–31.

6. Speaking of 1.2 of *Hamlet,* David Bevington, *Action is Eloquence* (Cambridge: Harvard University Press, 1984), writes: "The stage is filled with richly costumed persons and (although the stage directions do not specify) the occasion would seem to demand a throne on stage, centrally located" (180). George F. Reynolds, "*Hamlet* at the Globe," *Shakespeare Survey* 9 (1956), also calls for the King and Queen to be seated in 1.2 (51).

7. See C. Walter Hodges's drawings for 3.2 in Philip Edwards, ed., *Hamlet: Prince of Denmark,* New Cambridge Shakespeare (Cambridge: Cambridge University Press, 1985), 51.In both his suggested stagings, Hodges places Hamlet and Horatio near the stage right post, suggesting no difference between Hamlet and Horatio as observers.

8. Styan, *Shakespeare's Stagecraft,* 81 ff.

9. Beckerman, *Shakespeare at the Globe,* 155.

10. Alan C. Dessen, *Elizabethan Stage Conventions and Modern Interpreters* (Cambridge: Cambridge University Press, 1984), 90.

11. The positioning of the players is problematical. Placing them in the middle of the stage, with the King and Queen upstage center, would have them playing with their backs to the downstage center theater audience. However, if the players played to the theater audience only, the King and Queen could not see their faces, and the dramatic illusion here is that the players are entertaining the court party. Perhaps the players could have played in profile, turning occasionally to the side and front audiences.

12. Dieter Mehl, *The Elizabethan Dumb Show* (Cambridge: Harvard University Press, 1966), 117.

13. Harold Jenkins, ed., *Hamlet,* The Arden Shakespeare (New York: Meth-

uen, 1982), suggests that ll.183–208 (Arden; 186–211 in Bevington, 4th ed.) may be the most likely candidates for Hamlet's inserted lines, while admitting that no set of lines has been universally accepted by scholars (507). But why must we assume that Hamlet's lines are in the inner play? Perhaps Hamlet interrupts "Gonzago" before it gets to his own lines.

14. Regarding the King's question, "Is there no offense in't?" Robson writes: "But what is the offense? The King cannot be referring to the murder. How could he ask such a question about a crime known only to himself, without admitting his guilt? What the King wants to find out is whether Hamlet intended the first scene of the inner-play to be an insult to his mother" (13–14). Robson's comment is perfectly logical, and indicates that Claudius is a stern, defiant adversary for Hamlet. Harley Granville-Barker, *Prefaces to Shakespeare: Hamlet* (1930; reprint, London: B.T. Batsford, 1968), sees the Player Queen's lines about "second marriages" and "A second time I kill my husband dead / When second husband kisses me in bed" (3.2.182–83) as Hamlet's "petty, superfluous triumph" against Gertrude, but he sees these lines nevertheless as encouraging "thereby the King's growing certitude that here is a trap laid for him, no mere coincidence" (89).

15. In an earlier draft of this essay, I called Hamlet's labeling Lucianus "nephew to the king" erroneous. Regarding this label, Philip C. McGuire commented in a personal letter that "Gonzago" is a mirror of both a past event (the killing of Hamlet's father) and a future event (Hamlet's killing his uncle). Thus, in McGuire's words, the Mousetrap "mirrors Hamlet's unenacted desires as well as Claudius's hidden crime. Which of these facets prompts Claudius's response?" Considered as a mirror of the future, Hamlet's label is not erroneous; the king will be killed by his nephew. But as an immediate, unpremeditated response to the moment, Hamlet's outburst is erroneous in that Gonzago is a Duke (Ham: "Gonzago is the Duke's name" [3.2.237]), not a King, and Lucianus's relation to this Duke is nowhere identified in the inner play. Professor McGuire's comments crystallize the complexity of Hamlet's remark here.

16. M. R. Woodhead, "Deep Plots and Indiscretions in 'The Murder of Gonzago,'" *Shakespeare Survey* 32 (1979), 159.

17. Seltzer, "The Shape of *Hamlet*," 177.

18. Recall Derek Jacobi's sudden intrusion into the players' space in the BBC *Hamlet*. For a brilliant psychoanalytical and theatrical analysis of Jacobi's performance and the BBC "Mousetrap," see H. R. Coursen, "Jacobi and the Players," *Shakespearean Performance as Interpretation* (Newark: University of Delaware Press, 1992), 103–21.

19. At a reading of an earlier draft of this paper at the 1991 Ohio Shakespeare Conference, Paul Gaudet noted a feature of my staging I had not previously realized. Within the symbolic "space" of the stage throne sit court members who will die: Claudius, Gertrude, Polonius, Ophelia, (presumably, as in Folio), Rosencrantz and Guildenstern, and Hamlet. Horatio, whom I place outside this space, will live.

20. Granville-Barker, *Prefaces: Hamlet,* observes that Hamlet forgets his "promised joining of judgments with Horatio" (91).

21. Stephen Booth, "On the Value of *Hamlet*," in Norman Rabkin, ed., *Reinterpretations of Elizabethan Drama* (New York: Columbia University Press, 1969), 152.

22. Robson, *Did the King See the Dumbshow?*, 21.

# Bibliography

Adelman, Janet. *Suffocating Mothers.* New York: Routledge, 1992.

Artaud, Antonin. *The Theater and Its Double.* Translated by Mary C. Richards. New York: Grove Press, 1958.

Barber, C. L. *Shakespeare's Festive Comedy.* Princeton: Princeton University Press, 1959.

Barish, Jonas. *The Antitheatrical Prejudice.* Berkeley: University of California Press, 1981.

———. "The Turning Away of Prince Hal." In *Shakespeare Studies,* Vol. 1. Edited by J. Leeds Barroll. Cincinnati: University of Cincinnati Press, 1965.

Barton, Anne Righter. "*As You Like It* and *Twelfth Night:* Shakespeare's Sense of an Ending." in *Shakespearian Comedy.* Stratford-Upon-Avon Studies No. 14. Edited by David Palmer and Malcolm Bradbury. London: Edward Arnold, 1971.

———. *Shakespeare and the Idea of the Play.* London: Chatto and Windus, 1962.

Bean, John C. "Comic Structure and the Humanizing of Kate in *The Taming of the Shrew.*" In *The Woman's Part: Feminist Criticism of Shakespeare.* Edited by Carolyn R. S. Lenz et al. Urbana: University of Illinois Press, 1983.

Beckerman, Bernard. *Dynamics of Drama.* New York: Drama Book Publishers, 1979.

———. "Shakespeare and the Life of the Scene." In *English Renaissance Drama: Essays in Honor of Madeleine Doran and Mark Eccles.* Edited by Standish Henning et al. Carbondale: Southern Illinois University Press, 1976.

———. *Shakespeare at the Globe.* New York: MacMillan, 1962.

Bentley, Eric. *The Life of the Drama.* New York: Atheneum, 1970.

Berger Jr., Harry. "Theater, Drama, and the Second World: A Prologue to Shakespeare." *Comparative Drama* 2 (spring 1968): 3–20.

Bergson, Henri. "Laughter." In *Comedy.* Edited by Wylie Sypher. Garden City, N.Y.: Doubleday, 1956.

Berry, Ralph. *Shakespeare and the Awareness of the Audience.* London: MacMillan, 1985.

———. *Shakespeare's Comedies: Explorations in Form.* Princeton: Princeton University Press, 1972.

Bethell, S. L. *Shakespeare and the Popular Dramatic Tradition.* London: P. S. King and Staples, 1944.

Bevington, David. *Action Is Eloquence.* Cambridge, Mass.: Harvard University Press, 1984.

Bevington, David, ed. *The Complete Works of Shakespeare*. 4th ed. New York: Harper Collins, 1992.

Blatherwick, Simon, and Andrew Gurr. "Shakespeare's Factory: Archaeological Evaluations on the Site of the Globe Theatre at 1/15 Anchor Terrace, Southwark Bridge Road, Southwark." *Antiquity* 6 (June 1992): 315–33.

Boose, Lynda E. "Scolding Brides and Bridling Scolds: Taming the Woman's Unruly Member." *Shakespeare Quarterly* 42 (summer 1991): 179–213.

Booth, Stephen. "On the Value of *Hamlet*." In *Reinterpretations of Elizabethan Drama*. Selected Papers from the English Institute. Edited by Norman Rabkin. New York: Columbia University Press, 1969.

———. "*Twelfth Night* 1.1: The Audience as Malvolio." In *Shakespeare's "Rough Magic."* Edited by Peter Erickson and Coppélia Kahn. Newark: University of Delaware Press, 1985.

Bradbrook, M. C. *The Growth and Structure of Elizabethan Comedy*. London: Chatto and Windus, 1955.

Bradley, A. C. "The Rejection of Falstaff." In *Oxford Lectures on Poetry*. 1909. Reprint, London: Macmillan, 1965.

Brennan, Anthony. *Shakespeare's Dramatic Structures*. New York: Routledge, 1986.

Bristol, Michael D. *Carnival and Theater*. New York: Methuen, 1985.

Brockbank, Philip, ed. *Players of Shakespeare*. Vol. 1. Cambridge: Cambridge University Press, 1985.

Brook, Peter. *The Empty Space*. New York: Atheneum, 1978.

Brooks, Harold F., ed. *A Midsummer Night's Dream*. The Arden Shakespeare. London: Methuen, 1979.

Brown, John Russell, ed. *The Merchant of Venice*. The Arden Shakespeare. 1961. Reprint, New York: Routledge, 1989.

———. *Shakespeare and His Comedies*. London: Methuen, 1957.

———. *Shakespeare's Dramatic Style*. London: Heinemann, 1970.

———. "The Theatrical Element of Shakespeare Criticism." In *Reinterpretations of Elizabethan Drama*. Edited by Norman Rabkin. New York: Columbia University Press, 1969.

Brunvand, Jan Harold. "The Folk-Tale Origin of *The Taming of the Shrew*." *Shakespeare Quarterly* 17 (autumn 1966): 345–69.

Bryant, J. A. "Shakespeare's Falstaff and the Mantle of Dick Tarlton." *Studies in Philology* 51 (April 1954): 149–62.

Bullough, Geoffrey, ed. *Narrative and Dramatic Sources of Shakespeare*. Vol. 2 London: Routledge and Kegan Paul 1958.

Burt, Edmund. *An Approved Treatise of Hawkes and Hawking*. Rpt. London, 1891.

Calderwood, James L. *Metadrama in Shakespeare's Henriad*. Berkeley: University of California Press, 1979.

———. *Shakespearean Metadrama*. Minneapolis: University of Minnesota Press, 1971.

Cartwright, Kent. *Shakespearean Tragedy and Its Double: The Rhythms of Audience Response*. University Park: The Pennsylvania State University Press, 1991.

Cavell, Stanley. "A Matter of Meaning It." In *Must We Mean What We Say?* New York: Charles Scribner's Sons, 1969.

Chambers, E. K. *The Elizabethan Stage.* 4 Vols. Oxford: Clarendon Press, 1923.

Champion, Larry S. *The Evolution of Shakespeare's Comedy.* Cambridge, Mass.: Harvard University Press, 1970.

Charlton, H. B. *Shakespearian Comedy.* London: Methuen, 1938.

Cohen, D. M. "The Jew and Shylock." *Shakespeare Quarterly* 31 (spring 1980): 53–63.

Cole, Douglas. *Suffering and Evil in the Plays of Christopher Marlowe.* Princeton: Princeton University Press, 1962.

Coolidge, John S. "Law and Love in *The Merchant of Venice.*" *Shakespeare Quarterly* 27, no. 3 (summer 1976): 243–63.

Cooper, John R. "Shylock's Humanity." *Shakespeare Quarterly* 21 (spring 1970): 117–24.

Cope, Jackson I. *The Theater and the Dream: From Metaphor to Form in Renaissance Drama.* Baltimore: Johns Hopkins University Press, 1973.

Coursen, H. R. *Shakespearean Performance as Interpretation.* Newark: University of Delaware Press, 1992.

Craig, Hardin, and David Bevington, eds. *The Complete Works of Shakespeare.* Rev. ed. Glenview, Ill.: Scott Foresman, 1973.

Crutwell, Patrick. *The Shakespearean Moment.* New York: Vintage Books, 1960.

Daniell, David. "The Good Marriage of Katherine and Petruchio." In *Shakespeare Survey.* Vol. 37. Edited by Stanley Wells. Cambridge: Cambridge University Press, 1984.

Danson, Lawrence. *The Harmonies of the Merchant of Venice.* New Haven: Yale University Press, 1978.

David, Richard. *Shakespeare in the Theatre.* Cambridge: Cambridge University Press, 1978.

De Marinis, Marco. "Dramaturgy of the Spectator." Translated by Paul Dwyer. *TDR.* 31, no. 2 (summer 1987): 100–114.

Dessen, Alan C. *Elizabethan Stage Conventions and Modern Interpreters.* Cambridge: Cambridge University Press, 1984.

———. "The Elizabethan Stage Jew and Christian Example." *Modern Language Quarterly* 35, no. 3 (September 1974): 231–45.

Donno, Elizabeth Story, ed. *Twelfth Night.* The New Cambridge Shakespeare. Cambridge: Cambridge University Press, 1985.

Edwards, Philip, ed. *Hamlet: Prince of Denmark.* The New Cambridge Shakespeare. Cambridge: Cambridge University Press, 1985.

Elton, W. R. "Shakespeare's Ulysses and the Problem of Value." In *Shakespeare Studies.* Vol. 2. Edited by J. Leeds Barroll. Cincinnati: University of Cincinnati Press, 1966.

Evans, Bertrand. *Shakespeare's Comedies.* Oxford: Clarendon Press, 1960.

Fraser, Russell. *The War Against Poetry.* Princeton: Princeton University Press, 1970.

Garner, Shirley Nelson. "*The Taming of the Shrew:* Inside or Outside the Joke?" In *Bad Shakespeare.* Edited by Maurice Charney. Rutherford: Fairleigh Dickinson University Press, 1988.

*Geneva Bible, The.* 1560.

Gilbert, Miriam. *Love's Labour's Lost.* Shakespeare in Performance. Manchester and New York: Manchester University Press, 1993.

Girard, René. "The Politics of Desire in *Troilus and Cressida.*" In *Shakespeare and the Question of Theory.* Edited by Patricia Parker and Geoffrey Hartman. New York: Methuen, 1986.

Goldman, Michael. *Shakespeare and the Energies of Drama.* Princeton: Princeton University Press, 1972.

Granville-Barker, Harley. *Prefaces to Shakespeare: Hamlet.* 1930; Reprint, London: B. T. Batsford, 1968.

Greenblatt, Stephen. "Invisible Bullets: Renaissance Authority and its Subversion, *Henry IV and Henry V.*" In *Political Shakespeare.* Edited by Jonathan Dollimore and Alan Sinfield. Ithaca: Cornell University Press, 1985.

Greene, Gayle. "Shakespeare's Cressida: 'A Kind of self.'" In *The Woman's Part: Feminist Essays on Shakespeare.* Edited by Carolyn R. S. Lenz et al. Urbana: University of Illinois Press, 1983.

Greif, Karen. "Plays and Playing in *Twelfth Night.*" *Shakespeare Survey.* Vol. 34. Edited by Kenneth Muir. Cambridge: Cambridge University Press, 1981.

Gurr, Andrew, and John Orrell. *Building Shakespeare's Globe.* New York: Routledge, 1989.

Gurr, Andrew. "The Rose Repertory: What the Plays Might Tell Us About the Stage." In *New Issues in the Reconstruction of Shakespeare's Theatre.* Edited by Franklin J. Hildy Jr. New York: Peter Lang, 1990.

———. "The 'State' of Shakespeare's Audiences." In *Shakespeare and the Sense of Performance.* Edited by Marvin and Ruth Thompson. Newark: University of Delaware Press, 1989.

Halio, Jay L. *A Midsummer Night's Dream.* Shakespeare in Performance. Manchester: Manchester University Press, 1994.

Hallinan, Tim. "Jonathan Miller on *The Shakespeare Plays.*" *Shakespeare Quarterly* 32 (summer 1981): 134–45.

Hapgood, Robert. *Shakespeare the Theatre-Poet.* Oxford: Clarendon Press, 1988.

Hartwig, Joan. *Shakespeare's Analogical Scene.* Lincoln and London: University of Nebraska Press, 1983.

Hattaway, Michael. *Elizabethan Popular Theatre: Plays in Performance.* London: Routledge and Kegan Paul, 1982.

Hawkins, Sherman. "*Henry IV*: The Structural Problem Revisited." *Shakespeare Quarterly* 33 (autumn 1982): 278–301.

———. "Teaching the Theatre of Imagination: The Example of *I Henry IV.*" *Shakespeare Quarterly* 35, no. 5 (summer 1984): 517–27.

Hazlitt, William. *Characters of Shakespeare's Plays.* 1817. Reprint, London: Oxford University Press, 1959.

Heilman, Robert B., ed. *The Taming of the Shrew.* Signet Classic Shakespeare. New York: The New American Library, 1966.

Helgerson, Richard. *The Elizabethan Prodigals.* Berkeley: University of California Press, 1976

Hibbard, George R., ed. *Love's Labour's Lost.* The Oxford Shakespeare. Oxford: Clarendon Press, 1990.

———. *The Making of Shakespeare's Dramatic Poetry*. Toronto: University of Toronto Press, 1981.

———. *"The Taming of the Shrew*: A Social Comedy." In *Shakespearean Essays*. Edited by Alwin Thaler and Norman Sanders. Knoxville: University of Tennessee Press, 1964.

Hillman, Richard. *Shakespeare's Subversions: The Trickster and the Play-Text*. New York: Routledge, 1992.

Hodgdon, Barbara. *The End Crowns All*. Princeton: Princeton University Press, 1991

Holderness, Graham. *Shakespeare: The Merchant of Venice*. Penguin Critical Studies. London: Penguin Books, 1993.

———. *The Taming of the Shrew*. Shakespeare in Performance. Manchester: Manchester University Press, 1989.

Honigmann, E. A. J. *Shakespeare: Seven Tragedies: The Dramatist's Manipulation of Response*. London: MacMillan, 1976.

Hosley, Richard. "The Playhouses and the Stage." In *A New Companion to Shakespeare Studies*. Edited by Kenneth Muir and S. Schoenbaum. Cambridge: Cambridge University Press, 1971.

———. "Sources and Analogues of *The Taming of the Shrew*." *Huntington Library Quarterly* 27 (1963–64): 289–308.

Howard, Jean E. *Shakespeare's Art of Orchestration*. Urbana: University of Illinois Press, 1984.

Hubert, Judd D. *Metatheater: The Example of Shakespeare*. Lincoln: University of Nebraska Press, 1991.

Humphreys, A. R., ed. *The First Part of King Henry IV*. The Arden Shakespeare. 1960. Reprint, London: Methuen, 1974.

Hunt, John Dixon. "Grace, Art and the Neglect of Time in *Love's Labour's Lost*." In *Shakespearian Comedy*. Stratford-Upon-Avon Studies. No. 14. Edited by David Palmer and Malcolm Bradbury. London: Edward Arnold, 1971.

Hunter, G. K. *John Lyly: The Humanist as Courtier*. London: Routledge and Kegan Paul, 1962.

Huston, J. Dennis. *Shakespeare's Comedies of Play*. New York: Columbia University Press, 1981.

Jackson, Russell, and Robert Smallwood, eds. *Players of Shakespeare*. Vol. 2. Cambridge: Cambridge University Press, 1988.

Jenkins, Harold, ed. *Hamlet*. The Arden Shakespeare. New York: Methuen, 1982.

———. "Shakespeare's *Twelfth Night*." Rice Institute Pamphlet 45 (January 1959): 19–42. Reprint. In *Twelfth Night: Critical Essays*. Edited by Stanley Wells. New York: Garland Publishing, 1986.

Jensen, Ejner. *Shakespeare and the Ends of Comedy*. Indianapolis: Indiana University Press, 1991.

Jones, Emrys. *Scenic Form in Shakespeare*. Oxford: Clarendon Press, 1971.

Kahn, Coppélia. *Man's Estate: Masculine Identity in Shakespeare*. Berkeley: University of California Press, 1981.

———. *"The Taming of the Shrew*: Shakespeare's Mirror of Marriage." *Modern Language Studies* 5 (spring 1975): 88–102.

Kernan, Alvin B. *The Playwright as Magician.* New Haven: Yale University Press, 1979.

———. "Shakespeare's Stage Audiences: The Playwright's Reflections and Control of Audience Response." In *Shakespeare's Craft.* Edited by Philip H. Highflll. Carbondale: Southern Illinois University Press, 1982.

King, T. J. Review of David Wiles's *Shakespeare's Clown: Actor and Text in the Elizabethan Playhouse. Shakespeare Quarterly* 39 (winter 1988): 518–19.

Knutson, Roslyn Lander. *The Repertory of Shakespeare's Company* 1594–1613. Fayetteville: University of Arkansas Press, 1991.

Latter, D. A. "Sight Lines in a Conjectural Reconstruction of an Elizabethan Playhouse." *Shakespeare Survey.* Vol. 28. Edited by Kenneth Muir. Cambridge: Cambridge University Press, 1975.

Leech, Clifford. *Twelfth Night and Shakespearian Comedy.* Toronto: University of Toronto Press, 1965.

Leggatt, Alexander. *Shakespeare's Comedy of Love.* London: Methuen, 1974.

Levin, Richard A. *Love and Society in Shakespearean Comedy.* Newark: University of Delaware Press, 1985.

Levin, Richard L. "Performance Critics vs. Close Readers in the Study of English Renaissance Drama." *Modern Language Review* 81, no. 3 (July 1986): 545–59.

Levin, Richard L. *New Readings vs. Old Plays.* Chicago: University of Chicago Press, 1979.

Logan, Thad Jenkins. "*Twelfth Night*: The Limits of Festivity." *Studies in English Literature* 22 (spring 1992): 23–38.

Lynch, Stephen J. "Shakespeare's Cressida: 'A Woman of Quick Sense.'" *Philological Quarterly* 63 (summer 1984): 357–68.

Mahood, M. M., ed. *The Merchant of Venice.* The New Cambridge Shakespeare. Cambridge: Cambridge University Press, 1987.

McFarland, Thomas. *Shakespeare's Pastoral Comedy.* Chapel Hill: University of North Carolina Press, 1972.

McGuire, Philip C. "Egeus and the Implications of Silence." In Marvin and Ruth Thompson, eds. *Shakespeare and the Sense of Performance.* Newark: University of Delaware Press, 1989.

———. and David A. Samuelson, eds. *Shakespeare: The Theatrical Dimension.* New York: AMS Press, 1979.

———. *Speechless Dialect: Shakespeare's Open Silences.* Berkeley: University of California Press, 1985.

McMillin, Scott. *Henry IV: Part One.* Shakespeare in Performance. Manchester: Manchester University Press, 1991.

Mehl, Dieter. *The Elizabethan Dumb Show.* Cambridge, Mass.: Harvard University Press, 1966.

Montrose, Louis Adrian. "The Purpose of Playing: Reflections on a Shakespearean Anthropology." *Helios* n.s. 7, no. 2 (1979–80): 53-74.

Mooney, Michael E. *Shakespeare's Dramatic Transactions.* Durham: Duke University Press, 1990.

Morgan, Maurice. "Essay on the Dramatic Character of Falstaff." In *Eighteenth Century Essays on Shakespeare.* Edited by D. Nichol Smith. Oxford: Clarendon Press, 1963.

Mullaney, Steven. "Brothers and Others, or The Art of Alienation." In *Cannibals, Witches, and Divorce: Estranging the Renaissance*. Selected Papers from the English Institute. Edited by Marjorie Garber. Baltimore: Johns Hopkins University Press, 1987.

———. *The Place of the Stage: License, Play and Power in Renaissance England*. Chicago: University of Chicago Press, 1988.

Neely, Carol Thomas. *Broken Nuptials in Shakespeare's Plays*. New Haven: Yale University Press, 1985.

Nelsen, Paul. "Reinventing Shakespeare's Globe? A Report of Design Choices for the ISGC Globe." *Shakespeare Bulletin*. 10 (fall 1992): 5–7.

———. "Sizing up the Globe: Proposed Revisions to the ISGC Reconstruction." *Shakespeare Bulletin* 11 (fall 1993): 5–13.

Nevo, Ruth. *Comic Transformations in Shakespeare*. New York: Methuen, 1980.

Newman, Karen. "Renaissance Family Politics and Shakespeare's *The Taming of the Shrew*." *English Literary Renaissance* 16 (winter 1986): 86–100.

Novy, Marianne. *Love's Argument: Gender Relations in Shakespeare*. Chapel Hill: University of North Carolina Press, 1984.

———. "Patriarchy and Play in *The Taming of the Shrew*." *English Literary Renaissance* 9 (spring 1979): 264–80.

Oliver, H. J., ed. *The Taming of the Shrew*. The Oxford Shakespeare. Oxford: Clarendon Press, 1982.

Orgel, Stephen. *The Illusion of Power*. Berkeley: University of California Press, 1975.

———. "Shakespeare Imagines a Theater." In *Shakespeare, Man of the Theater*. Edited by Kenneth Muir et al. Newark: University of Delaware Press, 1983.

Ornstein, Robert. *The Moral Vision of Jacobean Tragedy*. Madison: University of Wisconsin Press, 1960.

Palmer, D. J. "*Twelfth Night* and the Myth of Echo and Narcissus." *Shakespeare Survey*. Vol. 32. Edited by Kenneth Muir. Cambridge: Cambridge University Press, 1979.

Palmer, Kenneth, ed. *Troilus and Cressida*. The Arden Shakespeare. New York: Methuen, 1982.

Peat, Derek. "Looking Up and Looking Down: Shakespeare's Vertical Audience." *Shakespeare Quarterly* 35, no. 5 (summer 1984): 563–70.

Phialas, Peter G. *Shakespeare's Romantic Comedies*. Chapel Hill: University of North Carolina Press, 1965.

Quiller-Couch, Arthur, ed. *The Taming of the Shrew*. Cambridge: Cambridge University Press, 1953.

Rabkin, Norman, ed. *Reinterpretations of Elizabethan Drama*. New York: Columbia University Press, 1969.

———. *Shakespeare and the Problem of Meaning*. Chicago: University of Chicago Press, 1981.

Ranald, Margaret Loftus. "The Manning of the Haggard: or, *The Taming of the Shrew*." *Essays in Literature* 1, no. 2 (1974): 140–68.

Reynolds, George F. "*Hamlet* at the Globe." *Shakespeare Survey*. Vol. 9. Edited by Allardyce Nicoll. Cambridge: Cambridge University Press, 1956.

Richmond, Hugh M. *Shakespeare's Sexual Comedy.* New York: Bobbs-Merrill, 1971.

Robson, W. W. *Did the King See the Dumb Show?* Edinburgh: Edinburgh University Press, 1975.

Rose, Mark. *Shakespearean Design.* Cambridge, Mass.: Harvard University Press, 1972.

Rossiter, A. P. "Ambivalence: the Dialectic of the Histories." In *Angel With Horns.* Edited by Graham Storey. 1961. Reprint, New York: Theatre Arts Books, 1974.

Rutter, Carol, ed. *Clamorous Voices: Shakespeare's Women Today.* London: The Women's Press, 1988.

Saccio, Peter. *Shakespeare's English Kings.* London: Oxford University Press, 1977.

———. "Shrewd and Kindly Farce." *Shakespeare Survey.* Vol. 37. Edited by Stanley Wells. Cambridge: Cambridge University Press, 1984.

Salingar, Leo G. "The Design of *Twelfth Night.*" *Shakespeare Quarterly* 9 (1958): 117–39. Reprint. In *Twelfth Night: Critical Essays.* Edited by Stanley Wells. New York: Garland Publishing, 1986.

———. "Falstaff and the Life of Shadows." In *Dramatic Form in Shakespeare and the Jacobeans.* Cambridge: Cambridge University Press, 1986.

Seltzer, Daniel. "The Shape of *Hamlet* in the Theater." In *Perspectives on Hamlet.* Edited by William C. Holzberger and Peter W. Waldeck. Lewisburg: Bucknell University Press, 1975.

Shapiro, Michael. "Role-Playing, Reflexivity, and Metadrama in Recent Shakespeare Criticism." *Renaissance Drama* n.s. 12. Edited by Alan C. Dessen. Evanston: Northwestern University Press, 1981.

Shurgot, Michael W. "Gobbo's Gift and the 'Muddy vesture of Decay' in *The Merchant of Venice.*" *Essays in Literature* 10 (fall 1983): 139–48.

Sprigg, Douglas. "Shakespeare's Visual Stagecraft: The Seduction of Cressida." In *Shakespeare: The Theatrical Dimension.* Edited by Philip C. McGuire and David Samuelson. New York: AMS Press, 1979.

Stewart, J. I. M. *Character and Motive in Shakespeare.* New York: Barnes and Noble, 1949.

Stewart, Patrick. "Shylock in *The Merchant of Venice.*" In *Players of Shakespeare.* Vol. 1. Edited by Philip Brockbank. Cambridge: Cambridge University Press, 1989.

Stockwood, John. *A Sermon Preached at Paules Crosse.* London, 1578.

Styan, J. L. *Drama, Stage, and Audience.* Cambridge: Cambridge University Press, 1975.

———. "In Search of the Real Shakespeare; or, Shakespeare's Shows and Shadows." In Franklin J. Hildy, Jr., Ed. *New Issues in the Reconstruction of Shakespeare's Theatre.* New York: Peter Lang, 1990.

———. *The Shakespeare Revolution.* Cambridge: Cambridge University Press, 1977.

———. *Shakespeare's Stagecraft.* Cambridge: Cambridge University Press, 1967.

Summers, Joseph H. *Dreams of Love and Power.* Oxford: Clarendon Press, 1984.

———. "The Masks of Twelfth Night." *The University Review* 22 (1955): 25–32. Reprint. In *Twentieth Century Interpretations of Twelfth Night*. Edited by Walter N. King. Upper Saddle River, N.J.: Prentice Hall, 1968.

Swander, Homer. "In Our Time: Such Audiences We Wish Him." *Shakespeare Quarterly* 35, no. 5 (summer 1984): 528–40.

———. "Shakespeare and Beckett: What the Words Know." In *Shakespeare and the Sense of Performance*. Edited by Marvin and Ruth Thompson. Newark: University of Delaware Press, 1989.

Thompson, Ann, ed. *The Taming of the Shrew*. New Cambridge Shakespeare. Cambridge: Cambridge University Press, 1984.

Thompson, Marvin and Ruth, eds. *Shakespeare and the Sense of Performance*. Newark: University of Delaware Press, 1989.

Thompson, Peter. *Shakespeare's Theatre*. 2nd ed. London: Routledge and Kegan Paul, 1992.

Traversi, Derek. *An Approach to Shakespeare*. 3rd ed. Garden City, N.Y.: Doubleday and Company, 1969.

Van Laan, Thomas. *Role Playing in Shakespeare*. Toronto: University of Toronto Press, 1978.

Voth, Grant L., and Oliver H. Evans. "Cressida and the World of the Play." *Shakespeare Studies*. Vol. 8. Edited by J. Leeds Barroll. New York: Burt Franklin and Co., 1975.

Watkins, Ronald, and Jeremy Lemmon. *A Midsummer Night's Dream*. In Shakespeare's Playhouse. Totowa, N.J.: Rowman and Littlefield, 1974.

Weimann, Robert. "Bifold Authority in Shakespeare's Theatre." *Shakespeare Quarterly* 39 (winter 1988): 401–17.

———. "Performing at the Frontiers of Representation: Epilogue and Post-Scriptural Future in Shakespeare's Plays." In *The Arts of Performance in Elizabethan and Early Stuart Drama*. Edited by Murray Biggs et al. Edinburgh: Edinburgh University Press, 1991.

———. *Shakespeare and the Popular Tradition in the Theater*. Edited by Robert Schwartz. Baltimore: Johns Hopkins University Press, 1978.

West, Michael. "The Folk Background of Petruchio's Wooing Dance: Male Supremacy in *The Taming of the Shrew*." *Shakespeare Studies*. Vol. 7. Edited by J. Leeds Barroll. Columbia: University of South Carolina Press, 1974.

Westlund, Joseph. *Shakespeare's Reparative Comedies*. Chicago: University of Chicago Press, 1984.

Wickham, Glynne. *Early English Stages*. Vol. 2, pt. 2. London: Routledge and Kegan Paul, 1972.

Wiles, David. *Shakespeare's Clown: Actor and Text in the Elizabethan Playhouse*. Cambridge: Cambridge University Press, 1987.

Wilson, J. Dover. *The Fortunes of Falstaff*. Cambridge: Cambridge University Press, 1944.

Winny, James. *The Player King*. London: Chatto and Windus, 1968.

Woodhead, M. R. "Deep Plots and Indiscretions in 'The Murder of Gonzago.'" *Shakespeare Survey*. Vol. 32. Edited by Kenneth Muir. Cambridge: Cambridge University Press, 1979.

Worthen, W. B. "The Rhetoric of Performance Criticism." *Shakespeare Quarterly* 40 (winter 1989): 441–55.

Yoder, R. A. "'Sons and Daughters of the Game': An Essay on Shakespeare's *Troilus and Cressida.*" *Shakespeare Survey.* Vol. 25. Edited by Kenneth Muir. Cambridge: Cambridge University Press, 1972.

# Index

264

Holderness, Graham, 90, 228 n. 67, 232 n. 26, 233 n. 33, 234 n. 39
Honigmann, E. A. J., 218 n. 30
Hosley, Richard, 18, 218 n. 23, 220 n. 11
Howard, Jean E., 242 n. 12, 244 n. 33, 245 n. 44
Hubert, Judd D., 242 n. 13
Humphreys, A. R., 143, 235 n. 3, 237 n. 31, 239 n. 61, 240 n. 66
Hunt, John Dixon, 229 n. 13
Hunter, G. K., 229 n. 2
Huston, J. Dennis, 30, 220 n. 12, 221 n. 28, 223 n. 39, 224 n. 46

Jacobi, Derek, 253 n. 18
Jenkins, Harold, 245 n. 38, 252 n. 13
Jensen, Ejner, 99, 100, 234 n. 44
Johnson, Samuel, 237 n. 31
Jones, Emrys, 20, 62, 219 n. 31

Kahn, Coppélia, 220 n. 19, 221 n. 25, 223 n. 43, 227 n. 60
Kempe, Will: as Launcelot Gobbo in *Merchant of Venice*, 82; as Falstaff in *I Henry IV*, 104, 106, 111, 112, 120, 127, 130, 138, 140, 142–43. See also *I Henry IV*
Kernan, Alvin B., 17, 217 n. 19, 229 n. 11
King, T. J., 235 n. 6
King, Walter N., 244 n. 23
Kirsch, Arthur, 9
Knutson, Roslyn Lander, 216 n. 11

Latter, D. A., 18, 201–2, 218 n. 25
Leech, Clifford, 247 n. 57
Leggatt, Alexander, 219 n. 10, 234 n. 38, 235 n. 45, 246 n. 46
Levin, Richard A., 244 n. 24
Levin, Richard L., 215 n. 3, 219 n. 3
Logan, Thad Jenkins, 163, 168, 241 n. 1, 242 n. 7, 244 n. 29, 245 n. 36, 246 n. 48, 247 n. 53
*Love's Labor's Lost*: debate structure in, 58; dichotomies in, 67; mediated view of stage action during, 64–66; and *Midsummer Night's Dream* as experimental plays, 57–58; multiple perspectives during Elizabethan performance of, 61–67; Shake-

speare's use of inner play in, 61; stage audience, reaction to inner play during, 61–67; staging eavesdropping scene in, 58–60; staging pageant of Nine Worthies in, 61–67
Lynch, Stephen J., 192, 249 n. 13, 251 n. 37

Mahood, M. M., 79, 231 n. 11, 235 n. 47
Marowitz, Charles, 55
McFarland, Thomas, 126, 132–33, 236 n. 21, 239 n. 54, 240 n. 63
McGuire, Philip C., 13, 14, 68, 72–73, 174, 214 n. 3, 215 n. 7, 230 nn. 17 and 22, 242 n. 5, 246 n. 51, 248 n. 2, 253 n. 15
McMillin, Scott, 103–4, 235 n. 4, 239 n. 57
Mehl, Dieter, 206, 252 n. 12
*Merchant of Venice, The*: anti-Semitism among Venetians in, 78–99; dramatic tension during, 94–99; in Elizabethan theater, staging of, 92–99; judgment during, 95–98; *locus* as place of authority during, 92–99; multiple perspectives during performance of, 93–99; *platea* during performance of, 81, 83, 86, 92–93, 95–99; Portia's appeal for mercy during, 94–98; ring episode as coda to, 99–100; theatrical energies in performance of, 78–99; trial scene: divided audience at end of, 98; Shylock: as perceived outsider, 79; character of, 78–81, 85–92; relationship with Antonio, 79–81, 92–99; relationship with Jessica, 82–86, 91, 99–102
*Midsummer Night's Dream, A*: Pyramus and Thisbe playlet in, 72–74; stage audience, reaction to inner play during, 70–76; staging inner play during, 68–76
Miller, Jonathan, 144
Montrose, Louis Adrian, 17, 217 n. 20
Mooney, Michael E., 217 n. 16
Morgann, Maurice, 135, 237 n. 36, 240 n. 68
Mullaney, Steven, 104–5, 139, 234 n. 39, 236 n. 7, 237 n. 30, 240 n. 74